BROADEN
THE VISION
AND NARROW
THE FOCUS

BROADEN THE VISION AND NARROW THE FOCUS

MANAGING IN A WORLD OF PARADOX

JAMES R. LUCAS

Westport, Connecticut
London

HD
57.7
L817
2006

Library of Congress Cataloging-in-Publication Data

Lucas, J. R. (James Raymond), 1950-
  Broaden the vision and narrow the focus : managing in a world
of paradox / James R. Lucas.
    p. cm.
  Includes bibliographical references and index.
  ISBN 0–275–98592–X (alk. paper)
  1. Leadership.   2. Corporate culture.   3. Organizational effectiveness.   I. Title.
  HD57.7.L817 2006
  658.4–dc22   2005020942

British Library Cataloguing in Publication Data is available.

Library of Congress Catalog Card Number: 2005020942
ISBN: 0-275-98592-X

First published in 2006

Praeger Publishers, 88 Post Road West, Westport, CT 06881
An imprint of Greenwood Publishing Group, Inc.
www.praeger.com

Printed in the United States of America

The paper used in this book complies with the
Permanent Paper Standard issued by the National
Information Standards Organization (Z39.48-1984).

10 9 8 7 6 5 4 3 2 1

The following are trademarks of Luman Consultants International, Inc.,
with all rights reserved: APEX Diamond™, Be-In™, High-Performance Ethics™, ICE™,
Paradox-Based Leadership™, PassionCapital™, The Passionate Organization™, Play
Book™, Powersharing™, The Reality-Based Organization™, Strategic Planning Guide™,
The Teaching Organization™, Ten Key Elements™, The Thinking Organization™,
VMVB™, and VMVB Reference Guide™.

Advance Praise for *Broaden the Vision and Narrow the Focus: Managing in a World of Paradox*

"This is one of the best business books I've read in years! Wisdom leaps off nearly every page. I can't imagine anyone in the world of business not benefiting tremendously from its wealth of practical insights. Jim Lucas deeply understands the paradoxical balancing act that every great leader has to perform, and he clearly shows how, used appropriately, paradox is power. Open this book and meet a great teacher you'll be very glad to know!"
Tom Morris, Author
True Success, If Aristotle Ran General Motors, and *The Art of Achievement*

"Straightforward, direct and pragmatic, Lucas' latest book takes the mystery out of the everyday either/or challenges leaders face. It's both–and! His clear and insightful prose yields genuinely useful tools to successfully navigate these inherent contradictions."
Michael V. Harper, Consultant and Co-author
Hope Is Not a Method: What Business Leaders Can Learn from America's Army

"Jim Lucas' suggestion that leadership greatness is harnessed in understanding and managing paradoxes is very compelling. The concept is simple but not simplistic. This book arms a business leader with information on how to use the power of paradoxes and provides an approach to successfully applying the paradox principle in our organizations. I believe that developing a competency in managing paradoxes and creating a thinking organization is a leadership imperative. My leadership team and I plan to leverage these principles to access the power of paradoxes and develop a passionate and engaged thinking organization."
Glenn Hartman, Director of Customer Operations
Procter & Gamble, North America

"Jim Lucas has captured the key leadership issues in *Broaden the Vision and Narrow the Focus*. Too often leadership books are overly simplified, telling readers that if they only exhibit this one behavior, or perform this one action, then they will be great leaders. The reality is that leadership is based on simple principles, but it is a much more complex subject. This book treats leadership the way it deserves to be treated—thoughtfully, proactively, and with detail appropriate for the complexity of the issue. I certainly plan to keep this book within arm's reach."
Dave Hager, Chief Operating Officer
Kerr-McGee Corporation

"This is a must-read book for business leaders at any level. Whether you wish to simply improve the quality of your business operations or move your organization to a world-class level, managing through the power of paradox is both fundamental and provocative. Lucas shows us how effective organizations behave in flexible yet sometimes contradictory ways, and he provides leaders with eight simple steps to improve business decisions and master the paradox principle."
Robert Barrett, President & CEO
InCharge Institute of America

"Jim Lucas gets it just right in this provocative book. You can't lead what you don't understand, and the only way to surmount the challenges of today's organizations is to master paradox—learning to lead with the heart and the head, in the present and the future. Lucas shows how in this readable and practical guide."
Lee G. Bolman, Marion Bloch/Missouri Chair in Leadership, Bloch School of Business and Public Administration, University of Missouri-Kansas City
Co-author, *Reframing Organizations: Artistry, Choice and Leadership*
and *Leading with Soul: An Uncommon Journey of Spirit*

"This is a remarkable book. It is relevant and rigorous, yet highly readable. Full of perceptive insights. It should be read by all concerned with the future of management, leadership, and organizational performance."
Bruce Lloyd, Professor of Strategic Management
London South Bank University

"We are inundated with advice—how to live our lives, how to raise our children, how to run our businesses. For all of our dilemmas there are a host of 'experts' willing to offer their opinions, but they often contradict each other. 'Fools rush in,' one cautions, while another warns us that 'he who hesitates is lost.' Ironically, almost all of this conflicting advice is true, but we wrestle with its application. In *Broaden the Vision*, Jim sums up contrasting views of organizational life and shows leaders how to implement paradoxical solutions. He offers leaders excellent guidance as they decide how to handle thorny problems, pulling from the best of a broad array of top-tier ideas."
Edward T. Reilly, President & CEO
American Management Association

"The topic of thought leadership in a world of paradoxes is complex. Understanding and dealing with this complexity is critical for leaders to unleash the 'power of both.' Jim Lucas takes on this topic in a very practical manner, using twenty examples based around four areas: leadership, culture, talent, and strategy. Without being prescriptive, the book helps leaders think about a diverse range of questions from 'What does it mean to be customer centric?' to 'Why does innovation and change need to be ubiquitous?' Readers will come away with a much deeper understanding of how to balance their brains, hearts, and courage."
Andrew K. Tipping, Vice President
Organization and Change, Booz Allen Hamilton

"Thought provoking. The idea of thinking of business issues as a paradox is very instructive. Learning to think in a way that gets to truth is the important issue here. And that's pure gold for the CEO or anyone who's in charge. We pay consultants millions of dollars to get at the truth. Learning to think in terms of the paradox and ask questions that flow out of that thinking makes getting at the truth much more likely. In a nutshell, I'm reading this book four years later than I would have liked. I needed it before I retired. It would have been a great help."
Wes Cantrell, retired Chairman, President & CEO
Lanier Worldwide, Inc.

"As always, Lucas inspires great leadership. He challenges leaders to continuously reinvent their leadership capabilities, yet at the same time reminds them to continue doing

what has been successful in the past. Another leadership paradox from one of the great minds in leadership training!"
Peter A. Luongo, Executive Director
The Center for Leadership and Executive Development
University of Dayton School of Business

"Jim Lucas has put his finger squarely on the key to the future of management: the rapidly increasing multitude of paradoxes one faces in this quickly changing world. The management truisms of the past decades no longer hold with any certainty. Virtually everything seems constantly up for grabs. Most valuable is Jim's ability to deal with the four primary realms of paradoxes in today's organizations: leadership, people's talents, the organization's culture, and its overall strategy. Interestingly, he wraps up the book by applying the paradox principle to creating wealth. If that doesn't grab the reader, probably nothing will."
Gordon Shea, Management Consultant
Co-author, *New Corporate Cultures That Motivate*

"*Broaden the Vision and Narrow the Focus* continues in the tradition of *Balance of Power* and *Fatal Illusions* in helping to develop the people that are the heart and soul of any organization. Jim Lucas helps each of us to be a better person—a balance of body, mind, spirit, and work—which, in turn, naturally makes us better managers, leaders, citizens, spouses, and parents. The world of paradox doesn't end at the office parking lot. The principles in this book challenge each of us to be more effective in our daily lives—indeed, the ultimate paradox."
James DeStefano, President & CEO
Occupations, Inc.

"As always, Jim Lucas sends an appropriate and timely message. He has again made the complex comprehensible."
Tobias W. Buck, CEO & Chairman of the Board
Paragon Medical Corporation

"Author Jim Lucas provides insight on the value of balancing opposing approaches, ideas, and strategies for leaders to create high-performance results. When weighing choices and business decisions, Lucas says don't choose either/or—think AND."
Annell R. Bay, Vice President Exploration, Americas
Shell Exploration & Production Company

"I always enjoy and learn from Jim Lucas' work! However, as a senior manager, *Broaden the Vision and Narrow the Focus* will have a permanent place on my bookshelf next to William Strunk, Jr. and E.B. White. *Broaden the Vision* will be my management and leadership bible!"
Bruce Muller, Director
Training Operations, New York State Office of Children & Family Services

"One of the greatest paradoxes for today's leadership is that success often depends less on taking charge and exercising management power than on the ability to listen, to inspire,

and to build a true partnership with the people who are ready to make a difference. Lucas has created an excellent framework for the thought process required to start mastering high performance. Understanding paradoxes and embracing their complexity will go a long way toward achieving progress and prosperity for any organization."
Adolf Haasen, Managing Partner
A&R Associates, Ltd.
Co-author, *New Corporate Cultures That Motivate*

"When you read Jim Lucas' books, it's obvious that he has actually been in the corporate trenches, as he writes about management *reality* and not about management theory. *Broaden the Vision and Narrow the Focus* explores the challenges of successfully executing against the day-to-day opportunities typically encountered in large organizations while juxtaposing the often contrary perspectives of planning, communicating and embracing a visionary view that is required to elevate your company to the next level."
Deborah McIntyre, Vice President
Card Services, Wells Fargo Bank

"There are no simple answers to the challenge of managing organizations. *Broaden the Vision and Narrow the Focus* provides an excellent roadmap for leaders in all sectors–public, private, and non-profit–as they chart a path for their organizations through the complexity and paradoxes of management in the 21st century. In the challenging decade ahead, as Lucas makes clear, leaders must deal effectively with the conflicting demands of leadership, culture, talent, and strategy in order to accomplish the mission of the organization."
Mark A. Abramson, Executive Director
The IBM Center for The Business of Government

This book is dedicated to the outstanding people at Luman Consultants International—a team that truly believes in the many serious leaders who know that it is not only possible but *necessary* to think deeply about their organizations.

And to thinking leaders everywhere—who know that maximum performance awaits those who combine their passion and commitment with richly textured thought.

CONTENTS

20 POWER PARADOXES

VICTORY WITH PARADOX

ACKNOWLEDGMENTS

I am exceedingly grateful to the many leaders who have invited us in to share with them, and help them implement, the critical concepts discussed in this book. In a world with far too many people who are willing to look for (and sell) cheap answers, simplistic solutions, soothing bromides, and threadbare ideas, it is refreshing and encouraging to work with leaders who know that the real cost of performance and excellence and legacy is thinking deeply and acting smartly. Their organizations can be found on our firm's Web site, http://www.lumanconsultants.com. I salute them.

The Luman Consultants team provided outstanding support—freeing up my time, helping with research, providing input, and reviewing and critiquing drafts of the book. I want to single out several people. Senior Consultant David Hughes provided both structure and content to the book, as he does so well with our clients. His passion and focus have greatly assisted in the development of *The Thinking Organization*, of which managing paradox is a centerpiece. Graydon Dawson, a brilliant consulting associate, gave incisive commentary and useful suggestions and oversaw the development of many of the related tools found on http://www.paradoxbasedleadership.com. My son Peter, a leader in our consulting operations, helped in many ways and personally ensured the effective launch of the book's Web site. My executive assistant, Maryl Janson, provided both support and encouragement along the way. And my daughter, Laura Lucas, somehow found time while finishing a Ph.D. and a book of her own to provide her usual peerless insight and editing. To them and the rest of the Luman team, I offer a hearty "Thanks!"

The team at Praeger/Greenwood Publishing Group has made this a pleasant journey. My editor, Nick Philipson, has been a strong believer and supporter from the beginning, and deserves much credit for bringing this work to you. There are so many others who have been involved in this project: James Lingle,

Lisa Webber, and David Wilfinger, just to name a few. I hope we get to do more together.

My agent, John Willig, gets my highest thanks. He kept me on the "thought-leadership" trail and off all of the interesting side paths. He helped to frame this work and believed in it without flagging. John (all too rare among agents) had this idea that you could actually think. And I think he's right.

No one knows better than an author's family what they have to put up with during the writing of a book. Thank you for your patience, understanding, support, commentary, and humor—for the fourteenth time.

"I owe a real debt to those who introduced me early on to rational, logical, complex thought and how to transform it into something useful. The rigorous and demanding program in Engineering Management at the University of Missouri-Rolla (the first of its kind in the United States), and the premier faculty throughout that university, left no room for squishy or rosy thinking. Bernard Sarchet, the visionary founder and first chair of the program, showed me both that complex organizations and systems could be managed intelligently *and* that engineering design thinking could and should be "baked into" intelligent management. Further training in business and economics at the University of Missouri added to that foundation. And a grateful salute is offered to the in-comparable teachers at St. Louis University High School, men who believed that young men could be developed into people of the mind, people unafraid to face truth and facts and convert them into service to others.

Peter Drucker has been an intellectual mentor since my undergraduate days. From the time when we first shared the platform at a program in 1998, my respect for him and his work have only increased. Thank you for showing us that business is no place for sloppy thinking, and that good results are almost always preceded by good thinking.

Finally, my thanks to L.D. for your inspiration and encouragement.

CHAPTER 1

THE TRUTH
ABOUT PARADOX

*First, a word on paradoxes. Leadership is loaded with them. . . .
Performing balancing acts every day is leadership.*[1]

—*Jack Welch*

*The paradox is the source of the thinker's passion . . . the thinker
without a paradox is like a lover without feeling: a paltry mediocrity.*[2]

—*Søren Kierkegaard*

So you're in charge.

You're the president, or CEO, or COO. Or you're running a business unit or
division or department or project team. The buck stops with you. Or maybe
you're the founder or owner, and *all* of the bucks stop with you.

You've got the power. If you're secure enough in your role or strong enough in
your personality, few are likely to challenge you.

And that's a huge paradox—the overarching paradox of power. Everyone who
works for you *owes* you the truth, but almost no one who works for you will
actually *give* you the truth. Respect and fear get strangely intermingled.

Here is an astonishing reality: The key to leadership greatness is understanding the paradoxes of power—and the power of paradox. Weaving the power
of paradox into your approach to leadership gives you a shot at creating a lasting
imprint and widespread wealth.

What are paradoxes? We see them all around us. We're told by some to
challenge our people with high expectations, and by others to allow for human
error. We're instructed by one authority to take charge and by an equally
credentialed authority to empower our people. In our left ears, we hear encouragement to be General Pattons, and in our right ears Mother Teresas.

What are we going to do with all of this conflicting advice? When we get contradictory suggestions, are we going to follow Plan A or Plan B? The answer is, Absolutely.

We're going to follow both. We're going to do it all. We're going to have high expectations and high tolerance. Strong leadership that takes a back seat. Crisp alignment with anarchic creativity. A take-no-prisoners execution with a clear understanding that soft skills are in fact hard skills.

And to do it, we're going to have to think.

We want to go beyond the executing organization and the learning organization, to The Thinking Organization. This book is for the thinking leader who wants to perform at exceptional levels, and who knows that performance originates in the mind.

THE DUALITY OF LEADERSHIP

One writer observed, "Every situation for a leader is a composite of conflicting and opposing considerations, each of which is valid from a certain point of view. Each has its pros and cons, which have to be evaluated. The leader must be able to hold opposing ideas in mind and balance them judiciously. Otherwise, decisions become extremist answers with disastrous results."[3]

Great leaders understand that leadership is a duality, a paradox, a both–and rather than an either–or game. A paradox is a seemingly contradictory statement that may nevertheless be true. Most people believe that the two points of view are mutually exclusive, so they choose one position and discount the other. It doesn't look on the surface like you can do both—for example, taking more risks while eliminating risks—but great leaders can and *must* do both.

Two experts have written, "Fundamentally, paradox embraces clashing ideas. [It] involves contradictory, mutually exclusive elements that are present and operate equally at the same time."[4] Paradox does embrace clashing ideas. But paradox does not contain "contradictory, mutually exclusive elements." This flawed definition of paradox can prevent us from maximizing the value of paradox. Paradox is not contradiction, but only *apparent* contradiction. With thought, we recognize that the elements of a paradox are not only mutually inclusive, but mutually enhancing and generative.

It is important for us to know that each of the two sides of a paradox is valid. If we do not work hard to hold both of these opposing ideas in mind, we are destined to go to one side or the other and to produce imbalanced answers with out-of-whack results. Freedom without boundaries is as bad as boundaries without freedom. A half of a truth is not the truth—it's a lie.

World-class leaders know that a paradox is only an *apparent* contradiction. Average leaders fall for its trap and say, "I've got to pick one of these two approaches." Great leaders see the trap and say instead, "I've got to pick both approaches and build my leadership on the tension between them."

Charles Handy suggested that we need to "reduce the starkness" of the two sides of a paradox.[5] But the power comes from increasing the starkness, from amplifying each side to its full volume, and then bringing the two fully-developed sides into collision and merger.

Paradox is not compromise, or lowest-common denominator, and it is not the resolution of a problem. It is balancing two competing ideas at a high level—and more: growing a third truth out of the intertwined relationship, a tapestry of unique and differentiating ideas.

One expert has suggested that organizations move in a formulaic manner from the negative on one side of the paradox to the positive on the other side (using it as a cure). Then, when that side is overemphasized and becomes a negative, the organization moves to the positive on the other side.[6] But this simplistic approach misses a number of unfortunate realities. We might do both sides badly at the same time. We might erroneously use the negative side of one as a "cure" for the negative side of the other.

Instead, why not work consciously to repair the negative on both sides at the same time? Why not push ourselves toward doing one side well even if we're already doing the other side well?

The successful management of paradox involves five steps:

- *Embrace*—determine to fully accept and "live" both sides of the paradox
- *Eliminate*—rid ourselves of bad ideas and actions on each side of the paradox
- *Enhance*—develop the good ideas and actions on each side of the paradox
- *Engage*—merge the two sides into a cohesive "whole" consciously and systematically
- *Explore*—work to discover what grows out of the merger of the two sides

"Always act first to raise the lower rated side," advised two writers. "Get the two sides in balance before attempting to raise both of them."[7] But this advice imposes an artificial constraint. Why not do whatever we can to move each side along as quickly as possible, and work both sides simultaneously? This is exactly what we will do with the paradoxes in this book.

As we engage with paradox in the following chapters, you will see more clearly than you ever imagined the paradoxes inherent in having and exercising power, and you will see how to hold the two sides in tension, so you can mine each paradox for every ounce of worth.

IS THIS IDEA OF PARADOX TOO COMPLEX?

Simplicity: Is it a bad thing or a good thing? Yes. Absolutely.

American philosopher and writer Henry David Thoreau said, "Simplify, simplify, simplify"—And he was right. We all feel the need to do this, in both our professional and personal lives. And yet the very encouragement to simplify implies that there is much out there that isn't simple. No one understood better than Thoreau the complexities we face.

Simplicity is a bad thing when it's all we have. If simplicity is as far as we've gone—because it's as far as we've looked—we've stopped well short of the gold standard. There are a lot of reasons that people settle for cheap "solutions." Bad simplicity is selecting one idea because it fits our personalities and ignoring its opposite because it does not.

This kind of simplicity isn't looking for deep answers, mostly because it isn't asking deep questions. It comes in a variety of forms—leaving out whole areas of thought, ignoring ideas that seem to contradict the current "wisdom" or plan, squelching dissenting opinions because they are taking us off our linear path, paying for templates and models to superimpose on our organizations in fruitless attempts to get to the top cheaply. This kind of simplicity demands shortcuts.

Because of this, most writers and consultants offer to highly intelligent people mere pabulum in a tin cup. They try to get people ready for mind-numbing change with parables about mice. They have sixty-second solutions for problems that take a lifetime to master. They talk about how to go from decent to outstanding using plans that have already failed some of the highlighted companies while ignoring most of the companies that have been profitable for the last thirty years. These consultants offer keys to excellence that have failed many of the companies that are touted as excellent and that even the author says were just "made up."

We have books written in this millennium that tell us the key to leadership and creativity is to be just like Enron, and we have CEOs and other leaders writing books that are nine parts ego trip and one part lightweight content. This approach may sell books, but it is monstrously inadequate for the task at hand.

"I believe that many programs in management training today are moving us in the wrong direction," one expert wrote, "because they fail to appreciate the complexity and paradoxical nature of human organizations. Thinking loses out to how-to-do-it formulas and techniques, if not to slogans and homilies. . . . But the manager who can appreciate the absurdities and paradoxes of business relationships and organizations is surely going to be far less vulnerable to fashion, and therefore stronger as a leader."[8]

Authors and consultants will often tell you, "This"—things like customer-centricity, or growth, or innovation, or execution—is the key thing, the thing you should focus on if you want to win or be the best. Mark Twain's dictum applies: "To every difficult problem, there is a solution that is simple, easy, and wrong."

Ultimately, bad simplicity isn't simplicity at all. It's simplistic. Yet, it's what the vast majority of leaders and organizations settle for. It isn't "simple thoughts for simple minds," but "simple thoughts for *complex* minds."

On the other hand, simplicity is a good thing when it is the *result* of hard work rather than a *substitute* for hard work. We want elegant simplicity, which comes from the thoughtful integration of apparently competing ideas, from the synthesis of the two. If we accept complexity as a given, then we can see that the only way to get to meaningful, elegant simplicity is *through* the complexity that surrounds us and our organizations. We don't permanently stop at the first rest area and forget the rest of the trip.

This kind of simplicity—complex simplicity—recognizes that real leaders are faced with serious questions about apparent contradictions all the time. Is it our job to exercise authority over these people or to share power with them? Are we supposed to encourage our teams as catalysts of inspiration or make them face the ugly truth as prophets of doom? Should we take more risk or minimize risk? Should we centralize or decentralize? Should we move faster so we don't get killed, or should we move slower so we don't get killed? Are we desperate for more information, or are we desperate for less?

In his Nobel prizewinning book *One Hundred Years of Solitude*, Marquez described a couple who "lamented that it had cost them so much of their lives to find the paradise of shared solitude."[9] The concept of "shared solitude" is a paradox, simple but not simplistic, full of complex simplicity.

To simplify is to make something "easily understood."[10] That is the goal of this book. Something simple is "not complicated or elaborate."[11] The conclusions and recommendations will not be "complicated or elaborate," but to understand what they mean and how to use them, we first have to make our way through the complexity. The simple answers that grow out of *embracing* the journey through complexity are much different—much deeper, much more usable—than those that grow out of *avoiding* the journey through complexity.

On this topic, an executive summary is just not enough.

HOW CRUCIAL IS PARADOX FOR BUILDING HIGH-PERFORMANCE ORGANIZATIONS?

Simplistic management generally produces suboptimal results. The reason is not that complexity is valuable in itself. Rather, the kinds of situations we face are complex and require thoroughly reasoned answers.

The untrained mind works to reject these and pick easy extremes, but paradoxical leaders study and embrace these apparent contradictions—these paradoxes. The greatest leaders deliberately think in both–and ways and reap the powerful and profitable results of that choice.

Our design will fully determine the results we get. Apple trees produce apples, not oranges. Wanting and defining and describing the results we desire won't get us there if the design is faulty. Managing by paradox gives us a design worthy of the results we want.

There was perhaps a day when an organization could achieve market mastery by mastering one side of a paradox—taking risks without eliminating risk, narrowing the focus into a niche and ignoring the broader field, establishing strict policies and procedures and devaluing individual freedom, benchmarking competitors to be a "fast follower" and glossing over the need for a unique value proposition. That day is over.

Please take a moment to scan the table of contents. Ask yourself, "Does this look like a result I need in my organization? Do I need to spread optimism and give people hope, and spread ugly truth to give them a needed dose of reality? Do I need to have a team that thinks fully about both the now and the future, never losing sight of either one? Do I need to put more pressure on my team to perform, while finding a way to keep the wheels from coming off? Do I need to get everything moving at a faster clip and ensure that all important issues get full deliberation?"

If any of these power paradoxes looks like a combined result that you need (and I suspect that at least some will), then you are ready to master them.

And here's another paradox. These twenty paradoxes are both the results that mark a high-performance company and the design that produces those results.

Mastering paradox is not only crucial for achieving high performance, it is the main ingredient.

WHAT'S OUR PLAN?

We will cover twenty of the most powerful paradoxes in this book. These are paradoxes that provide us great opportunity if we are aware of them and manage them well—and great frustration if we don't. We've divided the twenty into four major areas that every leader must focus on:

- Leadership Paradoxes—These are some of the "make-or-break" components of leadership. They will destroy your effectiveness if they are mismanaged. We consider how great leaders balance hope and reality, deal with truth, encourage and manage risk, zero in on results, and address both the facts and the feelings when dealing with complex human beings.
- Culture Paradoxes—We examine how great leaders balance the big picture and current objectives, keep one eye on now and the other on later, create value-add communication, distribute power, and unleash passion throughout their organizations.
- Talent Paradoxes—We explore how great leaders high-grade their teams, instigate freedom that is effective, manage tension, let loose directed creativity, and build harmony devoid of unhealthy consensus.
- Strategy Paradoxes—These paradoxes get to the heart of process and execution. We look into how great leaders manage customers, relate to competitors and "best practices," allocate resources, balance speed and deliberateness, and use a changeless core to drive constant change in everything else.

Power itself is a paradox, a double-edged sword. In itself it is neutral, merely the ability to get work done. It can be used for great good or for great harm—to liberate or dominate, to create wealth or destroy value, to nurture or cripple excellent work.

This book is not a litany of world-class leader "best practices." This book is about *you* becoming a world-class leader. It is a book of principles that have been applied by others just like you, principles that will let you manage paradoxes and access their power.

You can learn how to use the power of paradox, and the twenty Power Paradoxes, to build a dominant organization unlike most on the planet. You can use it to make an indelible imprint on your organization. You can cultivate the growth of widespread wealth, in every way that the term "wealth" can be defined.

If you're ready, let's get the fields ready for a fresh planting—it's time to think, and to let our thinking fertilize our actions.

20 POWER PARADOXES

CHAPTER 2

SPREAD OPTIMISM AND SPREAD THE UGLY TRUTH

We pride ourselves on rationality, while avoiding reality.[1]

—*Ralph Peters*

Optimism. There's nothing like it.

It encourages people to try for high, and even extraordinary, goals. It carries us through tough times, problems, obstacles, and losses. It is a key element of all winning teams. It improves relationships. It even has, according to many studies, positive effects on health and longevity.[2]

Work needs a positive framework. People will conquer mountains if they believe they can and that there is a point to the battle. They can change if they are encouraged about better tomorrows and the role they can play in creating them. Great leaders know the power of optimism, of pointing people toward hope.

But with hope, people also need the unadulterated truth—the ugly truth, if necessary.

Truth encourages people to face the real reasons that they aren't achieving their goals. It, too, is a key element of all winning teams. If handled properly, truth improves relationships because we're addressing the issues that are actually dividing us. And the truth, according to the old proverb, will indeed set us free.

So organizations need both optimism and the ugly truth. Few leaders act on this paradox. Perhaps some don't understand this need. For most, it may be that we simply haven't developed the skill set.

SPREAD OPTIMISM

Optimism is "an inclination to hopefulness and confidence . . . the theory that good must ultimately prevail over evil in the universe."[3] Optimism is the opposite of pessimism, the "tendency to take the worst view or expect the worst outcome."[4]

David McCullough wrote about the tenacious optimism of John Roebling, the man behind the Brooklyn Bridge: "'He was never known to give in or own himself beaten,' one of his employees would recall. Another would quote a saying of his they all knew by heart, 'If one plan won't do, then another must.'"[5]

In a world full of challenges and problems and losses, optimism is a weapon of a great leader. If we aren't inclined to "hopefulness and confidence," if we don't believe that our good ideas and actions can overcome the problems that confront us, how can we possibly hope to stir our teams to positive action? How can we expect to prevail?

There are, however, a number of things we can do that are certainly not spreading optimism, regardless of any short-term gain we might receive. We can:

- Lie—Whenever we are faced with less-than-stellar news, the temptation to cover it up with untruths naturally arises. The problems with this are manifold: no one has a good enough memory to be a liar, people are smart enough to see through it, and the bad news gets worse.
- Spin—Closely akin to lying, spinning is deforming truth to make it appear more positive or favorable than it really is. People hate being "spun," which they take as patronizing and insulting to their intelligence.
- Deny reality—We can simply refuse to acknowledge that disaster is looming. It is easier to incorporate people into denial than into lying or spinning, because bad news is hard to hear and denial promises short-term relief. Denial is using a pain reliever to fight cancer, with obvious results.
- Make excuses—We can attempt to explain away the problems as the by-products of something that is beyond our control. "We lost our biggest customer because of a major reorganization, but that shouldn't affect these other three major customer relationships."
- Promise saving events—One of my favorite "bad management" practices is to use some version of the following statement: "There's nothing wrong with us that _____ [breakthrough product, new discovery, cutting-edge process, sharp COO, etc.] wouldn't cure." Great leaders don't wait for saving events; in fact, they don't talk about them—or let anyone else talk about them either.

None of this is spreading optimism. These tricks are a magician's sleight-of-hand. It's getting people to look at something *other than what they really need to be looking at.*

So what can we do to spread optimism effectively?

Keep people focused on opportunities, possibilities, and strengths rather than on problems, limitations, and weaknesses. I am continually amazed at the amount of managerial time that is spent on the latter: "I'm here to fix problems, set boundaries, and improve or eliminate weaknesses." But these activities seldom add value; at best, they may slightly reduce the slow drain-off of value created elsewhere.

Affirm our belief in people by steadily increasing our *trust and* their *authority and responsibility.* We usually think of these things discontinuously rather than incrementally—a person is performing at one level until we promote her to a whole new level. This gives an espresso shot of optimism, to be sure, but misses the gain that comes from a steady, relentless increase in authority and responsibility on a weekly or monthly basis.

Celebrate. What should we celebrate? We can celebrate the arrival and commitment of new people and the wisdom and commitment of the veterans. We can celebrate necessary intelligent mistakes, a rite that will dispel fear and highlight opportunities to learn and grow.

Eliminate negative measurements. Quality, for example, is almost always measured in negative terms—number of defects, customer complaints, and so on. How can this approach build an optimistic culture? We need to turn these terms around—number of successful parts made, number of successful customer interactions. People are much better equipped to make good numbers great than bad numbers less bad.

Encourage people to see their potential. Everyone is born with a seed of greatness. Great leaders find that seed and nurture it. If we recognize that our people can make unique contributions—that no one else can do what they can do—our cultivation of their greatness can grow into improved performance and better results.

Optimism isn't a trait—it's a little-used leadership tool. You can put it to work.

SPREAD THE UGLY TRUTH

Spreading the ugly truth is critical to the long-term health of the organization.

This isn't just true for failing organizations. Often, the organizations that have been the most successful become the most resistant to truth and reality. Studies have shown that "people are less likely to make optimal decisions after prolonged periods of success."[6]

If we have serious problems, avoiding the ugly truth is probably the best way to ensure the organization's disintegration.

So is it always a good idea to tell the truth?

If you're nodding, I respectfully but heartily disagree.

We need to be clear up front that there are some actions we can take that look like they are spreading the ugly truth when they are really just spreading ugliness. We can:

- Slander—Telling the truth provides no advantage to the organization when it involves tearing down someone on the team. Many organizations have a lot of this kind of "truth-telling," and the ones that do seldom have any other kind.
- Tear down competitors—Even if we have some negative information about our competitors, using it to belittle them will do little or nothing to help us. It is

almost guaranteed to make us arrogant. We need to humbly learn from what they are doing well, and humbly learn from their terrible mistakes.

- Tear down customers—Customers are *not* always right. Sometimes they are not even *rational*. Better to fire them than keep them around as internal whipping posts, an approach that lowers or destroys a strong customer-service ethic in our organization. Of course customers have problems—that's why they need us.

- Focus on bad news that is irrelevant—There are many negative events and actions that take place every day. Constantly talking about the ones over which we have no control—"What can we do given this terrible economy?" "No one is making money in this market"; "All the major economic indicators are pointing downward"—is distracting to the critical task at hand, which is to profit from and exploit these conditions. The best way to make irrelevant bad news into destructively relevant bad news is to make it our center of attention.

- Take the worst possible view—Some believe that assuming the worst means that we will never be surprised and will always be prepared. The problem with this pessimistic "tendency to take the worst view or expect the worst outcome"[7] is that we waste lives and resources preparing for events that have almost no chance of occurring. Saying that something is uglier than it really is isn't spreading the ugly truth—it's spreading a different kind of lie, a lie driven by gloom.

- Make anonymous complaints or critiques—Spreading the ugly truth (or at least your version of the ugly truth) without accountability is an invitation to pettiness and cheap shots. Some book reviews are examples of this problem. When reviewers get to hide in a "cloak of anonymity,"[8] how can readers judge the reviewers' competence to offer opinions or the validity of the opinions they give? Anonymity intended to provide a "magisterial, objective, authoritative source, unsullied by personal biases,"[9] is more likely to provide opinions that are "every bit as quirky, perverse, and prone to bias as they are in publications where the writers must take responsibility for what they say."[10]

Organizations can be destroyed if one or more of these "methods" makes up their version of "telling the truth."

I have believed for many years that facing and spreading the truth, no matter how ugly—in fact, *especially* if ugly—is a critical business attitude and skill. It should be obvious from the failures filling the news that "confronting reality has to become a leadership priority of the highest order—a nonnegotiable behavior for everyone at all levels of the organization."[11] So what can we do to spread the ugly truth effectively?

Start by spreading the ugly truth about ourselves. We've got to set the example. Telling the ugly truth about someone else—middle management, for example, if you are a senior leader—is a lot easier than telling it about ourselves, but it won't resonate with people. It will smack of self-righteousness and hypocrisy. This personal truth-telling shouldn't be too hard. In a recent study of organizational disasters, one article reported that "a close study of corporate failure suggests that, acts of God aside, most companies founder for one simple reason: managerial error."[12] One analyst quoted in the study attributed failure to leaders' "incremental descent into poor judgment."[13]

Tell the ugly truth about our organizations. A sociologist has noted that leaders "may puzzle over contradictory evidence, but usually succeed in pushing it aside—until they come across a piece of evidence too fascinating to ignore, too clear to misperceive, too painful to deny, which makes vivid still other signals they do not want to see, forcing them to alter and surrender the world-view they have so meticulously constructed."[14] We've seen this so many times: clients who tell us that something cannot possibly be a major problem, and then slowly watch the shoreline of their conviction erode under the pounding waves of incontrovertible truth.

Tell the ugly truth about our specific problems during the hiring process. I encourage you to ask this question during your hiring process: "Here is a problem we are having—what would you do about it?" This is a hard question to dodge. In addition, we are teaching people at the front door that we have problems, that it is not only all right but mandatory that we discuss them openly, and that we expect everyone to face and fix problems that arise.

Create a process with formal mechanisms and tools that force us to get past the reality-impairment that is always growing back like mold. "All organizations need a discipline that makes them face up to reality," wrote Peter Drucker.[15] We can't just say to our people, "Let's just tell each other the truth, okay?" We have to build truth-finding and truth-telling into the core of who we are and what we do. For example, we survey clients using our "illusion checklists," to find how willing organizations are to face reality in twelve critical areas, and then work out practices that improve both willingness and ability to deal well with truth.[16]

Listen to those closest to the process. Often it is the people who are the farthest down the hierarchy who are in the best position to pick up early warning signals, but without an organization-wide commitment to spreading the ugly truth, they are also the least likely to be heard. One organization has a staff systems analyst who "grew up in the savannahs of East Africa, where small movements in the grass may suggest a predator. 'What may be fatal is what is not so obvious,' he says."[17] His attention to a faint signal saved a major drug for his pharmaceutical company.

Resist conjecture that isn't based on facts. It is too easy for people to offer suppositions that are not founded in available knowledge. When an idea sounds too good to be true, it almost always is, but we've got to keep our wits about us so we don't give in to its seduction. "A whole lot of folks do not invest the time to truly remove inference and introduce fact," says Toby Buck, president and CEO of Paragon Medical.

Ugly truth, like optimism, is a leadership tool. You can use it to build a colossus.

THINKING AND RESPONDING PARADOXICALLY

How will we navigate this paradox? How can we spread optimism *and* the ugly truth?

We have to be realists and optimists at the same time.

Realists often don't see the possibilities. Optimists often don't see the disasters. The best leaders are realistic optimists. They hope that things will be better than they are, even as they face without flinching how those things really are right now and what the true barriers to constructive change will be.

These pragmatic idealists have learned how to release teams into the future with a solid grounding both in the present situation and in the likely scenarios for the future.

One important approach to take in managing this paradox is to differentiate between *hoping* that things will be better than they are and *thinking* that things are better than they are.

If we hope things will be better than they are, we certainly have to find the courage to hold dear a bit of unreality. Things are bad, but we believe they don't have to be so. In fact, we believe that we can change reality. If our attempt doesn't work, we will be disappointed, but not disillusioned. We want to be realistic optimists—we have hope, but we face the ugly truth squarely and without flinching.

If we think things are better than they are, we have moved into the realm of total unreality. We don't think we need to change anything, because we believe that the situation is already as it should be. If things don't work, we will be disappointed, but we will also be very disillusioned. Our goal should be to face and define reality. We're not even in the ballpark of being able to solve the problem if we aren't committed to acknowledging it.

Hope is a terrible substitute for the truth but an indispensable part of being able to accept reality and change it. Likewise, truth is a terrible substitute for hope but is an indispensable part of making our hope viable.

We have to create an optimistic culture in which the ugly truth can be heard without destroying us. A general environment of optimism provides a healthy context for hearing and learning from bad news and allows us to approach the ugly truth with a redemptive attitude. For example, Eli Lilly has initiated a Project Phoenix, "which gives every failed Phase I compound not just a second, but a third pass."[18] It takes a lot of optimism to believe that we can continue to learn and profit from a series of mistakes, but great leaders "shape cultures that are open both to the possibility of failure and to the need to learn when problems do occur."[19] That openness is only possible in a context of optimistic resilience.

A big part of effectively managing this paradox is to realize that there are two distinct ways to tell any story—one that reinforces the positive elements in our current situation, and one that reinforces the negative elements. "We have the power to idealize or denigrate those characters that inhabit our life stories," wrote

Gordon Livingston. "We just need to experience both alternatives as reflections of our current need to see ourselves in certain ways, and to realize that we are all able to color our pasts either happy or sad."[20] In a robust organization, both stories are told—and interwoven.

Timing is so crucial. We want to spread the ugly truth, but only when we are prepared to provide some optimism at the same time. For example, a big project that had a rocky start deserves a postaudit, but unless we need to know what we've learned immediately, it would probably be best to do the review after we've had a victory or the project has come to a successful conclusion. We spread the ugly truth, but only in a context of optimism; otherwise, we could discourage the very attitudes that will be necessary for our team to overcome the start and finish strong.

My team was once doing a proposal for a major engagement with a new client. The proposal process had development snags and serious timing glitches, leaving us in a rush at the end. We saved the postaudit on the process until after we had won the contract. We were much better able to process what we had learned in the glow of success. If we had lost the contract, we would of course have had to do the postaudit anyway, but by waiting until the conclusion we had a chance to practice optimistic realism.

Timing often means we should delay the spread of recently uncovered ugly truth until we are sure that it is true—and sure that it is ugly. In wartime, people talk about the "fog of war," "a place where fact, fiction, and battlefield exaggeration merge into a muddle . . . [and where] 'Almost all first reports that we get turn out to be wrong.' "[21] One military expert noted that "The antidote to erroneous battlefield reporting might be to hold back and digest events before broadcasting them."[22] The reverse is often true—often we should delay the spread of recently fueled optimism until we are sure that it is good news, and sure that it is worthy of our optimism.

Spreading optimism and spreading the ugly truth at the same time requires leaders who have a balance of confidence and humility.

People who make a difference have to have enough confidence to know that they can make a unique contribution, and enough humility to know that other people can help improve and magnify that contribution. These leaders explore opportunities as though they own them, even as they set up constant alerts to minimize the effects of their fallibilities and lunacies.

Surprisingly, confidence isn't critical to spreading optimism—but confidence does allow us to spread the ugly truth. We are sure enough in our abilities and the abilities of our team to believe that no truth is too frightening to face, too difficult to conquer, too dreadful to exploit. We shouldn't look at admitting mistakes as a sign of weakness. "In most cases," writes Pat Croce, "your staff, clients, and others will forgive a miscalculation, a case of undisciplined exuberance, or a *faux pas*. But they will never forgive or forget a decision to cover up a mistake."[23]

"The line between confidence and arrogance is thin," wrote Carlo D'Este.[24] We want to stay on this side of that dreadful line, and humility is the way to do it. All arrogance is ultimately founded on ignorance. Observers of one television network head's failures noted that the cause was "not just his lack of a golden gut for the next big hit or a groundbreaking idea ... it's also arrogance.... [One hit] made executives more confident, and they didn't address the [underlying] problem."[25]

Arrogance can lead us to take credit where none is due and to delegate blame where none is warranted. When a boom market provides an unearned boost, the confident leader spreads that truth while the arrogant leader says, "Are we fantastic or what?" When a poor strategic direction causes a decline, the confident leader takes responsibility while the arrogant leader says, "It was an unanticipated market decline." Behavioral scientists talk about "attribution bias," which is "the tendency of people to credit themselves unduly for successes that are heavily influenced by external factors ... and to blame external factors disproportionately when they fail."[26] Executive suites are fertile ground for attribution bias.

Confidence keeps our humility from discouraging us, and humility keeps our confidence from destroying us.

Andy Grove reminded us that "only the paranoid survive."[27] There is truth in this statement—but only if we have the optimism to believe that we can convert our legitimate fears about ugly truth into resounding victory.

CHAPTER **3**

DEMAND THE
TRUTH AND HAVE
IT FREELY OFFERED

The greatest and most dangerous turbulence today results from the collision between the delusions of the decision makers ... and the realities.[1]

—Peter Drucker

In most organizations, people are penalized—or at least they *believe* they will be penalized—for telling the truth.

Leaders claim to love the truth dearly, but they often look like they're in the process of divorcing it. In spite of clear statements from notable executives that the first thing a leader has to do is face and define reality,[2] most organizations are perfectly designed to smother the truth.

We know instinctively that we are in trouble if we don't face the truth. But leaders often don't even get a chance to *meet* the truth because they resist hearing it, believing it, and acting on it. When forced to confront it, they frequently "shoot the messenger" and develop a rationale for dismissing it. The net result is that many organizations are severely reality impaired.

However, even leaders who actually *want* to know reality are often sheltered from it simply because they hold positions of power. They are hampered by the truth-filtering activities of people who won't tell it to them straight. James Surowiecki cites a study of young executives that found that the more ambitious people are, "the less accurately they communicate problem-related information." Another study "found that there was a correlation between upward mobility and not telling the boss about things that had gone wrong. The most successful executives tended not to disclose information about fights, budget problems, and so on."[3]

This is frightening. The people who are the *most* ambitious and successful are the *least* likely to tell us the truth? Our best and brightest are the most resistant to telling us bad news? Maybe the reason so many reports and responses seem so unintelligent is that the really smart people wouldn't talk even under torture—and they've filtered the input from everyone else.

Hearing the truth also becomes victim to an inverse relationship. The worse the news—and thus the more important that we hear it fast—the less likely that we will hear it at *all*. If and when we finally do hear it, it will be a lot later and a whole lot worse.

Great leaders design their organizations to hear bad news fast. If we want to know the truth, it's going to take a lot to overcome all of the forces driving the organization toward silence.

DEMAND THE TRUTH

The culture in most organizations instructs people in so many ways that truth-telling will bring them trouble. We have to create an environment in which truth-telling is the norm, and where *not* telling the truth will bring them trouble.

Right off the bat, we can think we're demanding the truth when we are doing anything but. Here are some very poor ways to insist on the truth:

- Require our people to "keep us informed"—Often we define a requirement to tell the truth as "you must tell me everything you know." There is no way any human being with a real job can keep another human being "fully informed" and do any real work at the same time. We'll have more on this in chapter 9.
- Require a fail-safe "early warning" system—Many managers make it clear that if anyone else in the organization hears about bad news before they do, heads will roll. This puts the focus on problem management rather than problem solving.
- Push people to give a clear-cut answer when they just don't know—When we require people to tell us clearly what they don't know clearly, we've changed the definition of truth from "what is really so" to "what I'm supposed to say so you won't hurt me." The freedom to say "I don't know" is a rare but powerful ally.
- Expect detailed incubation reports—Ernest Hemingway said that the best way to take all of the energy out of an idea was to talk about it too much while it's being developed. Creative work, new product or service ideas, ruminating about process changes—all of these require a stretch of time when our people are left alone.
- Review and edit every process—The problems caused by inserting ourselves along the way are many and include causing the truth to be "adjusted" to keep us satisfied (or at least off their backs). By becoming part of the process, we change it. This produces the irony that the more truth we demand along the way, the less truth we will probably have at our destination.
- Browbeat people in front of their peers—We can say, "I was only trying to get them to be honest," but there is a huge difference between demanding the truth and extracting the truth.

We have seen all of the above countless times. If we want a truth-telling organization, we've got to lose these broken tools.

When we demand the truth, we need to let people know that anything less than their best approximation of reality at every point in time is unacceptable. We have to understand that it is hard to speak the truth to power, even as we are adamant that people will be penalized for *not* sharing the truth, rather than for sharing it (as happens in most organizations).

While writing the book *Fatal Illusions*, I discovered a quirk of English: the word "disillusioned" is in the dictionary, but "illusioned" is not (yet). But how can we be disillusioned unless we were first illusioned? The only way to be disillusioned is to have believed something that wasn't completely true or accurate in the first place. We set ourselves up for disillusionment by our steadfast refusal to face the truth.

We have to fight the often-quoted lie that "perception is reality." This gives people a ready-made excuse to shade the truth. After all, isn't truth subjective? There is "your" truth and "my" truth. But although people will act as though their perceptions are reality, they are not. Reality is reality. It is uncompromising, and it will not dance to our tune.

The fact is that there is actual truth out there. Our customers are buying more or less for a reason, employees are coming or going for a reason, we are getting commitment and creativity from our people (or not) for a reason. We may not know the reason, and it may be hard to come to a rough approximation of what is going on (especially if it is a complex reality, affected by multiple drivers, or changing rapidly), but there *are* reasons. Our perceptions are only valuable if they align closely with reality.

How do we go about demanding the truth?

Seek truth from the bottom up. We must eliminate the reviewing and filtering that goes on as information works its way up the "chain of command" (a perfectly descriptive term, as chains bind people). We have to help our leaders understand the difference between reports that add value and reports that remove truth. Finally, it would generally be a good idea to have in the room not only someone who worked on the project (in research terms a "primary source," not just the "secondary sources" of managers in the middle) but also someone who specifically has a lot of objections to whatever is being proposed.

Seek truth from side to side. Most organizations are cluttered with silos or stovepipes that are designed to keep the truth "in here" and the spin "out there." We need to create ways for people in one silo to talk truthfully to people in others. This might be as simple as giving one unit or department a proposal prepared by another and asking, "What do you really like about this?" and "What to you looks incomplete or irrational?" It doesn't matter that it's a marketing document and you're talking to accountants—indeed, the fact that you are talking to people who have not only a different background but perhaps a different personality type is wonderfully conducive to hearing truth.

Get truth to value centers. A huge percentage of decisions in organizations are suboptimal for the simple reason that the people making them don't have access to the truth that is residing in someone out there somewhere. Any time anyone is working on a new idea, our second question (right after, "How are you using this to add or create value?") should be, "Who have you told about this and how are you helping *them* to use it to add or create value?"

Seek truth from the top down. One of the worst transfers of ideas from the military to all other organizations is that people will hear the truth on a "need to know" basis (we'll discuss this more in chapter 9). A communication plan that might be necessary in a military setting, where information leaks could lead to death, mayhem, and global reordering, is clearly not well-suited to a setting in which the exchange of information is critical to the bottom line. One of the deadliest questions ever asked by senior leaders is, "How do we say this to the troops to minimize their reaction?" Why shouldn't we want a reaction? Why shouldn't we want them to panic with us if the news is really bad?

Ask questions about the truth. Where is our market? Where is our market heading in the next five years? What is our face to the customer? What should our face to the customer look like? What's wrong with the way we're delivering results? "To manage in turbulent times . . . means to face up to the new realities," writes Peter Drucker. "It means starting with the question: 'What is the world really like?' "[4]

Never punish truth-telling. We have to be extremely careful not to punish people for telling us the truth. Even worse is to order people to tell the truth and then punish them for telling it. If they tell it badly—ungraciously, in the wrong forum, with the wrong wording—let's correct the deficiency, but let's be careful not to throw out the truth with the package it came in.

HAVE TRUTH FREELY OFFERED

If we want people to offer truth to us freely, we have to create a "safe place for dangerous truth."[5] There are some awful ways to go about getting people to want to tell the truth:

- Pretend to create a safe zone—In the early part of my career, I went to work for a CEO who actually used the word "love" (as in "we want to have a loving environment") in annual reports and meetings. This made people think, "Wow, this company will be a safe place to say what I think." It didn't take long to figure out that "love" meant "if you say anything I don't want to hear I will kill you."
- Bribe—We can try to use external incentives for people to tell the truth. Things like "suggestion boxes" and rewards will never get at the whole truth.
- Extort—Too often we can rely on threats. "If you don't tell me what she said . . . ," People are very creative, and will take many precautions to ensure that they are never put in that position again—and they will resent us for our coercion.

- Make false promises—"If you tell me exactly how you feel about this idea, I'll be in a position to help you in the future." To say something like this, knowing that if the feelings are negative or contradict our own we will be very unhappy with the person and unlikely to help them, is manipulation of the worst sort.
- Offer ways to "take shots" without accountability—Collecting general organizational truth in an anonymous survey can get at truth that would otherwise stay hidden. But letting people fire away at someone who is not in the room and who will not get a chance to counter, for example, is a formula for warfare, not truth-telling.

Instead, we have to put mechanisms in place that will work against the normal inclination of people to tell us what we want to hear or cover up their mistakes. Here are a few ways to coax the truth from your organization.

Invite the dangerous. Instead of keeping the rabble-rousers and "disagreeables" out of meetings, make a special point of inviting them in. The driving question should be, "Who is the person most likely to make us uncomfortable on this topic?" For a board of directors, it might be rephrased: "Who would the CEO least like us to have in for a discussion or presentation?" Then we invite that person and give her "permission to speak freely."

Celebrate the prophets. We have to distinguish between the naysayers and the naythinkers. Some people are pessimistic by nature and like to wallow around in bad news—or gossip or rumors. Some people, though, are thinking about our business all of the time and want to eliminate obstacles to success. "Smart people in any organization who are quick to recognize impending change and cry out early warnings should not be ignored," says Intel's Andy Grove. "Listen to them."[6]

Designate a formal devil's advocate. Whether the person is a regular member of your team or someone assigned to a major program or project, anoint one person to serve as the loyal opposition. Set some ground rules—you can't be petty or disrespectful, your criticism must be presented in a positive or constructive manner—but in the main unleash this person to skewer the team's fatal illusions.[7]

Create "Safe Zones." Give people actual forums where telling the brutal truth graciously is a risk-free proposition. This could be a ten-minute block at the end of certain meetings, or a specially designated section in a formal report.

Share the work and risk of acting on the truth. If people believe that sharing the truth will earn them nothing but more assignments—"I think you're right, so please do X"—we could be in trouble. If they are already overloaded, they have a large incentive to keep quiet.

Perform "Reality Checks." Use interviews or focus groups or surveys to get at the reality of your market, customers, competitors, and people. Compare the results of successive surveys to determine whether you are becoming more or less truth-friendly.[8]

Befriend bad news. One leader defined great leaders as people who have bad news get to their desks fast. We all hate bad news—who wants to hear that we've damaged a customer relationship or lost money?—but we have to make it our friend if we don't want it to slaughter us.

Instruct people on how to identify and tell the truth. Part of getting people to tell the truth freely is helping them to understand what is true and what isn't. Education is an important component of getting at the truth.

Clear out bad thinking. We have to understand what people are saying that they believe to be true but that isn't actually true: the salesperson who is convinced prices are too high when the sales approach is flawed; the manager who believes he needs to replace three people when it's his leadership style that has crippled them; the leader who is convinced that people are cowardly in meetings when it is her blunt interruptions that are shutting conversation down.

THINKING AND RESPONDING PARADOXICALLY

If we just demand the truth but don't create a free-offering zone, we are trying to manage half of this paradox and people won't respond. If we create a free-offering zone but don't make it clear that truth is not optional, the busyness of life combined with natural self-protectiveness will stifle the truth.

We have to create more incentives for telling the truth than for not telling it. The incentives for not telling it are many: past organizational responses, memories of abuse, personal experience where friendships were damaged over an honest conversation, fear of displeasing someone who holds our careers in their hands.

The incentives for telling it have to be many to overcome all of the forces arrayed against it. We have to say to our people, "Here are a dozen things we've done to make it easier for you to tell us the truth—and you *must* tell us."

We should tie our demand for the truth in with our hard work to create a safe-for-truth zone. Whether we are demanding the truth or creating ways to have it freely offered, we have to accept it and use it if we want the flow to continue. Geoffrey Parker reminded us "that military intelligence usually fails not through defective acquisition but through the inability of governments to analyze and accept what has been found."[9]

In this whole truth-telling business, we need to be concerned as leaders about our relationship to praise and blame. If we're in charge, we generally won't have to demand praise; it will be freely offered. But we will have to demand less pleasant truths. We'll have to find ways of asking so that it will become easy and normal for people to tell truth (e.g., "Here are ten leadership traits—please rank them in order of strength to weakness and then tell me five things I can do to improve number 10").

We need to be willing to take blame and disparagement to earn the praise that counts. "He who would acquire fame," wrote William Simms, "must not show himself afraid of censure. The dread of censure is the death of genius." Pythagoras reminded us to "Rest satisfied with doing well, and leave others to talk of you as they please."[10]

One writer notes that, "We live and work in a world where organizational failure is endemic—but where frank, comprehensive dissections of those failures are woefully infrequent; where success is too easily celebrated and failures are too quickly forgotten; where short-term earnings and publicity concerns block us from confronting—much less, learning from—our stumbles and blunders."[11]

The truth we need to know resides in the people who surround us. We can demand that they tell it to us—and make them glad that they did.

CHAPTER 4

ELIMINATE RISK AND TAKE MORE RISKS

If you can keep your head when all about you
Are losing theirs and blaming it on you,
If you can trust yourself when all men doubt you
But make allowance for their doubting too,
If you can wait and not be tired by waiting,
Or being lied about, don't deal in lies,
Or being hated, don't give way to hating,
And yet don't look too good, nor talk too wise: ...
If you can make one heap of all your winnings
And risk it all on one turn of pitch-and-toss,
And lose, and start again at your beginnings
And never breathe a word about your loss;
If you can force your heart and nerve and sinew
To serve your turn long after they are gone,
And so hold on when there is nothing in you
Except the Will which says to them: 'Hold on!'
...Yours is the Earth and everything that's in it.[1]

There is something very appealing about Rudyard Kipling's challenge, especially to people who have worked their way into even an entry level of leadership.

You might say, "I'm a leader, but I don't have any responsibility to manage risk. That's for our general manager, or risk management department, or the CEO." But you would be wrong.

Why? *Because leadership is an inherently risky way to spend your life.*

You exercise authority over people who have a fundamental aversion to having someone exercise authority over them. You have responsibility for people who are vastly unpredictable. You have accountability for things that are outside of your control and perhaps even resistant to your influence. You probably won't have sufficient resources to do an excellent job, but you will be expected to deliver top-level results anyway. And regardless of how well you perform against all of these odds, your ship might be sunk because you don't know the right people—or because the wrong people know you.

Regardless of your level of leadership, you are given an apparently contradictory relationship with risk. You are told to be willing to be counted, stick your neck out, challenge the status quo, step up to the plate. You are also told to mind your Ps & Qs, watch your back, stay out of the line of fire, and avoid rocking the boat. You are told to take more risks, and you are told to eliminate risk.

So this is a very personal paradox. It starts with individuals, and it eventually becomes an organizational contradiction. Many organizations today want "intrapreneurship" and people who will keep them on the cutting edge, even as they teach people to play it safe personally and follow the rules.

To complicate matters, the world we inhabit pushes this contradiction at us. The market clearly rewards risk-takers, and it clearly destroys risk-takers. It rewards the ones who win and destroys the ones who don't. The problem is, we don't know before taking the risk whether we will win or not—or even if our definition of "win" will be the same as the market's or our customers'.

So from every angle, we are encouraged to take more risk and warned against it. If we want to be successful leaders, we need to find a way to do both.

ELIMINATE RISK

We can take steps to eliminate risk that do not actually eliminate risk. Some of these are:

- Warn about risk continually—If we talk about risk too much, we can make taking a risk psychologically and emotionally impossible. These warnings usually concern known (or at least anticipated) risks, but the problem is that they produce a mindset that says "risk is bad." This has the effect of eliminating risk-taking while dramatically increasing the risk of doing nothing. There is a huge difference between eliminating risk and eliminating risk taking.
- Reduce discussion about risk—We can try to convince ourselves that if we stop talking about risk, and talk a lot about being "conservative" and "cautious" and "preserving our market share," that we will reduce risk. Actually, this approach makes the risk we do take less transparent, more ad hoc, and much less likely to benefit from a concentration of resources.
- Rely on spending authority and limitations—We can operate under an illusion that controlling how much people can spend will control the overall level of risk. This is wrong on at least four counts: first, the money that is spent at almost any level can open up the door to unacceptable risk; second, the money can be spent on things that are risk-free (either to the person or the organi-

zation) in the short term but unacceptably risky in the long term; third, the limits can provide a person just enough authority to fail; and fourth, the authority can be voided in practice by people who won't take action until there is a consensus.

- Micromanage to eliminate risky decisions and actions—We can waste inordinate amounts of time and resources, and drive ourselves crazy, trying to eliminate the stray conversation, letter, e-mail, idea, or behavior that might cost us a market advantage or customer. Better to take a few small hits than risk missing a grand prospect.

At the same time, it is crucial that we eliminate risk, so we can have enough risk-taking ability and resources left to serve and grow and profit. So what can we do to eliminate risk intelligently?

Wait. The first and easiest way to eliminate risk is to wait. Intelligent, planned procrastination may be one of our best friends. Typically, the longer we wait, the better our knowledge and experience and perspective. "[O]nce we act, we forfeit the option of waiting until new information comes along. As a result, not-acting has value. The more uncertain the outcome, the greater may be the value of procrastination."[2] We may risk losing an opportunity by waiting, but often (as uninteresting as it might be) waiting is the best way to manage risk.

Stop worrying about being a "first mover." We might get "first mover" advantage by being first to market, but we might lose more on some "first mover" tries than we will ever regain with a "first mover" win. The cost of creating an entirely new product, service, or market can be incredibly high. But even more to the point, most "first mover" tries fail: "The truth is, the failure to consistently produce dramatic and successful innovations [is a] comment on the nature of innovation itself. . . . It's tough to score once, much less repeatedly."[3]

Define and avoid unnecessary risks. We also have to eliminate all risk that is unnecessary. What is an "unnecessary" risk? It is any risk that:

- Does not clearly pertain to a core excellency, or make a significant improvement in a core competency, regardless of the "numbers"
- Cannot produce a substantial return, after a sizable allowance for all of the unexpected costs is factored in
- Relates to an opportunity so small that any resources spent on it could be better spent on a number of other ideas
- Cannot be reduced to acceptable levels through the acquisition of more knowledge or competence (i.e., cannot be brought more under our control over time)
- Cannot be managed effectively by the available staff or with the available resources or infrastructure
- Has the potential for serious and unacceptable collateral damage (e.g., attractiveness to investors, damage to brand, loss of credibility, hit to morale, etc.) if the risk fails

Plan for the possibility of unintended reactions. We know from physics that every action produces an equal and opposite reaction. And the reaction may truly be entirely contrary to our expectations. As a military historian wrote of the bloody battle for Italy in World War II, "The crux of the great dilemma facing . . . the Allies in Italy was one that plagued the Allies throughout the war: namely that the Germans usually failed to do what the Allies assumed they would."[4] The only safe assumption is that our competitors and others who are affected will react differently from our expectations. Only then can we prepare intelligently. "This is the essence of risk aversion—that is, how far we are willing to go in making decisions that may provoke others to make decisions that will have adverse consequences for us."[5] We can eliminate many risks simply by inaction, by not moving others out of a state of inertia and creating a momentum that does not currently exist.

Clearly delineate—in advance—what can't be done without clearance. We can't define all of the risks that are *proper,* but we can define all of the risks that are *unacceptable.* By taking the time to do this, we create clear "fences," within which our people can take personal and professional risk safely and with a high degree of confidence and creativity. We need to create safety nets to increase people's willingness to take risk, and one of the best safety nets is a clear understanding of the boundaries.

Reduce the threat of personal loss associated with risk taking. Studies have shown that people are not so much risk-averse as they are loss-averse. This means we have to reduce the fear of loss associated with risk. We need to put limits around potential losses and then make those limits transparent to our people. We might say, for example, "If this program falls short of our goal of a 10 percent increase but gives us at least 5 percent, we will keep the program intact and let your team lead the refinement effort." Such statements involve our people in the world of uncertainty and the understanding of risk while reducing the threat that their projects or teams or positions will disappear if their first attempt at a risk does not produce the level of results they anticipate.

TAKE MORE RISK

We need everyone taking more risk. Because of this need, we can find ourselves doing things that appear to be opening everyone up to taking more risk when they are really doing quite the opposite. What are some of those things?

- Highlight and associate risk taking with certain functions—We can't just limit risk taking to new product or service risks. When we talk about that as though it is the "real" risk, we diminish all other kinds.
- Highlight and associate risk taking with certain people or groups—We have "risk management" departments, as though we have any departments that *aren't* managing risks.

- Encourage people to take risks only when they have knowledge—We tend to do what we know, because that is in our comfort zone. The problem is that valuable risk is often beyond what we know and way out of our comfort zone.
- Encourage people to take risks only where they have competence—We also tend to do what we can do well. This is effective if we are trying to maintain value but ineffective if we are trying to create it.
- Encourage people to take risks that won't bring criticism—Most of us tend to do things that don't get criticized. The problem is that the things that are most worthy of being done are also the most likely to be criticized. Criticism doesn't mean we have a great idea, but the absence of criticism often means we don't.

Instead, we should push people to do "scary" stuff—things that are outside their current knowledge and competence. How can we do this?

Redefine "accountability." In general, people think of "accountability" as being responsible for getting results while following the rules and not making any mistakes. We need to redefine it as being responsible for getting improving results, while following the nonfoolish rules and not making any unnecessary mistakes, and while breaking all of the foolish rules that lower value and making all of the necessary mistakes that raise it. Accountability must include taking risk, not just delivering error-free results.

Ask people regularly what risky items they have on their agendas. Only a few of these ideas will prove to have any long-lasting value, but they have to have a number of them in process at any point in time if anything is going to result. They might take a chance on a new relationship risk (trying new connections with other leaders or functions or departments), a new content risk (changing the level or type of services being offered), a new delivery method (changing how internal or external customers access our offering), or a new process risk (such as removing questionable steps from the system). Whatever the case, we need to consider possibilities we haven't considered before, or we're not taking enough collective risk.

Ensure that people evaluate the benefit of taking a risk. Encourage people to ask, "Even though I am comfortable taking this risk, is this risk worth taking (or is it the best risk we could take)?"

Train people to think in terms not only of the cost of proceeding but also of the cost of delay. Many of the supposed risks of proceeding are merely conjecture, ghosts stirred up by an overactive imagination. But many of the costs of delay— lost opportunity, lost ability to define a market, lost sales, lost momentum, lost competitive advantage, lost relationships—are very real and heartbreakingly destructive.

Use questions to measure the amount of risk people are taking. "What are the three riskiest things you have taken on in the past year?" "What is the riskiest thing you are working on right now?" "What three things do you plan to take a risk on in the coming year?" Assessments, both formal and informal, can confirm whether risks are actually being taken.

Define risk templates. We're reluctant to take risk where our knowledge or competence is fragile. Daniel Ellsberg calls this "ambiguity aversion." But we need to be willing to make decisions and take actions based on limited information. All decisions involve risk, but at some point the increase in certainty that will come from an increase in information is too small to justify the delay. Where is that point? It will vary from situation to situation, but outstanding leaders work with their people to define templates: "In this kind of situation, as soon as you know these four things you have enough information to move ahead."

Gain knowledge to improve risk-taking ability. The question we should ask is not, "With what I know, am I comfortable with taking this risk?" Instead, we should ask, "Are there potentially valuable risks that we are not currently knowledgeable enough to be comfortable taking? If so how do we increase our knowledge?" Knowledge reduces fear and creates a willingness to take risk. Our first push shouldn't be, "we need to take more risk around here," but rather, "we need to learn more in this area so we can freely take more risk there."

Define and welcome "necessary" mistakes. We can think in terms of mistakes being "reasonable" or "unreasonable," but such assessments are highly subjective. More valuable is to think about "necessary" and "unnecessary" mistakes. There are some key questions: Is the possibility of making this mistake integral to progress? Will we learn more from making the mistake than from not making it? Will the mistake itself be a potential source of progress and profit?

Without risk taking, there is no modern world. And without it, there will be no modern organization.

THINKING AND RESPONDING PARADOXICALLY

There are some important questions to ask about risk before we decide to take it or eliminate it. These are valuable whether we're taking personal, "close-in" risk or organizational, "out-there" risk.

- *Is there the possibility of adding enough value to justify the risk?* Even if this decision or action will add some value, will it be enough? If it is just a small potential gain, the risk of change is probably not worth it. If we can't see a five times return (knowing that at least half will evaporate during implementation), we should be very hesitant about taking the risk. One of the myths of continuous improvement is that everything should be improved. Some things are simply not worth improving.
- *What is the return horizon?* Even if we can see a return for the risk, is that return close enough to the present to make its achievement a probability? The longer the time before the return is realized, the more difficulty can arise — from implementation issues, changes in capacities or capabilities, shifts in market or customer expectations, and so on.

- *Will our customers care about the added value?* If we offer additional value, will anyone care? We can improve specifications and performance, but if the cost is so high or the improvements so undesirable to our clients that no one will pay us for these things, we have just made a very poor bet.

The answers to these questions are unique to each organization. A different organization, with different core excellencies and competencies and incompetencies, might come to very different answers. The important thing is to have a dialogue with our teams and to come to the best approximation of the future we can. Failure is not having the dialogue.

Another way to take more calculated risks is to eliminate the unnecessary risks that surround our proposed action. Every new path has core risk that cannot be eliminated, but that risk is amplified when we don't address contextual risk that can be reduced or eliminated. To launch a new product is risky, but it would be foolish to risk it without full assessment of probable customer response, likely competitor reaction, potential operational or cost variables, or needed infrastructure to support it. "Of two things we cannot sufficiently beware," said the great German philosopher Goethe, "of obstinacy if we confine ourselves to our proper field, of inadequacy if we desert it."[6]

The essence of risk management lies in maximizing the areas where we have some control over the outcome, while minimizing the areas where we have absolutely no control over the outcome (and the linkage between effect and cause is hidden from us).[7]

So we find that this paradox leads us toward some significant couplets:

- Necessary vs. unnecessary risk—Necessary risk must be taken because of the vision and mission we have set for ourselves. We have to be prepared to take it if we expect to achieve our dreams and goals. Unnecessary risk is avoidable risk, risk that is not integral to our drive to fulfill our vision and mission. We have to be prepared to avoid it if we expect to achieve our targeted dreams and goals.
- Manageable vs. unmanageable risk—Because of our knowledge or experience or time to research, some risks are manageable. When we are missing the necessary knowledge or experience and cannot significantly influence the outcome, the risk is unmanageable.
- Core risk vs. contextual risk—Core risk is essential—it can't be avoided if the decision or action is taken. If the reward is worthy, we should always be open to taking more core risk. Contextual risk is risk that can be managed, reduced, or avoided by investigation, analysis, and time. It has great potential to make the total risk unacceptable.

We need to take necessary risks that are manageable and essential to our core mission and eliminate unnecessary risks that are unmanageable and contextual.

One way to eliminate poor risk is to focus the organization on more high-quality risks. In a competitive world, we might have resources for fewer tries, so we'd better try more radical things. Because many attempts won't work or will produce suboptimal results, we need to push beyond the ordinary, where the real profits lie, with the attempts that we do make.

Taking or eliminating risk is in large part a question of timing. If the risk of delay is greater than the risk of moving ahead, we should move. If the risk of moving ahead is greater, we should procrastinate. We need to place the risk in the right "time zone"—the place in time where, because of our greater knowledge or experience or certainty or opportunity, the risk is at its nadir and its potential reward is at its highest level—or at least where the difference between the two is significant.

After the analysis is done, much of this is intuitive and requires the best judgment of our people: Do we hire this person or team before or after getting the new contract? Do we replace this product before or after its predecessor has lost ground? Should we make this acquisition before or after we introduce our related new services? We need the collective wisdom of the team to go beyond analysis and know when to place our bets. "'A model ... doesn't necessarily get you to the truth.' Eventually, math stalls out and something more human— intuition, experience, wisdom—has to take charge."[8]

Another way to act paradoxically is to take more of the smaller risks that can eventually be parlayed into greater risks with a credible "history." For example, General Electric took "an entrepreneurial gamble on a small hospital ... it contracted to maintain all of the equipment and guaranteed the hospital that it would save money. Once it succeeded, GE Medical was able to go to potential customers with a track record."[9]

We can break big programs into phases and sell them a phase at a time, learning from the first phase how to make both later phases and other programs better and lower risk. We can get experience on cutting-edge products or services on a small scale before betting the farm. At these levels, we can even afford to offer a contract or price reduction if specified results aren't achieved and a premium or bonus if they are.

Remember the "rule of the 90 and the 10." Roughly 90 percent of the population is oriented more toward certainty and security than toward ambiguity and risk. In spite of the sense that we live in a mobile world, 90 percent of the people on the planet live within 100 miles of where they were born. In the United States, arguably the most entrepreneurial large country in history, 90 percent of the people work for someone else. This means that we must use the 10 percent who are built to be out on the ledge to prompt and push the 90 percent who are cautiously considering whether they should even open the window, and we have to use the 90 percent who are more realistically assessing the dangers to challenge and restrain the 10 percent who think they can fly.

Finally, we have to talk about risk and fear. *Good* fear makes us ask questions, do research, root around until we find the truth, make sure we know what the scope and scale of the risk really is. *Bad* fear causes us to respond emotionally, react instinctively, trade analysis for action or inaction, and exaggerate the likely damage.

We manage the fear associated with risk by looking not only at the possible injury but also the likelihood that this injury will come to pass. "Fear of harm ought to be proportional not merely to the gravity of the harm, but also to the probability of the event."[10]

Leaders are paid to be the voice of courage, the ones who pull their troops out of the trenches and on to the next objective. They have to be willing to take more, bigger, and more radical risks—but always risks that have real opportunity to deliver substantial results. And with relentless focus, they have to eliminate everything else.

CHAPTER **5**

FOCUS ON RESULTS
AND IGNORE RESULTS

The secret to success is constancy to purpose.[1]

—*Benjamin Disraeli*

Results.

Sales. Profits. Growth. Circulation. Wins. Goals. Runs. Touchdowns.

Even if we're not competitive by nature, we would be hard pressed to deny that the market demands results. Political leaders are rated by historians. Sports leaders are rated by journalists on their win–loss records and other stats. Business leaders are rated by analysts not on how their organizations change but on whether their organizations deliver good and growing results during their tenure. We may want to know about their leadership style and principles, their thinking, their vision, their strategy, their competitive drive—but only if they win.

Results are what we talk about, and for this reason it seems as though we're focusing on them. But in the real world there is very little actual focus on results, from "performance evaluations" at the individual level to progress reports at the organizational level. And because of this, most of the world falls miserably short of achieving meaningful outcomes.

Some individuals *really* focus on results. We define them, write about them, have meetings to discuss them (and dissect those who are not achieving them), offer rewards to those who achieve them and punishments to those who don't. We hammer away, but seldom does our hammering drive any nails home. We talk and talk about double-digit growth, but don't get close to it. We make reduced turnover a corporate objective, and it doesn't go down. We tell our mid- and front-line leaders that we want to see more energy and enthusiasm in the staff, but the place still feels the same. Somehow, focusing on results doesn't get the job done.

What's the problem? If we don't focus on results, we fail, but if we focus on results, we fail. There must be a systematic way to achieve the results we need, and this paradox provides that way.

FOCUS ON RESULTS

One of the most amazing things to observe in organizations is how quickly and thoroughly any focus on results evaporates. Midlevel and front-line managers, often lacking any real sense of what leadership intends, miss any message about results that is sent down from the top. When we want to counteract this lack of concentration, we often take actions that seem to focus on results while missing the mark widely. We are not focusing on results when we:

- Prioritize people's work—Reordering someone's "to-do" list is a lot different from focusing on results.
- Confuse action with results—When we say, "Somebody had better get some things done around here," we may introduce a flurry of activity, but any connection to results may be purely coincidental. People will focus on the things they can get their hands on—process, methods, tasks, controls, policies, and procedures.
- Confuse process with results—It is very easy to assume that efficiency will lead to effectiveness, but that connection is remote. At its worst, it is managing by nitpicking. We do this because we forget that a perfectly executed plan is worthless if it planned for the wrong things. History is full of examples of well-conceived military programs that missed victory on the battlefield—ultimately, the only truly important result.
- Treat urgencies like they're results—When people are ignoring results, they focus on whatever is urgent, whatever is burning a hole in their desks at the moment. The boss has asked for some information. No matter that he's asked five other people for the same thing and that none of the answers will help him add value. He's the boss. Important activities will have to wait.
- Confuse stated importance with results—In an organization with any size, there are a (probably growing) number of activities that are important to someone but worthless to the organization's results. In an organization with any maturity, there are a number of activities that were once important for achieving results, but something—the market, the customer, the product or service—has changed, and there has not been a corresponding change to our activities.

We have to reconnect old ideas and actions that are no longer closely tied to results in the world in which we are now living. For example, for a lot longer than most organizations even survive, Sears and Montgomery Ward produced outstanding results through their mail-order catalogues. No organization had better potential to capture the currently burgeoning trend of ordering products online. Only the methods—a computer screen instead of a catalog, an online order form sent by a click instead of a paper order form sent by post—changed. With a focus on process rather than results, these organizations let new competitors stake out the online market.

However, there are some actions we can take to effectively focus our organizations on results. To focus on results, we can:

Distinguish between results and targets. A result is something on which we stake our future. To satisfy our customers, to beat our competitors, to keep our best employees—whatever—we need to do X or Y or Z. A result has the force of reward and failure behind it. It is nonnegotiable. A result is a need. A target, on the other hand, is something that could enhance our future but isn't core to that future. Targets give the organization an edge and incentives. A target is a want. We might target 15 percent growth in a product or service line. We'll be happy to get it and thrilled to share the extra with those who helped. But we expect 10 percent growth and define that as a primary result. If we don't get the 10 percent result, we will start looking for people to share the pain.

Make sure the results we focus on will achieve our vision. We might focus on incremental market share growth and fail to realize that the future market will be in different products, as producers of 35-mm cameras and film discovered during the digital camera revolution. A military historian has noted that most generals focus on occupying enemy territory, which may be irrelevant to the goal of securing a more lasting peace. Great generals focus on a single result: to break their enemy's will to resist.[2]

Get agreement on the results. There is no way to focus on results as an organization unless 95 percent of our people understand, agree with, have prioritized and aligned their jobs with, and are actually working toward those results. Focus means that everyone is unwilling to be distracted by the countless items that can demand their attention.

Insist that people connect organizational results with their results. As leaders in organizations, we've got to make clear to people what results are needed, and then we have to work with them to develop group and individual goals that are aligned with the top-level results we are seeking.

Replace "roles and responsibilities" job descriptions. It might be possible to have a process and documents that are more distracting to individual performance, but it's hard to imagine. Why not *"results* and responsibilities?" The potential cumulative effect of everyone in the organization thinking about results is colossal.

Provide incentives to focus on results. We're not just talking about performance-based compensation, which can have some positive effect on focusing people's attention on results. In addition, the results we have defined need to be meaningful to our people. The key, of course, is focusing on results that are actionable (our people can do something about these) and valuable (if we hit the mark, new value is added or created). Worthy results have value for customers and clients and people we are trying to serve—results that our people can influence.

Make it clear that results are not optional. Leaders who focus on results and find ways to get their organizations to do the same are very likely to get what they expect. "Nothing so focuses a man's attention," noted Samuel Johnson, "as the prospect of being hanged."

Peter Drucker has recently said that one of the most important questions we can ask is, "What results were you hired to produce?" The number of people in most organizations who can answer this question at all, much less accurately, is astoundingly low.

IGNORE RESULTS

One of the great ironies of organizational life is that we can get our organizations so focused on results that they don't achieve them.

We have to get people's eyes off the finish line and get them to think about what they need to do this day, this week, this month, this quarter. If they are worrying about quota, it will be hard for them to do the things they need to do to achieve quota. If they are worrying about failure, it will be hard for them to take the necessary steps to have a smashing success. We can't have our minds cluttered with deliverables in assorted shapes and sizes. We've got to be able to ignore results.

But there are some terrible ways to ignore results that we have to drive from our repertoire:

- Develop results attention deficit disorder—In far too many organizations, no one has the attention span to keep long-term expected results in view at all.
- Sacrifice future results—If we're not careful, we can drive out any organizational ability to focus on long-term results. If people aren't given time and reason to focus on long-term results, they will be very much ignored.
- Keep the big picture private—Many managers take the position that people "down the line" don't need to know the organization's overall strategy or expected deliverables. "They'll be told what they need to know to contribute to the cause." But this lack of transparency disconnects people from results—people can't get excited about hitting what they don't know exists. Besides, managers don't have enough information to make all of the connections.
- Keep people "on task"—People who are overwhelmed can't think about results very well. When people can't get their arms around how to achieve results, they revert to the near and real. They focus on procedures and policies and duties and prescribed methods and limitations. By default, they're ignoring results, but not in a way that adds value to the organization.

We need to learn to ignore results productively, to get our people to stop looking at the top of the mountain long enough to take the next step along the dangerous path that leads to the summit.

What can we do to ignore results productively?

Define critical success factors (CSFs). Critical success factors are actions that move us toward the results (Key Performance Indicators—KPIs) we have defined. If we haven't agreed on critical success factors, we have no chance to allocate resources to them or concentrate forces around them. In the absence of this conversation, a huge portion of an organization's wealth is simply poured out on the ground. What do CSFs look like? For our clients struggling with high turnover, a critical success factor is to define motivation in a new way—turnover is more a matter of daily "incentives within the job" than of compensation. For the Department of Labor in New York state, under pressure to get trainees to show up for third-shift jobs, a critical success factor was to schedule the training at the same time as the shift—if trainees were willing to show up for the odd-hour training, they were more likely to show up for the odd-hour job. For baseball hall-of-fame pitcher Sandy Koufax, a critical success factor was to throw a strike on the first pitch—opponents' batting averages dropped dramatically when he got ahead of them on the count.[3]

Clearly connect CSFs to results. We need to help everyone see how excellent execution of CSFs will deliver or exceed the desired results, partly so they will be motivated to work on them, and partly so they can let us know if our connection is weak.

Measure and manage CSFs. If the connection of our selected CSFs to our desired KPIs is clear, we can focus on the CSFs and ignore the results.

Do "gut checks" on our CSFs. We should regularly evaluate the correlation between our CSFs and our KPIs. We can only safely ignore results if we know we are focusing on the things that produce those results. One of our clients had been sure that shorter lead times was an important CSF for customer satisfaction and sales growth, spent a lot of money shortening the process, and then found that their desired results didn't materialize. Another client had been certain that their product quality was a nonnegotiable CSF, worked to produce the most technically excellent product in their industry, and found that most of their customers were largely indifferent—inferior products worked just as well.

Remove "results anxiety." Our people need to know that we don't expect them to worry about results. That will only cause them to make poor decisions. We want them to worry about whether they are doing everything necessary, everything that is actionable, right now.

Great leaders and organizations learn how to ignore results, as those results are not actionable. Only CSFs are actionable.

THINKING AND RESPONDING PARADOXICALLY

We need to get our organizations and our people focused on results, but not so they (and we) can spend a lot of our time and energy thinking about those results, meeting to discuss them, and beating people for missing them.

Here's the problem. We have a KPI meeting to get everyone focused on the results we're expecting. We lay them out. Everyone seems to understand and agree (not very likely, but hey, they're all nodding and smiling pleasantly). But we don't talk about what our people need to do to achieve those results.

Without that discussion, everyone walks out into a real world that will not improve their chances of achieving the results we've just discussed. The actual world—full of ignorance and incompetence and distractions and bases to be covered and roles and responsibilities and other duties as assigned—overwhelms their efforts even to consider *how* to achieve the results.

So we've sent them out, thinking about results, talking about results, worrying about results. They know they need to achieve them, or else. But they don't know how. They don't know how to connect what they're doing to the results we've discussed. They know enough to be afraid but too little to be successful.

The alternative is to have a CSF meeting to identify actions our people can take to achieve the KPIs.

We can also focus on results to get organizational agreement and alignment about what is important. We have to agree where we're going or we're doomed not to get there. The Roman philosopher Seneca said, "If you don't know where you're going, any road will take you there." Then we can tie the results we want to achieve to the activities that will bring those results to pass.

Once we define critical success factors, we have to ensure that resources are allocated primarily to those factors. Everything else is white noise. We forget KPI meetings and start having CSF meetings. Are we making acceptable progress on our CSFs? Do they have enough resources and attention? What is distracting us from our CSFs, and how do we annihilate those distractions?

The goal is results, but we have to remind ourselves how focusing on them is only a small part of actually achieving them. Measuring CSFs (and their supporting drivers) and taking "as-you-go" corrective action is the only way to assure that our goals are met (and we need to remember that "drivers" does not mean methods or processes). Measuring our CSFs/drivers lets us know if our KPIs are working, while measuring our outcomes (KPIs) lets us know if we have the right CSFs.

And then, after we've made all of the necessary connections, we ignore results. Their real value to the organization's decisions and actions and nonactions is finished.

Results have two purposes. One is to provide a scorecard for our stakeholders—this is what they expect, this is what we'll deliver. The other is to define a destination and guide us into what we need to do to reach it.

Perhaps I want to lose a certain amount of weight and get to a certain sustainable weight. I might feel very motivated to attain the goal I have set, especially if the weight loss goal is tied to issues of health. My CSF could be never to eat more than 1800 calories per day. I can focus on this CSF right now, as I am eating a portion that brings me to 1750 for the day, and use my knowledge of this daily limit to guide me to stop. If I do this long enough, I will gradually but relentlessly lose weight. When I waver, my very large motivator—the long-term result—is still there to remind me. But no one ever lost weight by defining a weight result and then doing business as usual.

To be sure, we should periodically hold meetings to evaluate whether our CSFs are directly connected to the results we need or targets we want. Such meetings are not for the purpose of reviewing or changing our KPIs. We assume those targets are defined and clear and generally understood and worthy. Instead, CSF meetings should be called to review the alignment of CSFs and results. If we are advancing as agreed on our CSFs and still not achieving our results the solution is not to work "harder" or "smarter." The solution is to stop and see whether we have the right CSFs—or the right measurements of those CSFs.

At least once or twice a month, everyone should be asked four essential questions:

1. What are the primary results we can expect you to deliver?
2. What are the secondary results that we can expect you to deliver?
3. What are your CSFs?
4. How will you interact with others to ensure the delivery of your results?

Let's look at each of these items in turn.

Primary Results

Why do we even need this person or team or department or business unit? Why should they exist inside our organization and absorb capital? There should be from two to five critical deliverables.

Secondary Results

What should they do if they have additional resources and these secondary activities won't distract from their primary results? This is a lower-order set of deliverables.

CSFs

What are the things they must do to deliver their primary and secondary results?

Interaction

How are they going to work with others to achieve their CSFs and a direct line of sight to our results? How do we manage consensus so it doesn't get out of hand? How do we take advantage of diversity of thought?

"We collaborate by forming agreements," Stewart Levine wrote. "Usually, the cause of conflict is the lack of clear agreement. Either we did not take the time or we did not know what we needed to talk about to craft an effective, explicit agreement. . . . I believe everyone would benefit greatly if we embraced the idea of creating agreements for results and stopped negotiating agreements for protection."[4] If we get agreement on results, we can put the agreement in the drawer and go to work on doing the things that will deliver those results.

Leaders who manage through the power of paradox never take their eye off results—except when they ignore them.

CHAPTER 6

LEAD WITH THE HEAD AND LEAD WITH THE HEART

Method is much, technique is much, but inspiration is even more.[1]

—*Benjamin Nathan Cardozo*

In many organizations—in many people—there is a huge divide between rational and emotional leadership.

Good thinking and decision-making must include the best of both the intuitive and analytical points of view.

A double illusion could be operating in our organizations: Some may believe that consistently excellent results can be achieved without a commitment to process, whereas others believe that process alone can always produce the best results. We need to adjust our mindsets and eliminate the false either–or approach that tells us to rely on either intuition or analysis. Rather than "leading the business and managing the people," we need to manage the business and lead the people. We manage the business by leading with our heads, and we lead the people with our hearts.

LEAD WITH THE HEAD

It doesn't take a close reading of history to see that the absence of method and empirical analysis and reason has not been a friend of humanity. Ignorance (often willful), superstition, myths, tribal passions, group delusions, prejudice, and self-destructive greed have dominated eras and cultures. Leading with the head in the political, economic, social, technological, and organizational spheres has brought astonishing advance.

At the same time, there are some fairly stupid ways to lead with the head:

- Insist that everything be "fact-based"—We often don't have all of the facts (or at least some of the critical facts). It is arrogant to assume that everything can be driven by rational analysis and numbers when we often don't know how to make a complete analysis or are missing key numbers.
- Hold babies accountable to adult standards—Although rigorous analysis is generally a good thing, when we apply the same analytical standards to embryonic ideas that we apply to existing and long-standing programs, we are missing the mark widely.
- Value process over people—It's probably hard to have industrial and scientific revolutions and not get infatuated with their impressive knowledge and power. We need to remember that it was people that created the nuts and bolts of those revolutions. Selling people short is a good way to stop selling anything.
- Believe that everything that's important can be measured—Some of the biggest decisions leaders make either can't be measured at all or can only be measured indirectly by long-term results. Casting aside the important things that can't be analyzed is a common means of corporate suicide.
- Allow rationally skilled people into leadership positions—Early in my career in the corporate world, I watched as highly skilled engineers and scientists became highly incompetent managers. The arguments—"they're the only ones who understand the business," "they're smart and can learn," "we want to reward our best performers," "they're the only ones that people will respect"—are worse than wrong, they're foolish. If people don't know how to lead with the heart, they don't know how to lead.
- Abandon useful myths and traditions—We could assume that everything that can't be fully explained isn't worth keeping around. We would be wrong. There are many things that make us "us" but that cannot be defended on rational or financial grounds.

In contrast, a lot more "leading with the head" would do many organizations well. What are some effective ways to lead with the head?

Get widespread understanding. We constantly find senior leadership teams that don't even have a shared understanding of the *terms* they are using. "Strategy," for example, can mean everything from budgeting and resource allocation to visionary brainstorming. People say, "let's not get hung up on words," when that is the very thing they need to take time to do.

Secure alignment. People can understand a purpose without aligning themselves with it. Once, we were meeting with a senior leader to review a survey that would go out to all employees and that included this statement: "I am passionate about the vision of the company." We had asked people to rate the statement from "strongly agree" to "strongly disagree." The leader stopped us midreview. His comment? "Perhaps we should include a copy of our vision along with the assessment survey." At that point, we somehow knew that we didn't have to include this statement in our assessment survey to know how low it would be rated. After some dialogue, another leader suggested that it might be a good idea to include the vision in new employee orientation. These were great people who really wanted to see their organization go to the next level of success. But they struggled to understand how vision could possibly connect to "hard" business issues.

Honor process and analysis. If the results of a process or analysis are not respected, the entire system loses integrity and decisions will be considered illegitimate. A midlevel leader at one of our clients summarized a widespread frustration by saying, "I wish people wouldn't throw out the analysis just because they don't like the outcome." When a process or analysis is initiated by leadership, a clear directive should be given: all data—even those that might derail the project—must be included. For process to be honored, it will be necessary to debate vigorously and come to hard-fought consensus.

Handle exceptions thoroughly. When a process or analysis is overridden, a simple, one-page summary about "why" should be sent to all stakeholders. When more data or information are requested, a simple, one-page summary about "why" should be issued. Where the process is deemed faulty, a simple, one-page summary about the observed defects should be issued to all stakeholders. One client summarized widespread frustration: "In most cases, if we would just let the process work we would get high-quality decisions, but we tend to interrupt and frequently override it."

Establish a corporate philosophy that the biggest and riskiest decisions will get the most comprehensive level of analysis. This means in practice that the biggest decisions would in general have the most people involved, and that most of the smallest decisions would be made by individuals with no further review or approval required. Washington Mutual involves as many as one hundred frontline people in choosing targets and getting a fair price.

Create opportunities to challenge intuition at the extreme. Leadership should be especially careful to create opportunities for people to challenge a decision that overrides a direction clearly identified by the established process ("I know what the data say, but I think we should. . ."). This might take the form of direct dialogue. The direct approach can be effective only if the leadership opens up career-safe conversation and shows that it is comfortable with conflict. Alternatively, everyone with a stake in the decision could be invited to a "Mavericks' Meeting," where everyone is allowed to question or challenge a decision. All concerns should be included in a section of the final report to senior leadership.

Leading with the head means that we never leave reason out of the equation, even as we avoid making it the whole equation. We should lead with the head by using it as a thinking tool, not a battering ram.

LEAD WITH THE HEART

Success—the bottom-line result we desire—depends on the power of leading with the heart. However, there are some really poor ways to lead with the heart:

- Rely on gut feel—Decisions that can't be explained to intelligent people are not likely to be supported. They are also not very likely to be right.
- Ignore some or all of the facts—How many new ventures are begun with a lot of heart—but no plan or hope of success? Too often, when someone says, "I'm going with my heart on this," they mean "I'm going to do this no matter what anyone says, so don't confuse me with the facts." This is a stubborn act of the will, not a gutsy act of the heart.
- Defend irrationality—When we've made a decision contrary to all sound thinking and it doesn't work out, we don't improve the situation by defending our poor decision with the lame explanation that "it felt like the right thing to do at the time."
- Replace substance with cheerleading—Samuel Johnson was right: patriotism is the last refuge of a scoundrel. Likewise, when we have no plan or a bad plan, and simply try to get people "pumped up to do something," we are leading with trumpery, not with heart.
- Use emotional blackmail—What we are proposing is marginal or worse, but we use appeals to sentiment to get people to accept it. This is an abuse of good-natured people. "I need you to do this for me," "we go way back," "I hope I can count on you to watch my back," "if you care about the team you'll support me on this." It's done all the time, and it should be against the law.
- Push people to make decisions too soon—As leaders, we know we need to drive the organization, and we can be very impatient for action and results. This can cause us to push people to "go with your gut," even when they aren't procrastinating but are really waiting for important facts to come in.

It is too easy to run with a current enthusiasm when that's all we've got. Remember Churchill's definition of a zealot: one who's redoubled his effort when he's forgotten his goal.

So how *should* we lead with the heart?

Start with people. Leading with the heart tells us that getting people who care and commit eliminates the need for "management" and opens the door to better results. "Getting the right people in the right jobs is a lot more important than developing a strategy," wrote Jack Welch.[2]

Build around values. Shared values, and the mutual understanding and trust that go with them, can replace mounds of policies and procedures and regulations. Leaders often dismiss their importance and, in so doing, dismiss themselves as leaders. Geoffrey Colvin writes that "coalescing around shared values becomes a logical, effective organizing principle." He adds that many "now seem to understand that they will find competitive advantage by tapping employees' most essential humanity, their ability to create, judge, imagine, and build relationships."[3] "The reason people come to work for GE," said CEO Jeffrey Immelt, "is that they want to be about something that is bigger than themselves . . . to work for a company that makes a difference."[4]

Invite intuition into the process. Participants in decision making should invite into the process the intuition of leaders or others who can add value. This activity could be done along the way (guidance is sought before further work is done), or at the end (the decision-making process has not clearly identified the direction that should be taken). We should look for opportunities and invite a high level of wisdom, experience, and passion into the equation.

Use intuition on the "close calls." The goal is to eliminate the idea that "intuition is a necessary evil" and to incorporate intuition formally into the process, where the data are overwhelming and analysis leaves us with no clear answer. This would require narrowing the field of decisions brought to senior leadership from "all decisions" or "slam dunks" to those in which the decision is very complex or fuzzy (one of our clients termed these the "Solomon decisions").

Differentiate between using our instincts when the facts can't be completely known, and using our instincts in lieu *of the facts.* It is generally bad practice to make a decision before we have to, especially when analysis and debate are incomplete.

Understand the difference between the nonrational *and the* irrational. The nonrational includes such excellent commodities as faith, belief, hope, confidence, intuition, investment, and commitment. The irrational includes illusion, delusion, reality-impairment, willful ignorance, wishful thinking, greed, and bravado.

Set our hearts tenaciously on nothing less than victory. "There is one out of ten," wrote ancient Chinese philosopher Lao-Tzu, "who is so full of life, they say, that even wild tigers and rhinos avoid him, and their claws and horns do not know where to injure him, nor do weapons of war know where to kill him. How can this be? Because he has no death to die."[5] We lead with the heart well when we act with tenacity and dogged determination, when the failure that is staring us in the face is simply not an option.

The former president of the Disney Channel advised us, "The key ingredient in any decision-making process: passion. If you let passion inform your decisions, you'll make good ones."[6]

THINKING AND RESPONDING PARADOXICALLY

We need *intelligent intuition.* We need to understand that leading with the heart is most effective when our intuition is grounded in hard-headed analysis.

In the early days of our consulting practice, we had several key slots to fill to round out our core team. We did all of the required rational analysis. We defined the jobs and the results we needed from them. We wrote crisp advertisements, scoured hundreds of resumes, interviewed dozens of candidates, and after our usual deliberate approach worked its way to completion, found two people we wanted to bring on board. Some major work was about to come our way, which made our need for both people even greater. The only problems: we didn't have a contract for the work before we had to make the hiring decision, and we had already set a guideline that we would only hire each additional person *after* we had generated X dollars of additional revenue.

I knew these were the right people to invite in and that we needed them to do the new work, and I knew that if we didn't invite them in soon we would lose them. My head still had plenty of reservations, all of them logical, but my heart said "go!" We brought them on board and had a functioning system before the new projects came through the door.

Conversely, we need to understand that leading with the head is most effective when our reason is animated by our intuition. A good idea is dramatically more powerful when it is encased in fire.

In the example of our hiring decision, because we had excitement about future growth, felt that our time had come, and were thrilled to have these people available, we did our homework. We ran and reran the numbers. We reconsidered our revenue-versus-hiring guideline. We put the best of who we were on winning the new projects. We had the passion to do the intellectual work to support our decision.

This is the pattern for intelligent intuition. As much as possible, we think through what we need. We collect data and information. We filter and sort, getting down to the relevant facts and filling in any gaps that can be filled. We review and refine the facts and try to convert them into knowledge. And then we let it all percolate. We let what Malcolm Gladwell calls our "adaptive unconscious"[7] go to work, mulling, meditating, prioritizing, and making valuations. We let our hearts use intuition to convert our knowledge into truth, and perhaps our truth into some outstanding wisdom that will help us win big.

When we come to the moment of decision, we need to be well-informed, well-armed. When I am working on a book, I often read something related to the specific topic I am working on right before I go to bed. When a young woman asked composer Johann Sebastian Bach if he ever awoke with fresh ideas, he answered that he could hardly get to his study without tripping over them. My practice gives me at least a small experience of what he meant. Our background "head work" frees our hearts to make the decision. In other words, we can comfortably trust our hearts because we have drained, even exhausted, the intellectual process.

We have to recognize that there are problems that cannot be resolved with a "head only" or "heart only" approach. With "head only," we simply will not be able to get enough data or information to make a good decision. There are other times when we will get too much data or information, which can overload and even paralyze our thinking—and sometimes the information leads us in the wrong direction, like the taste tests that led to the fiasco of New Coke in the 1980s. When all of the data said "change it to taste more like Pepsi," Coca-Cola replaced its flagship product, and the data (however "accurate") turned out to be totally wrong.

The problems with "heart only" are just as severe. Sometimes, a lack of data can paralyze our intuition, and sometimes, our emotions can lead us in the wrong direction.

We have to acknowledge our mistake gracefully when we hit one of these two walls:

- There are times when the emotions are high, but the essential facts are unarguable. Pilots, especially over the water at dusk, can feel that their situation is very different from what is showing on their control panel, but if they follow their feelings they will die. In similar situations, we need to acknowledge and respect the feelings but reduce the conversation to the pragmatics of the situation. "Will this work?" is a better question than "How do you feel about this?"
- There are times when the thinking is at high levels, but as leaders we know we have to make the decision based on our passions. In fact, this might be the highest level of decision we are ever called on to make. Blaise Pascal said, "The heart has its reasons, which reason knows not of." At other times, the only way to break through is with an appeal to the heart. "When struggling to overcome maladaptive behaviors by the use of logic," wrote one psychiatrist, "one is often confronted with the fact that *some ignorance is invincible*."[8] To logic, yes, but perhaps not to the heart.

One of our clients called this needed balance a "war of equivalence." The key question is, "Is it possible to combine the experience and intuition of those at the top with the knowledge and intuition of those down the line to produce better decisions?" Another client defined intuition properly used as an *extension* of good process: "Wisdom is knowledge to the intuitive power."

In general, we need to practice passion directed by reason. High-performing companies are driven by passion at all levels of the organization. As an organization, and as individuals, we perform at our best when we are doing what we are passionate about. But the goal is heart in *front* of head, not heart in *lieu* of head. We have to ensure that our passions are constantly being checked by our reason. Checks can include rigorous final analysis of all major decisions before implementation, including all interested voices in all stages of the process, and welcoming more discipline in the way investment decisions are made.

We should avoid the very common trap of using intuition for the big decisions and process for the smaller ones. It is too easy to use intuition on the bigger (and perhaps riskier) decisions (like mergers and acquisitions [M&A] and major strategic directions—"I know we'll find a way to integrate these different cultures"), while using process to squeeze small amounts out of lesser decisions. It is easy, as one client said, "to find yourself saving pennies and blowing billions."

Replace binary thinking with nuanced analysis based on both intuition and process, both heart and head. Too much decision-making is done on a "go/no go" basis ("either this will work or it won't work"). Instead, we could use a reporting and evaluating format that allows the possibilities to be represented on a continuum. One question to ask is, "What makes this a better project than others that would use the same resources?"

Managing this paradox well is especially important on the crucial issue of responsiveness to change. In every great change initiative, the starting point has to be making the case for the change. But the case for change has *two* components:

- The head case for change—Let's look at the threats and weaknesses, our position in the marketplace, our standing with customers, and our various financial trends—the scarier the better. Let's do an intelligent extrapolation to show what happens if we don't change.
- The heart case for change—Let's look at the loss of purpose, the damage to our legacy, and the harm to our stakeholders if we don't change. The scarier the better here, too.

There has been much written on managing change. Aside from the fact that managing change is impossible, this approach has another major defect: it is too low a target. We don't need to manage change. We need to anticipate it, face it, cause it, and drive it, but even more we need to welcome it and relish it and exploit it. Logic can't drive out fear and anxiety and dislike, and a strong rational case can't instill curiosity and wonder and enthusiasm and passion. Only winning the heart case for change can do that.

There may be times when the head can make the decision alone, and that is fine. There may be times when that is perhaps even the preferred approach, as when an air traffic controller gives instructions to a pilot, or a surgeon to a nurse. But even when logic is in the driver's seat, we will still generally do better with a heart-led mind. A CEO who says, "Given our situation, I know that laying off 10,000 people is the reasonable thing to do, and I will be applauded by the Board and the shareholders or owners for doing it, but it just doesn't feel right," is expressing the heart-led mind.

This type of thinking could lead to intuitive reasoning: "This catastrophe is my fault and my leadership team's fault for not anticipating this situation and taking earlier steps. It is not the fault of the 10,000, so instead we will see how many people we can keep if my team and I take no compensation this year, cut out the headquarters 'extras,' reduce the pay of those at high levels who contributed to the bad decision-making, and enlist our people in a passionate effort to increase revenues and cut costs so we can save the rest." The fact that leaders who think this way will be able to feel wonderful about their decisions for the rest of their lives is just icing on the cake of the more resilient, passionate, and ultimately profitable organization their decisions will create.

In some organizations, the formal leadership is held in awe, if not in fear and dread. In other organizations, the formal leadership is felt to be warm, part of the team, and accessible. The first approach can lead to truth being squelched and filtered, whereas the second can lead to fuzzy accountability and insufficient focus on results.

Great leaders know how to work in both modes—how to keep a healthy distance and at the same time make a healthy connection. It is not only possible, but necessary, that leaders walk the fine line between excessive familiarity and excessive aloofness.

Paradoxical leaders present rational plans, even as they realize that those plans might be the smallest component of what drives productive action.

Then they check the level of passion and emotion — both positive and negative — in their teams and develop ways to maximize the positives and minimize the negatives.

Socrates said, "The unexamined life is not worth living." This reminds us to focus on the head to make sure that we miss nothing important while life ebbs and flows around us. Solomon said, "He seldom reflects on the days of his life, because God keeps him occupied with gladness of heart." This reminds us to focus on the heart to make sure we miss nothing important while life ebbs and flows around us.

To be successful in all that means, we need to do both. With head or heart alone, we are half leaders and truncated human beings.

CHAPTER 7

BROADEN THE VISION AND NARROW THE FOCUS

The granddaddy of them all is the short-long paradox, as in the question I always get: "How can I manage quarterly results and still do what's right for my business five years out?" My answer is, "Welcome to the job!"[1]

—*Jack Welch*

Don't limit yourself.

Stick to your knitting.

If we broaden the vision without narrowing the focus, we end up being all things to everyone and nothing to anyone. If we narrow the focus without broadening the vision, we end up executing perfectly against the wrong opponent. At either end of this paradox, organizational disaster lurks.

Great leaders will not allow too much of the future to be tied to too much of their past vision. They ask critical questions: What else are we passionate about? Where can we make a unique contribution, given the new rules of the game? What are our noncustomers up to right now? At the same time, these leaders know that resources are scarce and that they had better be spent on the best opportunities that are available. They eliminate distractions and will not allow the organization to wander into a strange land.

These leaders concentrate on values and results in equal measure. They know that there are visionary leaders who try to inspire their teams with calls to making a difference, and bottom-line leaders who try to inspire their teams with victories and shared rewards. Great leaders know that either approach alone—inspiration without performance, profits without meaning—is insufficient to building ethical high performance.

Organizations are often guilty of violating both sides of this paradox. An organization can have the worst of both worlds—a narrow vision and broad focus, playing on too small a field with too many balls.

To manage this paradox, we've got to broaden our vision at the same time that we narrow our focus.

BROADEN THE VISION

The starting place for an organization is answering the bigger questions broadly before trying to answer the smaller questions narrowly.

We encourage our clients to answer the bigger questions of vision, mission, values, and behaviors before the smaller questions of strategy, structure, process, and execution.

Of course, there are some approaches that seem to be broadening the vision but are actually doing the opposite.

- Rounding out the product offering—"We're offering 90 percent of what our customers need—doesn't it make sense to give them the other 10 percent?" This seems reasonable—as long as we don't think about the energy and resources it will take to launch in new directions, the distractions from other opportunities, or the harm to our message. At Luman Consultants International, we build passionate, thinking, high-performance organizations, but we don't consult on downsizing or legal issues. Those are real problems, but they're for someone else to solve. We believe that doing what we're doing will reduce the need to deal with the uglies, but we aren't going to get involved in things that are counterposed to our message.
- Becoming a "single source"—The lure of the "one-stop shop" can tempt most organizations. For most customers today, single-sourcing is far less important than choice, price, delivery, service, and quality.
- Growing by bolt-on acquisitions—We don't know how to grow? Buy something! Acquisitions can be an important part of our vision, but they are a terrible substitute for it.
- Moving into areas because they are "logical"—"This is a logical extension of what we're already doing" isn't broadening the vision—this is extrapolating the present. Does this have anything to do with why we exist? Does it enhance our current offering? Do we have the competence to make it a profitable part of our portfolio? E-learning, for example, might look to a university like a logical extension of face-to-face classroom learning, but it could take away from the institution's cachet, diminish its on-site offerings, and require the recruitment of people very different from the current faculty or team.
- Being enticed by peripheral success—One of our clients had a regional manager take the initiative to launch a new service, with some success. This generated a lot enthusiasm from others in this growth-oriented company. But

the service was largely unrelated to their core offering, required a lot of start-up resources, and took a clear brand into a foggy ravine. As we've learned from most motion picture sequels, just because you've done something well doesn't mean you should keep doing it.

Instead, we should find effective ways to concentrate on the big picture. How can we do this?

Ask big questions. These questions fall into four broad areas:

- Vision—Why should we exist and absorb capital? Where are we going with this thing? How will we know if we've won?
- Mission—What major things should we do to achieve our vision? What are our critical success factors? Our objectives?
- Values—What should our cultural design look like? What is our identity? What can we do to distinguish ourselves from everyone else who does what we do?
- Behaviors—What are the "rules of engagement" between people and teams and business units? How will we act and interact to secure our vision?

For our clients, we capture all of this in a *VMVB Reference Guide* ("VMVB" for vision, mission, values, and behaviors). Understanding the "organizational character made plain" can have an astonishing effect on passion, alignment, and the ability of people to add and create value. In our extensive experience with many organizations across a wide array of industries, few have invested themselves as thoroughly into the VMVB process as Kerr-McGee. This global oil and gas exploration and production company clearly saw the need to clarify, deepen, and extend the impact of their vision, mission, values, and behaviors throughout the organization. The opportunity to participate was given to every employee and contractor through a thorough process of engagement. The document that resulted from these efforts and the process itself began producing immediate positive effects on morale, commitment, decision-making, productivity, and the ability to deliver on the strategy. A large acquisition was absorbed into the process, which led to a much quicker and stronger integration of the two cultures. A 75-year-old company had the courage and wisdom to make these changes before being forced. "This process has met my very high expectations," said Dave Hager, Kerr-McGee Chief Operating Officer.

Connect the vision to the market. Broadening the vision has to be an externally oriented, not internally oriented, process. If something is a strength but the market doesn't care, why should we care? "The general environment is the same for every player," wrote Larry Bossidy and Ram Charan. "What differentiates the successful ones are their insights, perceptions, and abilities to detect patterns of change and relate them to their landscape, industries, competition, and business."[2]

Connect the vision to the strategy. Once the organization has defined a vision worthy of the lives and resources that will be invested in it, it needs to define the parameters of acceptable strategy will be. We call this critical document a *Strategic Planning Guide.* This lays out the "fences"—here's what any strategy that evolves from strategic conversation must include (or not include). A well-developed Strategic Planning Guide is a doorway to strategic flexibility and an incredible competitive advantage. It lets the vision dictate the bounds into which strategy must fall before we ever get to narrowing the focus through strategic planning.

Have a high-powered, cross-functional expansion team. No matter how often we are warned about the "tyranny of the urgent" and how the problems of today can swallow up tomorrow, it is very hard to act on the warning. Life is just too busy, and the demands of today are real. Creating a "team with teeth" to force talk about the future can be a perfect mechanism for broadening our vision.

Use scenario thinking to broaden the vision. Scenario thinking can be useful, but in the twenty-first century, it is usually applied to the wrong end of the paradox, to strategic planning. Scenario thinking at the vision level—envisioning multiple futures rather than multiple nitty-gritty plans—is where the real value is. Spending too much energy on the question, "What do we do if our competitors do that—or that or that?" takes our focus off the ability simply to notice the nuances of marketplace reality, whereas spending energy on the question, "Why are we here and what do we want that to look like in five to ten years?" can broaden our perspective. With a future so far out and filled with so many complexities along the way, how could there *not* be an array of possible visionary futures? This is what senior leadership teams should be engaged in, rather than the details of strategic and tactical planning. Creating a broad vision of the future—or really, a series of visions that can be evaluated and ranked—forces us to keep looking outward and prevents us from missing large-scale change and the opportunities or disasters that change represents. We find that "leaders tend to focus on the probable rather than the disruptive [because] 'Every president wants one scenario.'"[3]

In a global, hypercompetitive, disruptive, rapidly changing world, broadening our vision goes beyond growth and success. For many of us, it is the difference between life and death.

NARROW THE FOCUS

Narrowing the focus is an idea that needs definition. It does not mean "eliminating everything that does not add or create value" but, rather, "eliminating everything that distracts us from a concentration of forces, even if it does add or create value." Picking out the worthless for elimination is relatively easy compared with picking out the valuable activities that just don't fit.

Narrowing the focus is about what we choose to keep. Rather than scratching items off a list, this would be better begun by picking the most critical items off the list or ranking the list and zeroing in on the small group at the top. We can't start with the question, "Is this useful?" or "Is this important?" Rather, ask, "Is this the best thing we can do?" or "What would happen if we did mostly this and little of everything else?"

However, we have to be careful. Many leaders hold the illusion that they are narrowing the focus because they engage in one of these counterproductive activities:

- Sticking to the knitting—"This is what we've always done, this is what we know how to do, so let's not waste our time looking at a bunch of things that just aren't 'us.'" We can stick with what we're doing, until at best we miss a range of better opportunities, or at worst end up knitting a shroud.
- Using scenario planning to determine strategy—Scenario thinking is usually applied to the strategic planning area, but as noted earlier, its real strength is in the strategic visioning area. As someone has said, "Strategy is change management." There is neither the time nor the need to clutter it up with a wide range of scenarios and related processes. Strategic plans need to be ready to react quickly to any opportunities or challenges, whether previously anticipated or not.
- Cutting products or services—We can drop a product out of a very large line and still have a very large line. We can do away with a service without thinning the scope of our offering at all. Narrowing the focus is about concentrating on what's most important rather than on what isn't.
- Using a meat axe to carve out a future—Narrowing by edict is swift but not painless. It has the advantage of being simple and the disadvantage of being simplistic.

We know we can't be all things to all people. We know we need to narrow our focus. So how do we narrow our focus effectively?

Ask the right questions. Our dialogue at this point should help us to pare down the enormous range of possibilities before us. These questions should fall into four key areas:

1. Strategy—What should we do in the near term to advance the vision? How will we deliver results?
2. Structure—How should we organize ourselves to optimize our ability to deliver the strategy? How can we adapt to change that is certain to come?
3. Process—Given our organization's structure, which of the systems, tools, and procedures that might possibly work should we adopt to maximize our chances of delivering on our strategy? What tactics will allow us to make our strategy viable?
4. Execution—How will we ensure consistent discipline and clear accountability? What measurements will tell us both *how* to win and *whether* we're winning?

Use strategic planning as the vehicle for narrowing. Perhaps we should change the name from "strategic planning" to "strategic focusing." A thick strategic planning document is a testament to failure in narrowing our focus. "[T]he essence of even the most complex strategy can be expressed on one page. A good strategy process . . . makes the mind better at detecting change."[4] Robust strategic conversation should allow us to detect change and focus on the soul of that change.

Have a high-powered, cross-functional veto team. To leave the important action of narrowing the focus to annual strategy planning and budgeting processes is to leave it largely unattended. These events are designed to look backward before extrapolating forward. Worse, to leave narrowing the focus to the hoped-for attention of the senior leadership team and a "someday" offsite is far too ad hoc, puts too much burden on too few people (who—no matter how brilliant—are unlikely to be up to the task anyway), and handles narrowing as an event rather than as a mindset.

Make sure that what we do focus on gets attention. It is possible to *agree* that we will focus on a certain area and then not *actually* focus on it. Once we know where we want to concentrate our forces, we have to work relentlessly as a team to ensure that this occurs. "I think supporting the field means looking systemically to see what the barriers are to achieving goals," said a 9/11 Commission member. "Do they have the right strategy, and what are their obstacles to achieving their strategies?"[5]

There are too many options, too many opportunities, too many distractions, too many things to relentlessly devour our energies. We have to narrow the options.

THINKING AND RESPONDING PARADOXICALLY

This paradox is the marriage of adaptability and alignment.

Broadening our vision refers to our need to build flexible, change-exploiting, mobile, speedy, divergent-thinking organizations.

Narrowing our focus refers to our need to be a fixed, force-concentrating, penetrating, tenacious, convergent-thinking organization. We can only be this if we position ourselves to select—often with a fuzzy or incomplete picture—the best of what is available for development.

It is important to get everyone involved in opening up the options. "When I first took over as CEO," reported Bob Barrett of the InCharge Institute, "I worried about how I was going to build the work culture that I had long dreamt of. The beginning of my solution was to assemble all of our managers and ask them one question: 'What do we need to stop, start, and continue doing?' Once people realized I expected absolute honesty, the floodgates opened." They opened up over fifty new areas to explore and then began to focus on the ones that could be implemented to great advantage. Involvement does two things—it gets many more ideas on the table, and it secures investment on the part of those participating.

There is a necessary sequence—broaden the vision first, narrow the focus second. After imagining a broad array of visionary futures, leadership can engage in significant dialogue with the rest of the organization, synthesizing the results of this deliberation into a "better than all alternatives" picture of what the organization can be and do. Then, and only then, is it reasonable to narrow the focus.

An analogy comes from offensive military strategy. In the thirteenth century, the Mongols "broadened their vision" by using a multipronged advance to advance against several enemy strongholds at the same time. They kept their options open until the last possible moment, causing the enemy to divide its forces to defend multiple points. Then the Mongols combined forces quickly to concentrate them on a single point. This became an accepted doctrine in the West in the seventeenth century and was used effectively and repeatedly by Napoleon.

However, the broadening only worked if it was followed by effective narrowing. In explaining the failed advance on Amiens by the Germans late in World War I, military historian John Keegan faulted their "adoption of a three-pronged advance in which none of the prongs would be strong enough to achieve a breakthrough." They broadened their vision but didn't narrow their focus because they were distracted by the preliminary success of the various prongs.[6]

In a remarkable article on David Pottruck's dramatic termination as CEO of Charles Schwab, it was noted that "He felt the sheer number of projects he launched hurt the company by keeping it from focusing its energies on the best ones."[7] He broadened the organization's horizons, but without a corresponding process that would let people weed out the less valuable and focus on the more valuable. All of the ideas in the new vision may have been worthwhile, but they were stripped of any advantage by leaving out the opposite side of the paradox.

However, we don't want to narrow our focus too soon. If we narrow our focus before we have broadened our vision, we are winnowing from a much smaller field than the one that can be ours.

We help clients manage this paradox using our ICE process to identify

- Core Incompetencies—the things that we have done or are doing that we are not good at (and likely have little passion for). These are different from "weaknesses," which imply that a performance-improvement plan might save us.
- Core Competencies—areas in which we have developed capabilities or capacities that meet the norm for our market or industry.
- Core Excellencies—capabilities or capacities that far exceed the norm and that may be or become the "gold standard" for our market or industry.

We want to broaden our vision to include every core excellency (and every core competency that could reasonably be converted into an excellency), and then we want to narrow our focus to our core excellencies that match up with market demands. If we have no market-facing edge, we have no reason to go there.

We have designed our consulting practice around this very paradox. We are not focused on a specific industry or two but, rather, work with a wide range of organizations in a wide range of industries and fields, including not-for-profit and government. This allows us to have a broad vision of what can be done—one that is much broader than if we were "industry specialists." From this buffet, we work with clients to select those approaches that will allow them to focus their energies on a few core excellencies that are closely related to their industry or sector. We combine our breadth of vision with their necessarily narrowed depth of focus.

Most organizations are nearsighted and some are farsighted. We should want our organizations to see fully and well, both far and near, with breathtaking vision *and* relentless focus.

CHAPTER 8

LIVE IN THE PRESENT AND LIVE IN THE FUTURE

In strategy, it is important to see distant things as if they were close and to take a distanced view of close things.[1]

—Myamoto Masabi

To be successful, we have to live intensely in the present. Sloughing off the present to plan for and worry about the future is a chaotic way to live and a formula for long-term failure. Organizations with big dreams and plans for the future, but without short-term wins and critical cash flow, are not likely candidates for organizational old age.

To be successful, we have to live intensely in the future. We have to see the present as a flashback, where we are looking back on today from a point we can only imagine. "The empires of the future are the empires of the mind," said Winston Churchill.[2] Sloughing off the future is an unrooted way to live and a formula for unending short-term chaos. Organizations with a focus on execution and meeting the next quarter's expectations, but without a strong sense of the outline of the future and the demands it will make, are no more likely to make it to maturity.

The problem is simple: It is both hard and important that we find a way to occupy two places at the same time, the very real and tangible present and the no less real if slightly less tangible future.

Some leaders describe themselves as "hands on," "bottom-line" managers. Other leaders think of themselves as "visionaries" or "long-term strategic thinkers." Often, the CEO will take the "visionary" role while the COO becomes the "bottom-line" member of the act. But great leadership requires both perspectives, in all people, at all times. Splitting these activities and assigning the roles to separate people loses the advantages that come from a dual perspective in each person. If the "hands on" leader is a stronger personality, the organization will become obsessed with execution and detail. If the "visionary" leader is a stronger personality, the organization will become obsessed with brainstorming and scenarios.

Instead, we need to live on the "line" between present and future realities.

Simply put, here is the paradox: to achieve outstanding results, we must focus our organizations on short-term outcomes to the exclusion of long-term possibilities. To achieve outstanding results, we must prevent our organizations from focusing on short-term outcomes at the expense of long-term possibilities. How can we design our organizations to focus on the short term while ignoring the short term? And focus on the long term while excluding it from our thinking?

LIVE IN THE PRESENT

If we don't manage well today, there will be no tomorrow. Too many organizations and leaders live in the past, carrying past actions into the present (often regardless of whether they have been, or are, successful), and tweaking that past to make it fit the now.

We have to fully inhabit the present. The past is gone.

We can also spend too much time in the future. "What should we do with this line next year?" "How will we position this to take advantage of those trends we see converging in three years?" "What will we do if our top customer leaves us down the road?" All of these are legitimate questions, but we might never get to answer them if we're not around or don't have the resources to answer them well because we've ignored the present.

Although living in the present is critical, there are some ways to do it very badly.

- Focus everyone's attention on the present—The thrust of too many conversations and meetings is, "What are you doing now?"
- Make busyness a measure of value—"You can feel the energy in here." Busyness, even if it is about the right things, usually relates to getting something done, not getting something thought. Ironically, we live in a knowledge economy where almost no one has time to think.
- Fill the present up—Meetings, conferences, voice mails, e-mails, and "communication" can absorb most of our productive time and turn it into ash. If living in the present means everyone disturbs everyone else every time they have a stray thought, we are living in the present very, very badly.
- Give disproportionate incentives for short-term performance—Although it may be true that we "get what we expect" and that "what gets measured gets done," huge short-term incentives can skew even a great leader's perspective. When large, respected companies start giving quarterly bonuses, we can know without much analysis where people's attention is going to go.[3] Some organizations in effect only give incentives for short-term results.

- Mortgage the future because the present works so well—When we are going "flat out" to deliver our products or services in the present moment, and we seem to be doing well, it is hard to say "stop" and spend energy on the future.

In these situations, the future has no future. But we can live in the present very effectively.

Find ways to let everyone think. The present is almost always enhanced, at least a little, when we give people the opportunity to think about it. The chance to contemplate what you're doing, rather than just doing it, is an investment in excellence.

Take snapshots. Right before our eyes, the world is changing. Our markets, industry, customers—everything is changing just a little bit. What do those changes look like? How can we exploit these modest movements?

Build strong relationships. Even in very transaction-oriented businesses, relationships go a long way. The retail clerk who looks familiar and always seems to be helpful, the restaurant server who knows your face and gives you a friendly reception, the bank teller who asks how you are—all are building relationships. Almost nothing costs so little and has so much return. My executive assistant constantly reminds me to stay, even if it's just for a few minutes, at the end of a media interview to make it a little more personal, to find out what really connected with the interviewer and audience. It is amazing how often this delivers extra opportunities. It may not be "on point," but it could end up *being* the point.

Promote enjoyment. It's a lot easier to do what we do with passion when our frame of mind is positive. I have walked into organizations that felt like cemeteries. How can great work be done by people who have been entombed? It's a good day to be alive. If we can help our people know that, their present will come alive too.

The present is, in truth, all we really have. The past is gone, and the future is just outside our reach and unlikely to be exactly what we envision. But we have now. This is the day to make a difference.

LIVE IN THE FUTURE

"If in the long run we are the makers of our own fate," wrote Nobel Prize–winning economist F. A. Hayek, "in the short run we are the captives of the ideas we have created."[4] We must free ourselves from captivity to our own current ideas. What we know that is working has value, and the greater the value the more likely it will take us hostage. To use these ideas without being mastered by them is the key.

Although living in the future is crucial, there are some poor ways to take up residence:

- Being an unrealistic optimist—For many people, the future is always a better time—even if they aren't doing anything to make it so. Optimism, unconnected to nitty-gritty effort, is an insufficient basis for the future.

- Being a pessimist—Doomsayers will always have an audience, in part because the future always has some frightening elements, and in part because of basic human nature that likes to look at train wrecks. Pessimism causes us to spend our energies and resources to prepare for a future that is unlikely to occur, while we miss the opportunities that only the upbeat can see.
- Overpreparing—In an ironic twist, getting ready for the future can actually prevent us from being ready. There is always one more thing we could learn or study, one more course we could take, one more potential partner we could talk with, one more analysis to run. If I had waited to give my first keynote until I had learned everything there was to know about speaking, I would still be waiting to make my first presentation.
- Overplanning—At some point, the future interferes with all plans, no matter how carefully thought out or accurate they may be. The brilliant German plan for the invasion of France, put together from 1891 to 1906, had the details down to how many rail axles would cross a given point on the track. It didn't account for the generals in 1914 who would misunderstand the plan, or for the reactions of the French and British.

However, we can live in the future well.

Becoming realistic optimists. Great leaders are constantly searching for news and ideas that can give them hope, and they are searching just as hard for news and ideas that could take them down. Leadership is too tough to let this paradox get out of balance.

Understanding our passions. If we understand what we care about most, we have an excellent chance of finding ourselves working on the right things in five or ten years. For instance, if we care about cutting-edge products, we are less likely to wander into commodity products or to stay in a product that is commoditized and can't be revolutionized.

Understanding our critical success factors. A major cause of organizational failure is getting distracted and focusing on the wrong things. It takes great discipline to focus on the factors that will determine our success with the people we are trying to serve.

Combining imagination with real work. If we spend time picturing a better future and then do the work necessary to get there, we are actively living in the future, right here, right now. It is action that brings the future into the present. Whether that is testing a new product or service idea with customers, doing a pilot project on a new process, or calling in an ad hoc advisory board to road-test the idea, we're bringing the up-in-the-air future to the down-in-the-dirt present.

Figuring out what will make money (or access more resources). Ultimately, no future will work without the resources to make it go. Planning for and securing those resources gives us options. An organization with resource options and an eye on the future is one that has a solid chance of thriving there.

There are alternatives to living in the future. We can try to keep our heads down and do well in the present and hope that is enough. We can assume that no one else knows any more about it than we do and, thus given a level playing field, can ignore it. But the future is there, as real as today though less tangible, ready to be homesteaded by anyone bold enough to stake a claim today.

THINKING AND RESPONDING PARADOXICALLY

It takes deft leadership to design an organization that is comfortable living in two worlds—the one we see and the one we will help create—at the same time. Human beings have the ability to think clearly about the task at hand while processing plans about an upcoming event at the same time, but this incredibly useful ability has not been transferred successfully to the vast majority of organizational life.

Two business authors a number of years ago suggested that the way to manage this paradox was to form two teams, a "P" (present) team and an "F" (future) team.[5] Although this type of approach can be effective on certain types of projects or processes, it cannot address the demands of living in two eras at once. This paradox is too powerful to be solved by mechanisms and elite teams. It has to be solved by changing mindsets to embrace the paradox and by involving "ordinary people."

We need to let our view of the future inform our present. Many leaders believe that working on the future *has* to have a negative effect on the present. They think it will destroy focus and drain away energy. But the future has a lot to say to the present—if we find a way to listen.

Our teams need to understand that if we never work on the future, we will always have short-term problems. The future will keep transferring its unanticipated problems and opportunities back to an unprepared present.

We need to let our view of the present inform our future. What we are doing now is what we have a certain level of commitment to do—probably have a certain level of competence to do—and we are probably having a certain amount of success in doing it. What does that mean? What is both good about what we are currently doing and applicable to the future at the same time?

This is the test of duality. If it's good now, but we can't make a case for its usefulness in the future, we've got a bad plan no matter how good the numbers look right now. And if we have something that looks good in the future, but in which we have little or no current competence or practice, we've got a bad plan no matter how good the future might appear.

In one sense, the present represents order—we can see it and feel it and make some sense of it. And the future represents change—we can't see it or feel it and it's hard to make sense of it. To manage this paradox is to recognize that we must balance order and change, the stable and the chaotic, the relatively fixed with the largely unfixed.

What does this mean? We always have to connect the dots about how the present will affect the future and vice versa. "If we continue handling customer service this currently successful way, what will happen if our customers change and do X?" "If we change this process because of the short-term gains we have been able to highlight, what will happen if our competitors respond and do Y?"

This is different from scenario thinking, which is more fit for vision than for strategy and tactics and execution. This is not asking, "What are the possible pictures of the future that we can imagine?" but instead focuses on looking at specific actions (or changes in actions) and how those will play out over time.

Managing this paradox requires that we approach both the present and the future with passion and discipline.

The present needs our passion, for obvious reasons. We seldom have to stir people to be energized about what is right in front of them. If we don't deliver results now, there may be no future to worry about. However, the present also needs discipline—not just the obvious discipline of good execution but also the discipline to know what to avoid (even if it is attractive) because it will damage the future, and the discipline to know what to add in (even if it is unattractive) because it will enhance the future.

The future needs discipline, for obvious reasons. We are always "planning for the future" (perhaps not well, but we keep trying). We have offsite brainstorming sessions, strategic planning experts or departments, and we take time to picture and analyze various scenarios. But the future also needs passion—not just the obvious passion that we are "excited about the future" but also the passion that allocates people and time and resources to preparing for it, and the passion that will cause us to act today in a way that will maximize our chances of securing that future.

If we're not careful, our age and generation can affect our ability to live this paradox well. Often, the roles are strangely reversed: young people, with an expanse of future stretched out before them, can focus almost exclusively on the present (or the next near-term event or purchase); older people, with much less future remaining, can focus on leaving a legacy and making the future that they will not live to see even better.

If we are older, and especially if we are in leadership positions, we can leave a greater legacy by bringing our younger colleagues out of their busy present and into the future that they will actually inhabit and influence in person. They can help us connect their savvy about the present into a more robust picture of the future. If we are younger, we can live a more inspired present by engaging those who have lived longer and as a result can see further. Younger people will not just live in the future, they will make that future happen—if for no other reason than the ideas and preferences of their generation will someday reign supreme.[6]

We need to measure how well we are living in the present and living in the future. We have many measures of what we are doing in the present, but few measures of what we are thinking about and planning for the future. We generally measure from the present backward into the past, and at best we extrapolate that line into the future. Other than setting some growth, revenue, and profit goals, however, most organizations have done little to establish measurements for what we will be doing over a long period of time.

"We need to think through what performance is," said Peter Drucker; "we need both short-term and long-term measures. But management hasn't accepted this yet. That's because they're under short-term pressure from investors, who themselves are under pressure from their own management, who are looking for short-term results. . . . Management is a balancing act between the short term and the long term, between different objectives at different times."[7] There needs to be a roughly equal number of objectives, and related measures, for both now and later.

Many people talk about "balanced scorecards." What we need even more is a balanced timeline.

CHAPTER 9

COMMUNICATE MORE AND FILTER INFORMATION

It is not the quantity, but the pertinence of your words that does the business.[1]

—*Seneca*

I enjoy asking audiences, "How many of you are missing critical information that you need to do your job effectively?" Unless it's a group of CEOs, almost all of the hands in the room shoot up.

Sometimes, even CEOs know that they are missing important information. They may not be missing it "from above" like the rest of the people in their organizations, but they are missing it "from below." People are withholding information from them because there are more disincentives than incentives to sharing.

I also enjoy asking audiences, "How many of you are drowning in useless information?" The hands go up even faster, and the hands of the CEOs go up faster than everyone else's.

We're being shortchanged on what we desperately need to know while being overwhelmed with a flood of worthless data. We need knowledge, but we're getting noise.

I've heard a lot of leaders say, "We need to communicate more." But that's worse than half an answer, because without boundaries, a lot of the additional communication will add to the inefficiency. In fact, it is likely that people will freely share their garbage while fiercely protecting their gold. They will make more group distributions and "reply all" responses both to diffuse responsibility and to shred accountability.

I've heard other leaders say, "We've got to get this flood of information under control." But once again, without boundaries this initiative will cut far too little of the garbage and far too much of the gold. Often there isn't a cut at all, but merely a reorganizing of the data detritus into data graveyards (also known as data warehouses), new reports, and "streamlined" formats. Many people will use this fresh directive as a justification for holding back their important data.

If we're going to manage in a world of paradox, we have to communicate more and filter information, and we have to do both intelligently and at the same time. There's no way to communicate more unless we filter the vast empty information flows, and there's no way to filter unless we know what's important and what is a waste of time.

In a time when there are thousands of Web sites dedicated to discussing information overload—a delicious irony in its own right—we need to know how to harvest the good and weed out the bad.

COMMUNICATE MORE

In most organizations, knowledge is power when I know it and you don't. This is knowledge as zero sum: If you get more I have less. This is knowledge as a way of differentiating those "in the know" from everyone else.

We don't need to manage knowledge as much as we need to make it transparent. How do we get valuable information to the people who can use it for good? There are several communication strategies that are sure to produce chaos and ignorance rather than efficiency and wisdom—approaches we would do well to avoid:

- Have more meetings and conference calls—It is very easy to confuse "communicate more" with "meet more." Unfocused meetings are more likely to produce more useless ideas, opinions, and information than they are to enhance performance. Even focused meetings can use a lake of discussion to produce a pint of knowledge. "Business culture needs to be a carefully calibrated balance between creating participatory ethos and preserving your need for—and right to—privacy," wrote one expert.[2]
- Permit an unopposed grapevine—A problem related to the "need to know" mantra of many leaders is that people think they need to know everything. They are designed to want to know everything—not just information that might affect their jobs, but *everything*. If we won't tell them, they will fill in the blanks with made-up information that is likely to be inaccurate or unreasonable. The fact that people are talking isn't necessarily good.
- Encourage people to keep us in the loop—People can interpret this admonition in many different ways, telling us everything (including drivel) or just telling us drivel (which is always in sufficiently large supply to keep us occupied and out of their hair on the important things they want to keep to themselves).
- Encourage people to keep others in the loop—This directive provides, sad to say, a fine opportunity for people to spread responsibility and shred account-

ability. Too much communication is inimical to personal accountability. As the old saying has it, "When everyone is responsible for everything, then no one is responsible for anything."

- Use communication as an antidote to mistrust—When someone starts missing deadlines, working on the wrong priorities, or sending out poorly worded letters, our natural response can be, "Please copy me on everything." First we become editors, then auditors, and finally the doers of the work. The antidote to mistrust is more performance, not more communication. We need more agreement about (and measurement of) expected results—not more process data.

In outstanding organizations, knowledge is still power, but it is defined very differently: knowledge is power *when it is shared*. Knowledge can expand and multiply value, or it can die with us. And knowledge sharing usually comes down to, of all things, trust.

We need to be clear: knowledge sharing is not a one-time act—it's an *avalanche*. So how do we start a useful avalanche?

Adopt an attitude of openness. This doesn't mean that we actually do share everything with our people that is not restricted by a legal or other reason. It simply means that openness is our mindset. We're ready to give them everything. The standard position is "share." The exception is "don't share."

Ask the right opening question. Mediocre leaders ask, "Is there any reason that we should share this information with our people?" But great leaders ask, "Is there any reason that we *shouldn't* share this information with our people?" This implies that everyone has a *right* to know, as well as a need to know.

The simplest, most strategic answer is to get our people everything we can. We have to admit our own fallibility and finiteness. We have to acknowledge that we have precious little idea of what people can do with a little bit of knowledge.

Have confidence in people's ability to use information wisely—Speaking of the great success of Mao Zedong's Red Chinese army against the Nationalists in the 1930s, one military historian noted that "Communist leaders encouraged soldiers to solve various everyday problems and put much faith in the capacity of the individual soldier to understand his military task and carry it out. In a practice unheard of in other armies, leaders gave soldiers extensive precombat briefings about the tactical situation and battle plans and took pains to explain why orders they issued were important."[3] This was one of the intangible differences that helped an outnumbered and outgunned army to win decisively.

Build an environment of trust. We have learned after many years of working with organizations that what people define as a "communication problem" is usually a *trust* problem. If people trust each other, they'll communicate by carrier pigeon. If they don't trust each other, world-class technologies will die from underuse.

Tell people why you can't be open about certain information. Communicating more means that we should tell people as much as we can, and at least why we can't share the rest. People demand to be "in the know" but are usually understanding when they know why openness isn't appropriate. More communication about what and why we can't communicate more is crucial to an open society.

Especially communicate more about key topics. What are the most critical topics about which we should communicate more? Although the process of opening an organization to communication is one of the most difficult for leaders to do on their own, here are some good places to start:

- The way we define "victory"—It is too easy to focus on process instead of outcomes, means instead of ends, methods instead of results. Great organizations focus their people on delivering results and adding value, relentlessly communicate the definition of victory at very detailed levels, and leave the process to their people.
- How strategies are formed—In most organizations, once we get below senior leadership there is only a vague idea of the organization's strategy (and at times even senior leadership is unclear).
- The way we make sales—If our people don't know why people are using our offering, how can they help us find more ways to sell it? If they don't know what the sales process and cycle are, how can they enhance them?
- How customers or clients use our offering—All divisions—marketing, sales, business development, operations, production, quality assurance, and accounting—profit from awareness of how people are using what we offer. Knowledge can only serve to make us organically wiser about how to meet current, future, and unanticipated needs.
- The way we make money—Making money is a lot different from making sales. If our people don't know how we make money, how can they help us make money? If they don't understand where expenditures create value, how can they reduce less-necessary costs and increase spending where it can make a difference?

We'll never have a great organization until we have an organization that communicates lavishly. It will take a lot of work, and a lot of old habits will have to be changed. But the price of not communicating more is paid in failure.

FILTER INFORMATION

I love asking audiences, "How many of you think it is your job to keep your boss informed?" Invariably, almost all of the hands in the room go up. However, I heartily disagree. Without some definition, this job description means you would have to tell your boss *everything*.

Our people did not join our organizations to keep us informed. This bustle consumes way too much time, energy, and focus that should be reserved for much more useful activity. Instead, it is their job to get us every piece of information we need to enable us to add or create value.

Our obligation to them is the same. If information doesn't help them add value, how is it worth anyone's time to pass it around? Information that can't help them add value *has* no value. It soaks up resources that could be better spent on almost anything else.

Of course, there are a number of terrible ways to filter information, based on the illusion that "We can run this thing without sharing that information."[4]

- Practice omertá, the Sicilian Mafia's "code of silence"—We should not pledge people to secrecy when the information isn't really private or confidential.
- Underestimate what people can do with information—In my work with organizations, I have learned never to underestimate what an intelligent human being can do with even a scrap of newly available information.
- Communicate on a "need-to-know basis"—We need to turn the usual question, "Is there any reason that we should share this with our people?" around 180 degrees. This normal organizational question is arrogant and unproductive. One is reminded of the oracles who made erratic appearances to utter a few mysterious words. This question starts with the bad premise that information is "owned" by leaders, who then decide whether to be charitable with it or not. But knowledge isn't *owned* by leaders, it is merely *hoarded* by them. The driving force behind this behavior is the idea that we will only share with our people what they "need to know" to do their jobs. But how do we know what people "need to know" unless we know their talents and responsibilities as well as they do?
- Use screeners—Many leaders set up lines of defense against unwanted intrusions. The problem is that these screeners—people or processes—can screen out some of the most important news. They can do this directly, using their own judgment about what is important and just not knowing enough to make a good call, or they can do this indirectly, by their mere presence. Who would volunteer to face a question like, "And just exactly *what* is the nature of the problem you want to discuss with them?"

Instead, we should filter information intelligently. Wisely. How do we do this without killing the good stuff?

Ask the right question. The question we should be asking everyone with whom we interact is, "What information do you need from me that will allow you to add or create value?" And they should ask us the same question. Let's identify what's important, and let everything else fall away.

Silence the static so people can focus on important information. Less is really more. Once the husk of useless data is stripped, people can use what remains. When I am writing, I have to turn off much of the information around me. I can't check e-mail, listen to voice mails, watch the news, or read the newspaper before the writing for the day is finished, or my writing *is* finished.

Keep meetings relentlessly focused on progress. Meetings are a fertile ground for unnecessary communication and the frustration and waste that goes along with it. There are at least three major areas that need serious filtering in meetings:

1. The tendency for brainstorming, discussing, debating, and deliberating to focus on the obvious and redundant—We know that "in unstructured, free-flowing discussions, the information that tends to be talked about the most is, paradoxically, the information that everyone already knows."[5] Without structure, people tend to talk about the obvious, which is also the safest—the things that we all "know" and probably agree on. We need to create boundaries in meetings to work against this tendency. At some point, we need to prohibit the repetition of points already made (even with slightly changed wording). Items on which we have agreed need to go into an "asked and answered" category and not reopened, at least in that meeting, unless someone has a truly breakthrough thought about them.
2. The tendency for people to move to more extreme positions—Another problem with overcommunicating in meetings is that, "As a general rule, discussions tend to move both the group as a whole and the individuals within it toward more extreme positions than the ones they entered the discussion with."[6]
3. The tendency for conversations to become more negative the longer they go on—"Why are the sports-talk radio shows so negative?" one noted sports columnist was recently asked. His explanation? "When I write an opinion on a subject, I can state it in a few words and then move on. I'm done. I've got limited space to fill. But on these shows, they have hours to fill. The same opinion can be addressed and expanded until the problem seems much worse than when we started. It's a problem of too much time to fill."[7] We should never, under the guise of "not shutting off dialogue," allow a conversation to go on long enough that it takes the normal turn toward the negative. Better to drop the subject and pick it up again later.

Assign filtering duty to the right people. Who should do the filtering? The best approach is to let people guide their own filtering. We'll need to help with some incisive questions: "Is there anything you don't really need, but you're afraid to stop getting because you'll feel out of the loop?" "Is there any report or mailing that you rarely gain from getting, and if so, is there another way to capture that rare gain?"

Create self-managed communication forums. We need to ensure that our people have appropriate forums for information exchange, but that those forums are self-selected and managed. Only those passionate about communicating will participate, but in a peer-reviewed discussion, which gives us a much better chance of producing high-value information and knowledge: "[R]esearch suggests that Cisco's thousands of internal discussion lists, which employees typically spend half their interactive time using, encourage experts to emerge naturally."[8]

A well-filtered communication system is one of the most effective ways to maximize employee productivity and organizational performance.

French philosopher and mathematician Blaise Pascal once apologized for writing a long letter to one of his correspondents, claiming he did not have time to write a short one. Filtering is hard to set up, but once it is finished, what remains is something really worth reading.

THINKING AND RESPONDING PARADOXICALLY

From their birth until children turn three years old, they are building up a huge number of connections (synapses) between neurons. This is the equivalent of communicating more. But for the next decade, the brain begins a winnowing process, and—astonishingly—by the time the child enters the teens, the number of synaptic connections is only half of what it was ten years before. This is the equivalent of filtering information.

Great leaders understand that the relentless pace of economic and business life requires a lot of communication. At the same time, they ensure that communication is really strategic. They know that too much talk, like the many warnings on homeland security, can paralyze people, so these leaders take the time to make really short statements and insist that others do the same.

Leaders who manage this paradox communicate more really useful information, so their people will have incentive to filter everything else. The very valuable drives out the not very valuable. If we're focusing on critical information that advances our cause, there will be very little time to waste on trivial or petty "news."

Communicating more while filtering more means putting data through a "conversion process" to make it useful to an organization. The process includes five stages:

1. Acquisition of data—We have to find a way to access information. At this stage, it might be accurate or not, useful or not, value-adding or not. We acquire all the data available, then we begin filtering out the inaccurate and useless. At this point, if there is a question, the data stays in.
2. Conversion of data into information—After we've acquired the data and performed a minimum screen, we need to communicate about which chunks of the data are potentially useful. The rest are shuffled into a data graveyard.
3. Conversion of information into knowledge—Whether this mound of information concerns a program or project or initiative, we need to get it out to the whole team or selected teams to secure their advice on which pieces can provide the maximum value. This process is a priority filter. Not everything that can add value can add a lot of value. The information that gives us an edge—a legitimate competitive or service advantage—*this* information is knowledge.

4. Conversion of knowledge into truth—Truth is generally known, widely accepted, broadly applied knowledge. If people throughout our organization don't know something, we don't really know it at all.
5. Conversion of truth into wisdom—Wisdom is applied truth, truth tempered by experience (both good and bad). To build this type of wisdom into the fabric of organizations, our consulting team had to develop a twelve-part program of knowledge mentoring.

Managing this paradox means we have to get our arms around the idea of "seamlessness." While "communicate more" might mean we get the message out to more people (or everyone), "filter information" means we might have to scale back on the level of detail (and possible modify the language to make it resonate with each audience). But the key is seamlessness—giving everyone at every level the same core message. Communication becomes dysfunctional, and performance withers, when each group gets a different story. We can use different packages, but we'd better put the same product in each one.

In the final analysis, communication is only useful if human beings can turn it into worth. "Having a wealth of information is of little value unless it can be used for competitive advantage," note three information experts. "This is where many organizations fall short. . . . Firms have purchased the technologies that enable transformation of data into knowledge, but the human component necessary for this process has been given short shrift."[9]

The fact is, the "human component" is much more important than the "technologies." Herb Kelleher sketched out the Southwest Airlines plan on a napkin. "It's ironic," continue the authors, "that after accounting for all the technological advances of the past and future, sustainable competitive advantage will rely on two very human characteristics: insight and trust."[10]

We need to give people more information, and we need to give people less information, to open up communication and to cut the volume by 80 percent.

We need to communicate more on the really important things that add and create value, and filter more on everything else.

CHAPTER **10**

EXERCISE AUTHORITY AND SHARE POWER

Greatness lies not in being strong, but in the right use of strength.[1]
—*Henry Ward Beecher*

There are take-charge leaders, and there are consensus leaders.

Truly outstanding leaders are both.

Power is used as a tool and it is seen as a goal. It is used to liberate people and it is used to dominate people. The British Empire, with all its faults, finally used its power to end the slave trade. Totalitarians—Hitler, Stalin, Mao, Pol Pot, Idi Amin (the list goes on)—have used power to dominate and subjugate and annihilate untold millions. Far too many leaders have used their power to control and suppress and crush other untold millions.

So is power good or bad? *Extremely*.

In my book *Balance of Power*, I defined power as "a force for achievement or obstruction that can be used individually or collectively for the constructive good, or the destruction, of other people and organizations."[2]

All leaders and organizations, sooner or later, have to decide how they will use power. The approach we'll consider here is different from the "it's either you or me" style prevalent in most human transactions. This fresh approach says, simply, that *everyone* in an organization has power, and that it is the leader's job not to exercise or allocate it but to unleash it through what we call *power-sharing*.

Powersharing, the paradoxical balancing of all available power in the organization—formal and informal, coercive and influential, overt and tacit—is the way to success.[3]

EXERCISE AUTHORITY

There is a huge difference between exercising authority and throwing your weight around. Here are some terrible ways to use your authority:

- Micromanage—Do you have the opportunity to nitpick employees? Yes. Do you have enough power that they can't openly resist you? Of course. But is it a good use of the formal authority that you have?
- Send people on errands—One word from someone with formal power can unleash a flurry of activity, as ten people fly off to get the information or follow up on the suggestion. Someone once defined a team effort as "a lot of people doing what I say." While this approach feeds the ego, it saps the total power available to the team.
- Ignore input—We can show how much power we have by the quality of the people and the types of advice we can disregard. "He may know a lot, but I'm the one with the stick."
- Intimidate—The natural tendency for most people is to defer to the boss, politician, or celebrity. This creates an opportunity for insecure people to feel "bigger" than their admirers.
- Wage turf wars—Who has the biggest slice? Who can get and keep the ear of the CEO? Who can get control of the biggest program or largest number of resources? What a waste of good power. Frittering away the opportunity to accomplish something great for the opportunity to accomplish something petty is a miserable option.
- Impress—Because many people are impressed with power, it doesn't take a genius to use power to impress people. Extremely oversized offices, excessively expensive furniture, the ability to interrupt other people and have them scurry, the parking spot by the front door, name-dropping, insistence on being addressed formally—so many ways to impress, so little time.

All of these may make us feel important. They just won't actually make us *be* important.

Are there effective ways to exercise authority? Absolutely.

Distinguish between formal and informal authority, and then rely on the latter. Everyone in our organization has informal authority—even if it is simply the power to do nothing. But only a select few have formal authority, the power of being designated leaders. People respect the latter because they have to, but they respect the former because they want to. Which is the higher form?

Use authority to liberate rather than dominate. Power can be used either way, but great leaders use liberating authority and work very hard not to dominate. They ask: "How can I clear away the obstacles to performance? The detritus that makes decision-making tedious and ineffective? What am I doing to control bad impulses rather than to unleash magnificent ones?"

Insist that authority be exercised at the right level. Having the formal right to do something doesn't mean we should do it. If we make decisions that others who work for us can make nearly as well or even better, we are wasting a lot of power. While we are working on these delegatable items, there are things that only we can do that are being left undone (or are being done suboptimally). We are also overpaying people who have brains, because we're only paying them to do and not to think.

Exercise authority only when it adds or creates value to do so. Ultimately, the only legitimate use of power is to produce useful and honorable results. "Is making this decision going to help us achieve our vision? Will my involvement advance our mission? Can my attendance do anything to improve our strategy? Will our stakeholders be benefited by the actions I can choose to take?"

There are certainly times when we need to exercise authority, even if we are the only ones in the organization who think our decision or action is correct. But unless we are sole proprietors, if we're making more than about 5–10 percent of the decisions, we are making too many.

SHARE POWER

Why should we share power? We certainly don't have to. Most people in positions of formal authority don't.

We should share power because it is the right thing to do. It elevates human beings and unleashes their immense capacities. Is it fun to have celebrations and catered lunches and casual days? Yes. But it is vastly more enjoyable to be able to make a lot of real decisions.

Sharing power is also the effective thing to do. Powersharing produces an interdependence that has many benefits. It creates a higher level of commitment, as people feel more a part of the real life of the organization. It improves follow-through, as people feel invested in the decisions and outcomes. It elevates accountability, as people are not only responsible *for* results but also *to* other people.

It is also good for us to share power. If Lord Acton's belief that power corrupts was right, then moving away from a god-like status will be a very healthy direction. Unchecked power inevitably leads to hubris (overweening pride), and hubris inevitably leads to nemesis (fierce opposition). Or as Proverbs 16:18 puts it, "Pride goes before destruction, and a haughty spirit before a fall."

There are some very poor ways to share power:

- Empowering—Empowerment is based on a bad idea: "I'm the king or queen and you're not. But I'm a nice monarch, so I'll trickle some of my power down to you." Empowerment is something we do to, not with, people. And to most people on the receiving end, it feels like dumping.

- Selling—Too many leaders assume that all good ideas come from the top. Their role is then to "sell" those ideas to the staff to get their "buy-in." But informing is not involving, and selling is not powersharing. Selling is an honorable profession—but not when leaders are selling to their followers.
- Sharing the costs without the resources and rewards—We're not really sharing power when we delegate responsibility and accountability without commensurate authority and resources. Why do people do this? Because they get to keep the enjoyable part of power and pass along the painful part.
- Deferring to structure—We can think we're sharing power when we defer everything in a certain category to the structure of our organizations. If every team must be led by the highest-ranking manager, and every decision or action of a certain kind must be made by the marketing or purchasing department, we have a very truncated view of sharing power.
- Delegate all of the "dog" work—Although we have the right to delegate anything we want, and it is human nature to want to get rid of the junk, assigning everything bad and keeping everything good is poor leadership. We can lose touch as we no longer have to get our hands dirty. People will sense the inequity. Our direct reports will do the same with their direct reports. All of it will make delegated work something ugly to be avoided. In contrast, shared pain will gain a lot of ground with our followers.

The pressures that surround us can cause us to dismantle powersharing mechanisms. The director of the FBI admitted, "I struggle with micromanagement. . . . The big question is, 'Is this making us safer?' "[4] We often confuse micromanagement with attention to detail. In the fight against terrorism and criminal activity, there is of course a great need for concentration on detail—but not from the person at the top. Are we safer because he is looking at all of the minutiae, or would we be safer because he is focused on the big picture and is creating a structure that lets *many* experts focus on appropriate detail?

In the same speech, the FBI director said, "We don't have to spend a tremendous amount of time on values."[5] Really? Isn't this a place where the director could add immeasurable value? Wouldn't we have been safer if agents with information and concerns had been able to voice them openly before September 11, 2001? Values of openness and willingness to be challenged could have made a difference. The FBI director noted that (in regard to values) one-third of the organization doesn't "get it" and another third "needs to be persuaded." An exercise of authority to help these two thirds could unleash a flood of excellence.

As James Surowiecki notes, "Paradoxically, even as American companies became more hierarchical, more centralized, and more rigid, they paid increasing lip service to the idea that top-down organizations were oppressive and damaging."[6] This is probably not *paradox* as much as it is *contradiction*. People always cover up power-grabbing with talk of empowerment: The leaders of the French Revolution claimed to be the voice of the people (just before they embarked on the Reign of Terror). Modern political parties and politicians often request power so they can help the downtrodden, only to pursue a course of personal power consolidation and political infighting once elected. We should never allow the phony sharing of power, a sharing in language but not in reality, convince us for a moment.

What are some effective ways to powershare?

Fully involve people at the maximum level that adds or creates value. This is a way to move beyond the phony internal "selling to get buy-in" to an authentic "including to get *be-in*." Be-in leads to genuine commitment and follow-through.

Be approachable. It is very, very hard for most people to speak the truth to formal power. Formal power intimidates even when the holder of that power does not personally do so. We have to act on this important truth, or our blather about having an "open door" will mean nothing to our people and will frustrate us when they don't come through it. "Even a strong leader will falter if he ignores the ideas of subordinates . . . 'the leaders shouldn't be at the top of the pyramid, but rather at the center of a circle.'"[7]

Avoid the natural tendency to give gratuitous advice. If we've lived and managed long enough, we have probably developed opinions on just about everything. Aside from the fact that many of those opinions are probably not that remarkable, the very fact that *we* are giving them gives them the "force of law." If we want to see a thousand flowers bloom, we're going to have to keep our gardening tips to ourselves.

Survey the range of power available to us through our people. Our people have the power to invest, to commit, to care, to stay, to think for themselves, to use their own best judgment, to challenge and disagree, to add value, to create, and to build. If we could access just 50 percent of the available power in these ten areas, we would move ourselves into the ranks of the top organizations.

Create policies that move us toward powersharing. Most policies, in our experience, are designed to *restrict* people and *reduce* powersharing. We need policies that do the opposite. For example, we can create policies that defer whole classes of decisions to others—to people closest to the decision, people who have the most knowledge, people who can add the most value, people without formal authority.

Restrain formal authority. For informal power to be unleashed, formal power has to stand down. This means we don't open every meeting with our comments because we know that this will structure the rest of the dialogue. We advise certain senior leaders to stay away from an incubating project. We ask formal leaders to keep their input to themselves until others have time to brainstorm the idea. Nature abhors a vacuum; if those of us with formal authority create one, informal authority can flow in freely.

A key point is to realize that we are not abandoning our authority when we share power; instead, we are using our authority in another way—to enhance the authority of others.

THINKING AND RESPONDING PARADOXICALLY

To great leaders, power is the sum of everything available to accomplish work—to solve a problem profitably, to optimize an opportunity, to exploit change.

This "sum of all power" includes the leader's own formal and informal authority. There are times when we can go too far, intruding and micromanaging and disrespecting and neutralizing, until our power is diminished by the way it is spent and our team's power is diminished because there is no room for it. Or we might not go far enough, hiding and dithering and confusing, until our power is diminished by not being spent and our team's power is diminished because uncertainty almost always paralyzes.

We have to find the optimum point, the point at which our exercise of authority and our powersharing brings the total power available to the organization to the highest point. This can vary from situation to situation—here it will be best if I make the decision, there it will be best if I defer the decision to the team, and over here it will be best if we divide it up. The question is no longer, "Who should make this decision?"—who has the right, who has the prerogative, who "owns" the decision. The question becomes, "*How* can we best make this decision using the power we can bring to bear on it?"

A large part of managing this paradox is facing and answering the critical question, "How do we decide who decides?"[8] Good decision-making—the best decisions, made at the most effective level, at the appropriate speed—is a surprisingly scarce commodity in most organizations. It will only happen with design. In the absence of design, decision-making will be avoided or deferred to higher levels. Using our authority to decide the question, after powersharing to hear all valid input, is the only way to guarantee the efficacy of this powerful, fragile process.

We can insist that decisions get made and actions taken at the right level. We use our authority like a check and balance on the authority—both formal and informal—of everyone on our team. We make our authority the arbiter of power, nipping potential Napoleons in the bud, cutting show-offs down to size, refusing to let anyone's power become abusive. We liberate decision-making from positional and functional control and make it a tool of the masses. In other words, we exercise our authority to enforce the sharing of power.

The key is knowing where the leader can have an influence, make a unique contribution, or make a statement (traveling down the path of exercising authority and personal decision-making), and where powersharing can allow others to do the same. We have to know what's "ours" to do, what no one else has the full package of formal and informal authority, wisdom, experience, relationships, and whatever else to do.

Another key is knowing when others can have a greater effect than we can. Why would we make the decision when someone else could make it better?

In many situations, we need to find the middle ground between formal authority and powersharing. That middle ground is often the use of informal authority—the power of influence and character. We should be willing to use our formal authority when necessary (one author has noted that "The line between leadership by persuasion and the abrogation of responsibility is thin"[9]), but as a secondary rather than primary tool.

However, to manage this paradox, to find the balance, we must do something that typical career paths and succession planning do not usually prepare us to do: we have to rely primarily on our informal power and to use our formal power only when absolutely necessary. For example, we require a check-off on major decisions only when we are able to add value that no one else can add to the decision.

This is important, because formal power tends to shut down powersharing, whereas informal power tends to ignite it. If we want an engaged workforce that delivers high performance, we need to hold our formal authority in check. A little goes a long way.

For too long, there has been an organizational chasm between "line" and "staff." We need to obliterate this phony and destructive division. We need "line" people who step back from making decisions and leading efforts to study and evaluate, involve people, and operate as a "shared service" (saying, in effect, "I'm here to help you exercise your authority even more effectively"). And we need "staff" people who step back from making studies, evaluating others, and focusing on policies and transactions to operate as strategic partners who make value-adding decisions.

In a sense, we need to learn how to be both authoritative and laissez-faire at the same time. We need to call some shots. Five percent of the time we must have the last word, and 20 percent of the time we must use our words to influence. In those times, we need to know that what we say "goes." And we need to leave a lot of shots to others. Seventy-five percent of the time the word is theirs—and we need to know that what *they* say "goes." We need to be intensely focused on what is ours, and happily ignorant of the details of everything else.

We need to exercise our authority carefully, knowing that using it too much will deform us and debilitate the organization. An organization needs a leader "who simultaneously believes in using power and is keenly aware that its use is inevitably corrupting."[10] We're always on our guard against powermongers who might slip in—and against ourselves.

Amazingly, powersharing becomes the best thing for us as individuals. If we are spending more than 5 or 10 percent of our time fighting fires, answering detailed questions, and making decisions, we have not accessed the power of powersharing.

If we do this well, we will attract people who want to be leaders, the kind of people who can make our organization great. We can attract people "who would never be interested in an enterprise whose direction they couldn't affect. By making room for them, you attract people who aren't followers, who aren't looking for the kind of leader who will save them from the anxiety of responsibility."[11]

Because the astonishing truth is that, in the most passionate and high-performance organizations of the twenty-first century, there will be no followers—only leaders.

CHAPTER 11

CREATE PASSION AND EXPECT PASSION

We may affirm absolutely that nothing great in the world has ever been accomplished without passion.[1]

—*Georg Wilhelm Hegel*

Passion is a fabulous force. If two organizations are on the same playing field with roughly the same size, talent, and strategy, the one that has passionate people will ultimately destroy the one that does not. According to Gallup, if all "of your employees were 'fully engaged,' meaning playing at the top of their game and happy about it, your customers would be 70% more loyal, your turnover would drop by 70%, and your profits would jump 40%."[2]

And passion is a fearsome force. In the absence of positive passion, negative passion will flood and poison the culture. One of the lessons of history is how astoundingly zealous human beings can be when they are bent on destruction.

Organizations desperately need passion. What is passion? It is a choice to be wholeheartedly committed to achieving results and adding value. It is working with enthusiasm and energy and vigor to build something excellent. Although passion can include emotion, it is more a choice than a feeling—people can be quiet and still quite passionate. Passion is characterized by focus and intensity and persistence and commitment even more than it is by externally observable behavior such as constant activity, high animation, or simply putting in long hours.

I asked Maryl Janson, our longest-tenured team member at Luman Consultants International, to define what she has seen both within our organization and in the Passionate Organizations we have helped to build. She said that passion is "the burning desire to make things better for ourselves and others, the enthusiasm to make a mark and leave a legacy with our lives . . . the sense of purpose a person has when they know that they have insight or skills that can contribute to a process."

Passion, she went on to say is "the excitement a person experiences when they see the value of something they are involved in. The unleashing of energy in a person who is given the freedom and control to create a positive change. The ability to see the potential of doing something great that benefits people." At the highest level, it is "the moving realization that a person is involved in something bigger than themselves that will have impact beyond their lifetime."

Passion is *not* mindless enthusiasm or false hope in the face of stark reality. It is not hoping to make up with eagerness what we have lost through laziness, sloppiness, or inattentiveness.

But passion is the great differentiator. "Whenever I went to Crotonville and asked a class what qualities define an 'A' player," former General Electric CEO Jack Welch wrote, "it always made me happiest to see the first hand go up and say, 'Passion.' For me, intensity covers a lot of sins. If there's one characteristic all winners share, it's that they care more than anyone else. . . . Over the years, I've always looked for this characteristic in the leaders we selected."[3]

And so should we.

CREATE PASSION

Leaders are organizational designers, and one of the most important areas for design—along with strategic excellence—is the creation of an environment in which passion can flourish. In the absence of this kind of thoughtful design, few if any organizations will exhibit any passion (except the negative kind). If we don't create this kind of environment, we will get normal organizational behavior, and it will be bad.

But there are dangerous paths to take here. There are many ways to attempt to create passion that are doomed from the start.

- Motivational language—Many people think the key to moving human beings is to try to inspire them with motivational speakers, speeches, videos, banners—the list goes on and on. But this language, if removed from reality, is actually perfectly designed to produce cynicism. As the author of *The Passionate Organization*, I have been asked at times to provide this kind of superficial gloss. Regardless of the fee, we have declined until there was a stated willingness to face reality and make needed cultural changes.
- Motivational schemes—there are countless motivational schemes touted by speakers and books and articles. They seldom work well; they never work for long. They create an entitlement mentality, and they distract us from the things that really motivate high performance.
- Appeals to team "spirit"—Appeals can be made for the "good of the team" and a general spirit of loyalty (however unearned by the organization). But shirts and slogans and team outings and picnics are insufficient to produce a driving passion.

- Management by wandering around—There is nothing wrong with wandering around and being a "presence" with our people, and good can accrue from it. But the good will be fragmented and unable to produce cultural momentum if our wandering isn't tied to specific cultural elements. Brief contact may make people feel good, but it is not likely to make them feel passionate.
- BHAGs—The "big, hairy, audacious goals" of Collins and Porras[4] can give a passionate person or team a focus on producing results, but they can't by themselves (or automatically) generate the passion to actually produce those results.

Most of these attempts to motivate people are driven by bad questions and methods.

When you boil down all of the motivational books and schemes, they are trying to answer a single question: *How do we get people to do what, for some reason or another, they simply do not want to do?*

If we get down to it, this question is basically dumb. Great leaders don't waste their time trying to answer bad questions. They ask instead, "What is the fundamental reason that this person doesn't want to do this?" and "How do we create an environment that produces incentives *within* the job?" and "How do we find or create opportunities for this person to do what he or she *does* want to do?"

The methods many "experts" recommend are just as bad. Reward and recognition programs that single out the few (employee of the month, star-performers' club, etc.) predominate. They can drive performance at some level, but seldom can they create true passion even in the "winners." In many situations, they are just as likely to produce jealousy and backstabbing as they are to produce higher performance.

Many programs offer trinkets. "Do this and you'll get _____ (dinner for two, tickets to an event, etc.)." Although these can be fine and gracious gifts to show *appreciation*, they are terrible *motivators*. In effect, we are saying to people, "Do this really boring, meaningless task (namely, your job) and then we'll give you a chance to do something that is actually interesting and important to you." The very offer exposes the lack of value in the work we have assigned to the person or belittles the value of their work.

Great leaders know that they need to treat passion and commitment at a much deeper level than this.

It starts with the culture. Have we created an environment in which passion can naturally flourish? Or have we created an organization that is perfectly designed to erode it? Many organizations harbor systemic ways to squelch passion, and not a few are designed to produce *negative* passion (grapevines, gossip, turf battles, power plays, cliques, etc.). "Great organizations can ignite passion," wrote Jack Welch.[5] This is a great thought, but how do we do this? How can we create passion?

Design a passion-friendly environment.[6] In a joint survey of 755 organizations performed by Luman Consultants International and the American Management

Association, the results were not surprising but were still staggering. Here are the percentages of survey respondents who rated the passion of each level in the organization "very high" (a 6 or 7 on a 1–7 rating scale):

At the senior management level	60.0 percent
At the middle management level	34.8 percent
At the supervisory level	18.8 percent
At the professional/technical level	18.1 percent
At the hourly wage-earner level	6.1 percent
In the organization as a whole	21.7 percent
Among suppliers and vendors	12.2 percent
Among business partners	18.0 percent

Most of the people in our organizations are in the wage-earning category—the category in which just 6.1 percent are seen as highly passionate. How can we be world-class with that kind of indifference? Just think of the kind of performance we could have if just 30 or 40 percent of wage-earners were passionate.

Be very careful about who comes through the door. The only thing that can rival the influence of a good attitude is a bad attitude. We have to approach recruitment, hiring, orienting, and deploying in a radically different manner.[7] In the same survey quoted above, 68.7 percent of respondents rated very high a "passion for the organization and work" as an element of effectiveness in recruiting and selecting new hires. The only similarly high score was "prior performance," at 71.3 percent. Passion and performance—believers and winners. If we can find people who score high on these twin drivers, we are destined for good things. Rated lower were such things as "personal and career goals" (47.8 percent), which are not very meaningful if not fully aligned with the organization's goals, and "education and honors" (26.5 percent). Needless to say, most current recruiting and hiring is built around the lower-rated elements. This kind of valuation often leads to higher turnover (especially of the most passionate) but produces a deadened place to work for those who choose to stay.

Take a very different view of people. People are not costs (although they are reflected that way in financial statements), resources, or assets. If we think they are, we ask all sorts of bad questions, like "How do we get more out of this _____ (expenditure, resource, asset)? How do we use them more effectively?" People are actually investors—they can choose to care or not, contribute or not, create or not, add value or not, spend their finite lives in our organizations or not. If we think of them this way, our question becomes, "How can we create an organization that will be an attractive place for personal investment by passionate people?" In a number of industries that are having a very hard time attracting and keeping young people, this question takes on an even higher level of urgency.

Restructure work around passions rather than functions or skills. We need to match passions and assignments, rather than making mechanical linkages (like job descriptions to resumes). Why would we want people doing anything they don't inherently care about?

Remove hindrances to passion. Rigid structures, functional silos, politically driven and mindless meetings, overstuffed policy manuals, procedures and protocols for everything, tight restrictions around most actions, rules that serve as masters rather than servants, rewards that don't follow results, massive focus on the 5 percent of people who are terrible rather than the 95 percent who would like to care—we must chop our way through this jungle of management madness.

Tie passion to performance. This is a more natural connection than many suppose. In the Luman Consultants International and American Management Association survey, here is how survey respondents rated various activities for their effectiveness in building high-performance organizations (percentage rating a 6 or 7):

Element	Rating, as a Policy	Rating, My Own Organization
Committed Workforce	76.8%	37.6%
Strategic Planning	65.0%	21.2%
Reward/Recognition	59.2%	12.8%
Goals w/Measurement	58.9%	17.1%
Compensation/Benefits	50.6%	14.2%

These results illustrate the fundamental truth of the principle, "People first, strategy second." Let's get the commitment, and then let's have our committed team evolve a dynamic strategy. Even with all of the relative effort spent in most organizations on the last three items, note that none were rated nearly as high as a "Committed Workforce." In practice, all were rated at wretched levels. Compensation and benefits, the object of so much focus in most organizations, were only rated internally as "very high" by 14.2% of the respondents, even though leaders rely on these to reduce turnover, attract new hires, and motivate performance.

EXPECT PASSION

The question that it seems I shouldn't have to ask is, "Why on earth would we have anyone working for our organization who isn't as passionate about it as I am?"

If we aren't careful, we can fall victim to bell-curve thinking—"We'll have a few believers, a bunch of relatively committed people in the middle, and then the cynics." Although it may be that talent and competence fall along some sort of bell curve, passion takes its own stubborn shape.

We have seen organizations skewed way to the left, where the passion level is high and is almost all negative, and we have had the privilege of working with leaders and organizations to produce a passion curve skewed way to the right, where the majority of people are highly passionate and committed, we're still getting some on board, and the voice of negativism has been reduced to a whisper.

It is fair and reasonable for us to expect everyone in our organization to choose passion. To show up and do decent work is necessary but insufficient.

But we've got to be on our guard, because there are some very poor ways to expect passion.

- Demand it—We can insist that our people be passionate—or else. "I want to see some excitement around this program!" or "I'm sick of the lack of commitment in this office!" The problem is that passion has to be ignited from within, one person or team at a time. "The beatings will continue until morale improves" is not a formula for a passionate organization.
- Demand loyalty—"Loyalty,'" as too many people define it, is a poor substitute for passion. We need people who will commit to the vision and values and produce substantial results, not people who will make us feel personally secure. One CEO said about loyalty, "what too often happens is that CEOs surround themselves with sycophants, constructing echo chambers of agreement. Loyalty becomes a code word for intellectual servitude."[8]
- Use negative reinforcement—It is amazing that in the twenty-first century there could still be people who believe that criticizing people publicly and humiliating others in front of their peers or subordinates is an effective, spirit-building tool.
- Use fear—We might think we can "light a fire under" people by threats and people's related fear of loss, but the fire only heats performance as long as we keep stoking it. As always, the best people will get out of the skillet first.
- Tell people they're lucky—One of the most worn-out management attitudes is, "They are lucky to have a job." Or, "We're paying them a lot, so I want to see some fire in the belly in return." There is a difference in kind and degree between "feeling lucky" and being passionate.
- Vocally compare people to yourself—I once worked for the sole owner of a business who was proud of telling us frequently, "I am 100 percent committed to this organization." No kidding. We can use ourselves as examples to illustrate a point we are making, but we would be naïve to think we can use this example to spur commitment or enthusiasm.

These approaches are certainly quicker to implement than the ideas described below. The only problem is that they are also quicker to annihilate true passion.

There are some important things we can do as leaders to set an expectation for passion.

Measure potential hires on whether they are:

- Passionate about what we do—This means that they are not wanting to work for our organization just because they need a job, but because they need to do something worthwhile and believe they can do it best with us.

- Passionate about what they do—This means they aren't in their current career path because of inertia or path dependency but, rather, because what they are doing expresses who they are as human beings.
- Passionate about developing the people who work for and around them—This means they aren't trying to live a solo life in a community that needs them but, rather, have a genuine and consistent interest in enhancing other people's lives and work.

These are threshold expectations. If people don't strongly exhibit these, we gladly send them to a competitor. And in an ongoing way we evaluate our current team—full- and part-time employees, independent contractors, agents, whatever—on these same criteria.

Because passion requires mutual commitment, we can expect passion by taking the first pass at making that mutual commitment. We can expect commitment from our teams only if we make a commitment ourselves. To expect passion and "loyalty" from people to whom we have not made a commitment is simply folly.

Let people know clearly that high levels of passion are a condition of employment, advancement, and compensation. Nothing else will save them if they are missing it—not competence, knowledge, skills, experience, tenure, relationships. We can't accept those things as the core and hope we can add passion.

Treat people as though they have the passion. If we assume that people don't care, we won't take the time to give them what they need to participate in the life of the organization in an informed and meaningful way. We need to provide enough background to people that we and they know they can contribute and then lay out our expectations for contribution.

Set the example. We are passionate, whatever the obstacles or challenges or mistakes or losses. We are relentless in our passion, and we will accept nothing less from ourselves. Then we are in a position to expect that same relentless passion from everyone in our organizations.

We need to let our people know that "The passionless cannot change history."[9] We should expect everyone in our organization to be a vibrant agent of change.

THINKING AND RESPONDING PARADOXICALLY

Leaders who manage this paradox encourage their people to choose to be passionate about whatever task is before them. At the same time, these leaders design their organizations and train leaders to get people into areas where they can be the most passionate.

In other words, we expect people to choose to be passionate, even as we help them to find and pursue their passions. As we think of these two ideas together, creating passion and expecting passion, we begin to understand the passion paradox.

If people make more choices to be passionate, they earn more opportunities to work in areas that most interest them. We want to encourage people to *choose* to be passionate about whatever is in their area of responsibility and accountability. We tell people not to use boredom or "beneath me" thinking as a reason to slough off their work. They can choose, because it is part of their life and they are accountable for turning it into excellence, for pouring themselves into it because it is the right thing to do. It is never the wrong time to do the right thing.

If people choose to be more passionate, we make sure that they should earn more ready placement in areas of great passion. We want everyone to be moved into these areas in the long term, but the first people in line are the ones who—regardless of obstacles, regardless of boredom, regardless of anything—are working passionately on a daily basis.

At the same time, if we design our hiring and assignments around people's intrinsic passions, we will make it easier for them to choose to be passionate. We want to design the organization and train leaders to get people into areas where they can be the most passionate. Why would we want people permanently mired in work that doesn't use the best of who they are, doesn't stir their souls, doesn't make it easy for them to be passionate? Work restructuring is not as difficult as it might appear, and the potential payoff for the organization and the individual is enormous.[10]

We understand that if we do more to place people in areas and give them work about which they are naturally passionate, we'll make it easier for people to choose to be passionate. Passion is always a choice. We just want to make it the easy one.

It was said about all-time hockey great Wayne Gretzky that "Even in his prime, Gretzky wasn't very fast; his shot was oddly weak, and he was last on the team in strength training. As he said . . . 'Maybe it wasn't talent the Lord gave me. Maybe it was the passion.'"[11]

Just maybe.

CHAPTER 12

INVITE PEOPLE IN AND SEND PEOPLE HOME

It takes a wise man to discover a wise man.[1]

—*Diogenes Laertius*

The people we bring in aren't some peripheral part of our organizations, appendages to a monolithic machine. What we will be in three or five or ten years will be determined significantly—perhaps almost totally—by the people who have joined our organization. As I have worked with hundreds of organizations over the years, I have been amazed at the people they invite into their organizations and then decide to keep. The number of people who are operating at mediocre, value-draining levels is stupendous, and the capacity of organizations to put up with this mediocrity is astonishingly vast. Why organizations would tolerate this type of value-drain when there are excellent, driven, passionate people working in organizations right down the street is unanswerable.

Managing this paradox starts with believing that it is possible to have an organization in which people are not "normally distributed." Brilliant leaders can fall into stupefaction in a misguided effort to apply statistical tools to people and organizations. As we suggested in the last chapter, when we start with the mindset that people always fall along a bell curve (and accordingly even force rank them on a bell curve), it is amazing how easily that expectation will be met.

However, even in organizations that believe in bell curves, the distribution of people more closely resembles the feudal system of the Middle Ages than a well-constructed statistical model. The organizations have a passionate, power-enriched, well-compensated few and the clock-watching, disempowered, lesser-compensated masses. For many of us, if we could just get our organizations *up* to a normal distribution on passion and performance, we would see a significant upturn in organizational effectiveness.

Great leaders should want their organizations to skew toward passion and performance. At Luman Consultants International, we call this the "Rule of the 95 and the 5." We want to design our organizations to be places in which the vast majority of people are doing extraordinary things, and in which the sluggards are marginalized. For this design to work, it has to include controlled points of entry and exit.

The key to managing this paradox is to invite the right people in and to send the others home.

INVITE PEOPLE IN

There are a surprising number of very ineffective ways to invite people into our organizations:

- Focus on credentials—We are a credential-enamored world, in which what has been conferred on us is more important than who we are, what we know, and what we can contribute. Credentials are the most vastly overrated items on the criteria for the guest list.
- Focus on experience—Few things have the allure of experience. But is it useful? Is it transferable? Unless it has a relatively direct connection to what we need the employee to do, experience should be heavily discounted. Even then, people can have a lot of experience in something they loathe.
- Lure them—We see a person who looks great, and we go all out to get them. Whatever it takes. Up the ante. Throw more money at it. But this is the wrong reason for people worth their salt to go to work with us. We will find that if we invite them in for the wrong reasons, we'll have to keep furnishing the wrong reasons to keep them. And if they come for the wrong reasons, they're likely to leave for the wrong reasons as well.
- Use a speedy process—Hiring, like marrying, is a decision that should take more time than it usually does. Many activities in most organizations could be speeded up without harm. Hiring people is not one of them.
- Find people who "fit the budget"—Most of us have to live within budgets, but bargain hunting while building the heart of an organization is madness. We've found winners and believers, but our compensation limit is X and it will take $X + 20\%$ to get them. If our $X + 20\%$ will deliver a five or ten times return in short order, why are we fudging on fractions? If we just can't hire the best person, it's better to limp along and do the work ourselves than make a "reasonable" hire for X. Worse yet are the times we can't hire our $X + 20\%$ but can hire two for X, so we have two people performing below the level of our needs—and wasting time interacting with each other.

So how should we go about inviting people in? What are the standards for inviting people in?

Define the criteria for the guest list. Who really belongs here? What kind of person will thrive in this environment? Who will help us build something even greater around our shared core? We should take the time to produce descriptions of ideal candidates—regardless of the work they will be doing. Our decisions need to be built primarily on substantial, not superficial, criteria.

Focus on passion. This needs to be the central theme of our initial interview. Who cares whether they're competent, if they don't care? If what excites us doesn't excite them, we are in deep trouble. The proverb, "The one who is not with us is against us," strongly applies here. We can and should take steps to design a passion-friendly culture, but we get a tremendous head start if we ensure that people coming through the door already have it.

Think about the alignment of values. This is generally worthy of taking up the second interview (and yes, there should be more than two). If what is important to us isn't important to them, the trouble goes deeper. This can't just be a courtesy check ("What do you think of our statement of values?"). Some key questions: "Can you give me two examples of how you have practiced each of our values in the past?" "Can you give me two examples of how you have seen each of our values violated elsewhere, and what you did about that?" "Can you tell us about your personal value set, and then make the connection for us between those and our values?"

Look at authenticity. It is hard to discern authenticity without a long process of deepening conversations and shared experience. But we need to know if the passions and values and alignments are real. There are questions that can help, but plenty of time is the saving element here. We need to talk long enough that we have a real sense of who this person is. I don't know how you can do this in fewer than four or five discussions.

Evaluate competence. Credentials and experience aren't worthless here, but they are close. Real competence is all about *performance*. What you *know* and what you've *done* are tiny matters compared with what you've *delivered*. We've got to learn about accomplishments but also about the context and challenges that surrounded those accomplishments: "Tell me about the situation you were in, and how that affected your performance"; "What things made your performance more difficult, and how did you overcome them?"; "What was going well and made your performance a bit easier than normal?"

Look hard at the diversity they bring to the game. In addition to the obvious diversities of race, ethnic background, gender, and age—passive diversities—we need the active diversities of thought, perspective, and ability to create new ideas out of cultural odds and ends. Diversity is an elusive ingredient, and *useful* diversity falls somewhere between superficial differences and obnoxious disagreement about everything. Every useful difference fails to help us at a high level if the person won't insist on originality and excellence.

Use orientation as an extension of hiring. We are fallible, and some bad matches can still get through the door, but we need to keep them in the vestibule. Orientation in most organizations assumes that the person is a "done deal" and merely attempts to get the person *settled*. Orientation in great organizations assumes that the person might have slipped through the door when we weren't looking and attempts to get the person *rattled*. We have clients who have an orientation period of a week or more, and people at times either quit or are let go during that period.

Give people a lot of reasons to accept our invitation. One author noted that "When companies recruit, they often focus on attracting precisely those people who will be the most difficult to retain."[2] His solution was to lower our standards and find people who are less likely to leave. This is precisely the wrong answer. We want the people who are going to be a challenge to keep. We need to raise our standards. We need to make it harder to get in and make that difficulty part of the allure. And we need to draw them with our whole package—our vision, mission, values, strategy, offering, everything we have that makes us "us." If they come for a lot of reasons they will have a lot of reasons to stay.

Keep inviting people in. We need to keep the relationship fresh. "Recruit your people every day," noted a formal naval officer, "even though your crew is already on board."[3] We need to continue to invite them in. Would they come based on our relationship and what they are doing today? Is the level of commitment growing or shrinking? Are we still the best investment around?

To grow, we have to invite people in. To grow well, they have to be the right people.

SEND PEOPLE HOME

People get sent home from organizations all the time.

It is at times a sad thing to have to send them home. We might really like them. They might be "nice people." The team has gotten used to them. It can hurt to go through the trauma of final separation.

No matter. If they don't fit, they've got to go. And the sooner the better.

But we can err greatly if we send them home for the wrong reasons. Here are some lousy rationales for sending people home:

- They are disagreeable—There is a big difference between being obnoxious because you are a jerk and being obnoxious because you are disagreeing with a failing approach. The really frightening fact is that it is easier to keep the jerk around than the fussy person who cares, because although the jerk is annoying he isn't challenging the status quo.
- They refuse to be intimidated—People too easily confuse "respect for authority" with "you'll keep quiet if you know what's good for you." People that treat those in positions of formal authority—or for that matter, anyone—with disrespect should certainly have no place with us. But if they simply won't cave in to normal organizational fear, if they are unafraid to speak the truth, we have gold and should *never* send them home.

- They are mavericks—One of the biggest lies in the world of organizations is, "We really value diversity around here." If by "diversity" they mean, "willing to have women and men, people of all races and ethnicities—as long as they don't stray from the party line or take any risks," maybe so. But if they mean, "willing to think and act independently on a regular basis whether or not it annoys other people," probably not. Organizations think they are doing well when they "tolerate" mavericks. Great organizations nurture and celebrate them.
- They make mistakes—When there is failure, the natural response is to look for someone to blame. The natural response is wrong. It creates a whole organizational mindset that mistakes are terrible—even evil. The person being punished is often the wrong person—the primary people who ought to "get it" often do not, because they are the most powerful or have friends in high places or had the good fortune of not being "out front" on the program or initiative. And it takes our attention away from the potential value of the mistake—if we've made it and no one else has, that mistake gives us knowledge that our competitors have no way of gaining and a potential competitive advantage.
- They are threatening—Powerful people—meaning people who use power as a tool to make a difference, and thus will challenge the status quo—are profoundly threatening to some leaders and organizations. They can get squeezed out of boards, leadership groups, teams, and organizations. They are the very ones who will save us from disaster if they can avoid being dubbed "problems" for their relentless fight for the better way.

What we are saying here is that people shouldn't be sent home for obvious, superficial reasons, like embarrassing us with a good question (unless it was done to embarrass us). They should be sent home for the deep, disturbing, organization-destroying reasons that may not be so obvious. How many organizations drive out after six months the booming prophet who is annoying them with the truth, while granting lifetime tenure to the subtle disbeliever who is destroying them?

So how do we go about sending people home? What are the criteria for sending people home?

Give up false hopes. These hopes can be many: they may work out, they might be better than they seem after that third interview, we can improve this person, great leadership will stir them to better performance. Whatever the form, these false hopes are deadly. If it isn't a great fit from the start, it isn't likely to morph into one over time. The few that might aren't nearly enough reward for the pain of the many who won't.

Create a strong culture that rejects by its very strength those who don't appreciate it. Great leaders have learned that the *right* people to send home are the people who are *wrong* for you. And the earlier we can send them home the better—the first interview is better than second, second than third, third than orientation, orientation than a 90-day review. There is less damage to the person and the organization.

Send people home when there is substantial misalignment of passions, values, and expectations. It isn't safe to assume that these things, even if they were in alignment at the start, will stay in alignment over time. People and organizations change, and that change can move them very far apart.

Send people home when they are destructive. This includes far more people than those who steal or destroy company property. It includes people who focus on their own agenda at the expense of the organization, don't deliver consistent results, don't add value, shred our values by their behaviors, build empires, obstruct fresh ideas and change, disrespect and demolish other people, insist on rewards out of proportion with their contributions. In some organizations, this could be three-fourths or more of the people—at least of the people at the highest levels.

Much of this can be addressed by a deeply rooted process of organizational transformation. If we are in organizations that are struggling with weak cultures, misalignment, or destructive behaviors, we probably have an opportunity to initiate such a process. These things never improve by themselves but continue to follow the law of entropy until the energy is completely gone, until the window of opportunity is slammed shut.

Short of this type of initiative, we need to give decent people a chance to change before we decide to send them home. It's the right thing to do, more effective than starting from scratch with a new person and less traumatic to the organization that has absorbed them—but not too long. It isn't fair to the organization, and it isn't fair to the people. They need a chance to be invited into a place where they can be celebrated.

We need to give people a clear, consistent opportunity to self-select out of the organization. As we've discussed, it's tough to test values alignment, authenticity, competence, and diversity. Honeymoon periods often give way to the reality that this match is not all that one (or both) parties thought it would be. People can feel "locked in" for a variety of bad reasons—inertia, the difficulty of changing jobs, fear of losing relationships, fear of the unknown—so we have to help them.

Sending people home is incredibly important to building a passionate, high-performance organization. Laying out and enforcing this practice is a tier-one responsibility of senior leadership, not just of people staffers.

THINKING AND RESPONDING PARADOXICALLY

Paradoxical leaders bring in people who aren't limited by past golden ideas, flashy successes, or recent failures.

They know that the first order of business is to create an attractive "investment" opportunity for people to consider as they think about investing—their time, energy, knowledge, wisdom, experience, and lives. One research project concluded that "the majority of candidates move jobs because they are seeking a different working environment and corporate culture." In splitting the respondents into higher and lower income segments, they found that "Those in the upper earnings bracket ranked corporate culture above salary and benefits [while those] earning less...were more likely to cite money as a major motivator for changing jobs, but ranked culture as the next most important factor."[4] We create something that gives us a chance at the best possible people—for us.

And paradoxical leaders send people home who turn sour. These leaders rid their organizations of people who are problems rather than problem-solvers, who hang onto the past rather than invent new ways to add and create value, or serve customers, or conceive the future.

And they do these two activities at the same time, constantly asking, "Who should we invite in? Who are we missing? Who should we send home? Who is hurting us?"

But they do these two activities at a different pace. We invite people in very, very slowly. It's too easy to make a mistake and too hard to undo it. And we send people home very, very quickly. It's too easy to hope for improvement and too hard to get it. Note that this is the exact opposite of what most organizations do, which is to invite people in fairly quickly and to send them home very slowly. If we're not managing this paradox, we can take hours to make a hiring decision and agonize for months over ending a bad match.

One excellent byproduct of moving the wrong people out quickly is that it forces us to invite the right people in. The pain of terminating, finding time to interview, and investing in development can be a wonderful deterrent to sending out invitations to people who don't belong at our party.

Leaders managing this paradox start—and finish—at the core. They invite people in based on the degree of their alignment with the organization's vision, mission, and values. And they send people home based on the degree of their consistent inability to live in accord with those crucial elements.

Next, they look at the levels of passion and performance—whether or not each person is committed and delivering real results. Great leaders use assignments as a way of sorting the staff. They present large opportunities and problems as a challenge to be outstanding, and then they sort people by how they respond to the challenge. If we want a great organization, a consistently strong, passionate, value-adding response is the only one that is acceptable.

Turnover is a more complex issue than its treatment in most organizations would suggest. Frankly, we need to decrease some turnover (of the passionate performers), hold other turnover at current levels (of the passionate who aren't yet performing at expected levels but have the horsepower to get there), and increase some turnover (of those who aren't passionate and performing, even if they have great credentials and experience or high IQs). We need to segment turnover and ask different questions about the segments. We need people who will commit and add value, and we need to turn over everyone else until only these winners/believers are left.

In closing, let me give a sketch of the Luman Consultants International model for dealing with bad eggs.

- No to fast head count elimination—We don't want to take too long, but we want to make sure we're going after the real problem. When we move quickly, it's like making an ineffective strike at cancer. If we leave cells—the bad attitudes that have spread—the cancer will grow back and damage our culture.
- No to hatcheting while trying to build a Passionate Organization—This approach is confusing to the people who are still with us. The contradictory message—we value you, we value people, everyone is important, we're dumping X people—creates too much cognitive dissonance.
- Yes to using the good to drive out the bad—You can't beat something with nothing. Negative voices are powerful. We need to give people an alternate message that can appeal to the best in them. At first, bad eggs will still have a voice, but it will gradually be marginalized and eventually isolated. A few of the ringleaders might convert, and more will leave the organization. The remaining few will "go dark"—they will keep quiet because no one is still listening. If they don't perform, they can be sent home, and no cancer will be left behind.

It's never "too long" to find and invite in the right person. And few of us have ever fired anyone too soon.

The saying that dominated politics in the early 1990s was, "It's the economy, stupid." Paradoxical leaders know that "It's the people, stupid."

CHAPTER 13

CLARIFY BOUNDARIES AND INCREASE FREEDOM

*We do not expect you to follow us all the time, but if you would have
the goodness to keep in touch with us occasionally ...[1]*

—*Thomas Beecham, Conductor of The London
Philharmonic Orchestra, to a musician*

In the modern world, the power of freedom to improve lives and cultures and
economies is nearly irrefutable.

Not so in the modern organization.

In the modern organization, freedom is too often reserved for the people at
the "top"—often, for the few at the very top, and sometimes, for the lone person
at the head of the whole. He or she has freedom of movement. Everyone else is
constrained.

Freedom—the ability to safely exercise the free will that all of us inherently
possess—is the primary source of creativity and useful endeavor. Organizations
that refuse to access the power of freedom—right now this includes most of the
organizations embedded in free societies—are unnecessarily assigning themselves to lesser results.

But freedom is a dangerous thing. It acts in ways that we can't even understand, much less control. It makes people uncomfortable. It highlights and
magnifies differences when most people want conformity.

Eventually, freedom can even destroy itself. Adolf Hitler was freely elected to
the German chancellorship. The French Revolution destroyed the chains of
monarchy on the way to its own destruction by Napoleon. Rome sagged under
the load of decadent freedoms. All too many sins have been committed in the
name of freedom.

And because of this, societies have learned that boundaries are needed. In a
delicious element of this paradox, boundaries are actually needed to protect and

enhance freedom. Only boundaries can keep freedom from decaying and perhaps destroying itself.[2] We see in this paradox that freedom without boundaries is as bad as boundaries without freedom.

Great leaders know that the shackles need to go, because the organization will never exploit available opportunities with policies, procedures, accepted practices, rules, or regulations. They know that they desperately need good judgment and give great latitude to anyone who displays it for even a minute. They try to combine a free environment with well-exercised free will, a potent mixture that produces personal and organizational growth.

But great leaders also know that freedom from unnecessary restraint does not mean freedom to do anything. We have a chance to learn from history and do what few politicians have done—to increase freedom while clarifying boundaries, and not look at these as mutually exclusive activities.

CLARIFY BOUNDARIES

Boundaries are set for us from our first days. "Don't go out in the street." "Your bedtime is 8:00 p.m." "Don't hit your brother." "You can't watch television until your toys are picked up." "Don't go outside without a coat." "You can't have a snack until you finish your vegetables."

Some of these boundaries make perfect sense, and some may have been the product of parental neuroses, but all of them limited our behavior in some way. That's what boundaries do—they limit our behavior. In their absence, anything goes. One of the first things to go is respect for others and basic human decency.

There are some very prevalent, and very poor, ways to clarify boundaries.

- Confuse boundaries with "rules"—It is very easy to confuse a boundary with a rule. A boundary tells us what we *can't* do, whereas a rule tells us what we *must* do. Boundaries create zones inside which people can freely act. Rules create paths that must be followed to avoid certain consequences. "Any fool can make a rule," noted writer Jonathan Swift," and every fool will mind it."
- Make first boundaries overly constricted—When we don't know what a person or team can do, we often create rigid restrictions and gradually loosen them over time based on performance. There are several possible losses here: first, we lose much of the potential creativity and related value; second, we lose the value that only comes from experience and making necessary mistakes; and third, we lose the very best of our people.
- Try to address every exception—When we try to deal in advance with every possible boundary-buster, we can exhaust ourselves, fill up volumes, and still miss a thousand other ways that the boundary can be violated. General boundaries are usually more effective than specific ones.
- Punish modest violations—The only way to verify whether a boundary is useful or stupid is to test it. If the result is bad, we can reinforce the boundary. If

the result is good, we can stretch it. Good people will often test boundaries, whereas complacent people will consider them inviolable walls. If we punish modest violations, we'll teach everyone to stay far from the walls.

In societies, freedom is destructive without the rule of law. This idea is expressed in the formulation of Samuel B. Rutherford, who switched the word order of the traditional Latin phrase from *rex lex* (the king is law) to *lex rex* (the law is king).

The rule of law means that law should not be arbitrary and based on the preferences and whims of the "powers that be." Even the king—even the president, even the prime minister, even the premier, even the CEO—is under the law and has to answer to it. The law is there to protect us from wrongdoing.

We want to ask ourselves, "What should we put boundaries around to ensure the effective free action of the vast majority of our people?" So how do we clarify boundaries in a constructive manner?

Make boundaries known. If people don't know about or understand the boundaries, they will either run into them (like a dog with an invisible electric fence), or they will be so tentative that they will find a safe corner and stay there.

Clarify the goals of any policies or procedures we have, and describe when exceptions can be taken in the name of freedom. For example, an absence/tardiness policy should have as its goal productive endeavor, not merely requiring people to be physically present even when they are unproductive. This might mean an exception would be appropriate that would allow people to be "absent" or "late" if they are able to work more productively off-site than on-site in a given situation.

Insist on "the way" about a very small number of very large things. There can't be any core disagreement or misalignment with the vision and values of the organization. Treating people in an elevating and dignifying way is nonnegotiable. Taking responsibility and accountability for yourself and your results, making winning decisions, taking value-adding actions, sharing what you have learned and know—all of these are organizational "table stakes." Saying, "This is the way we do things around here," is not what turns us into micromanagers—it's saying this about the wrong things.

As leaders, set self-imposed boundaries on our own freedom of action. By the very nature of power, the people under formal power cannot unilaterally put restraints on our power. This is even so in nations, unless the people in power limit their own freedom to act, or the people form a government of their own or have a revolution. Because of the element of ownership, the options of self government and revolution are not available in organizations—so wise leadership will restrain itself. It won't do this because it is nice; it will do this because it is smart. Senior leadership needs to agree formally on its self-imposed limitations. In societies, this is called a constitution, which defines what the government can—and perhaps more important, cannot—do. Organizations need constitutions (whether published or not) and only wise leadership has the power to create them.

Define levels of decision-making, and steadfastly refuse to intrude or be involved any more than those levels allow. We approve strategies and leave tactics alone. We approve top-line budgets that have predefined levels of detail, with all levels below that reserved for others. We focus on leading our people and managing nobody.

Ask "bounding" questions. Serious questions about boundaries are worth a healthy series of dialogues. Some of the important questions are:

- How should we limit behaviors so that they replace infighting and territorial games with passion?
- How should we bound decision-making so that decisions are not made at the wrong level? This should address decisions that are made at either too high a level (which reduces the usefulness of the higher level) or too low a level (which abdicates responsibility of the higher level and puts undue stress on the lower level).
- How should we limit the allocation of resources so they can only be spent to add or create value?
- How should we define strategies to ensure that they are aligned with, and advancing, our vision and mission?
- How should we limit systems and processes so that they remain means and do not become ends in themselves?
- How should we limit our support staff to require them to really support rather than demand?

Put boundaries around fear. Scared people don't act freely—they don't innovate, they don't volunteer, they don't invest themselves. Deming was right—we need to drive fear from our organizations. We simply can't afford leaders who use fear as a tool. We need to identify them and move them out. The cost to the organization in performance is too high compared with the short-term gains they might produce. And we have to identify behaviors that produce fear. Public criticism (or the threat of it), chastisement for mistakes, erratic feedback, secrecy on topics that don't require secrecy, arbitrary goals set "on high," assignments given without adequate knowledge or experience or authority or resources, and performance evaluations based on bell curves and six sigma run amok—all are examples of organizational behaviors that are designed to produce fear.

Clarifying boundaries is telling the people in an organization what they can't do. The value of this is such that, given such clarity, people can operate with incredible freedom everywhere else.

INCREASE FREEDOM

While writing *Balance of Power: How to Fuel Employee Power without Relinquishing Your Own*,[3] I discovered that what I had observed first-hand in organizations for which I had worked turned out to be prevalent in most organizations: Everyone talks about freedom and "empowerment," but few believe that these concepts will actually work. They are abandoned early and often.

This disconnection between what we know to be true on our better days—that freedom is better than control, that liberty works better than slavery—and what we actually do (or allow our people to do), is certain to produce a stagnant organization. One of my surprising discoveries as a leader, including time as CEO in four different organizations, is that some people don't want to be free. Many more would like to be free, but don't think it is safe, and so willingly trade their freedom for security. Great leaders, however, *insist* on freedom, even for those who don't seem to want it or don't feel safe having it.

It is important for leaders to find out which people really don't want freedom (and who therefore can't be highly useful in a powersharing[4] organization) and which people don't want freedom because it isn't safe (and who therefore can be unleashed in a powersharing organization). The former might prefer to be sent to one of the many petty dictatorships that fill the planet. The latter need to be "detoxed"—they need to be shown the power and value of freedom, that it is safe to use it here, that it is *required* to use it here. We can assure them that in our organization, freedom isn't just possible; it is a condition of employment.

There are some things we can do that are very poor attempts at increasing freedom:

- Grant full trust too soon—Freedom ultimately depends on a number of factors, and among them is trust. We give children that we trust more latitude than those we don't. With a new person, some trust must be granted, but some must be earned. To unleash people too soon, without an understanding of how they will use their freedom, is a poor start to a bad finish.
- Let everyone set his or her own agenda—We can try to get agreement on the "big issues" and then wrongly assume that people will fill in everything they need to do to align with the overall direction.
- Eliminate monitoring—Although it is true that too much monitoring will stifle or kill freedom, too little can lead to very poor consequences. "Let me know if there are any problems" is a noble concept that would work if we were leading something other than people. There are a hundred reasons for people to hide or minimize problems.
- Assume that people are basically good—There is a humanistic streak in most of us that wants to believe the best about people. This idea, although noble, is fatally flawed. People aren't in general "basically" good. They aren't basically bad, either. They are basically both. Human beings are on a continuum, from "mostly good" to "mostly bad," but even the best of us can yield to things like unproductive anger, harming others (at least with our words), and fighting for our own way at the expense of others. We need to increase freedom in a way that doesn't increase the penchant for malevolence.

So if we want to increase freedom, we've got to take a broader view if we want to get it right. How can we intelligently increase freedom?

Focus on possibilities rather than on limitations. Great leaders know that people respond more effectively to the opportunity to score touchdowns than to the threat of reprisal after fumbles. Human beings are designed to respond with their best efforts to messages that offer hope, redemption, and victory, rather than restrictions, threats, and losses.

Ask freedom questions. There are some important questions we need to ask ourselves as leaders if we really want to see the fruit of freedom growing in our organizations:

- How can we replace the evolutionary process of "empowerment" with the radical, higher-level freedom of *powersharing*?
- What can we do to convince people that it is safer to be free in our organizations than it is to be an indentured servant anywhere else?
- How do we embed the principle, "It is never the wrong time to do the right thing," in our culture?
- What can we do to get everyone, including formal leaders, to focus on measurable results and stay out of dictating methods as much as possible? How do we create a mindset that *what* gets done is more important to manage than *how* it gets done, as long as the process is ethical?
- What formal processes and reviews should we put in place to reign in policies and procedures and ensure that they don't morph into people's masters?
- How can we reduce the number of meetings and reports so that people are free in practice, because they are free to spend more of their time on things that in their best judgment will advance the interests of other stakeholders?

Create safety nets. People need to know that a free act made on behalf of the organization, even if it leads to a mistake, will not be fatal to their jobs or careers. The price of freedom is always high. For the organization, it is the cost of mistakes and intermittent chaos that free people will certainly cause. Freedom is not practically meaningful to someone who doesn't feel safe. I once asked an African immigrant to the United States what he liked most about his new country. His answer suggested a fundamental freedom: "That I can go to bed and know that I will not be taken away in the middle of the night."

Give people the freedom to set boundaries for themselves. Boundaries set by the people who will be bound by those laws—the basic idea of representative government—are always the best and most effective boundaries, for a number of reasons:

- The boundaries are chosen rather than imposed, so they avoid natural resistance.
- Participating in boundary creation produces a natural sense of ownership, along with accountability for enforcement (related to both our own behavior and that of others).

- Boundaries will be clearly stated in language that everyone can understand, as they are written by those who will use them.
- The need for exceptions will be openly debated, clearly stated, and taken advantage of because of the openness and clarity.

THINKING AND RESPONDING PARADOXICALLY

This paradox drives us toward an interesting conclusion: We need to clarify boundaries to *increase* freedom rather than to restrict it.

Restriction is often the reason for boundaries. We fear that people will do the wrong thing, or fail to do the right thing, so we introduce boundaries to "help" them make their choices. And we end up with deformed boundaries. There are two types of warped, "restrictive" boundaries:

- *Manipulative* boundaries, which "encourage" people to comply, without a clear threat of punishment. "This is the province of purchasing," "Only HR can recruit," "Good employees are in the office early (or late, or both)," "Never go around your boss"—these are all examples of implicit boundaries, with unclear consequences (or consequences so bad that it isn't polite to mention them).
- *Coercive*—these boundaries tell people in withering detail what will happen to them if they violate them. Spending limits, equipment usage, attendance policies—all in all, these can make us long for the simplicity of the Ten Commandments.

We need to be especially careful not to set restrictive boundaries when we are faced with market turbulence, earthshaking competition, or other outside factors beyond our control. "Other factors equal," wrote historian Will Durant, "internal liberty varies inversely as external danger."[5] It takes great leadership to avoid this inverse relationship.

We also need to increase freedom to clarify our boundaries. Boundaries can't be tested in a laboratory. They can only be tested by free people who deem them "not sacred." The heresy of freedom can test the orthodoxy of boundaries—to see if they are good, to see if they are necessary, to see if they *add value*.

Freedom should be primary when it produces good and not harm. We can and should be tolerant of diversity of thought, disagreement, and constructive dissent because they open the door to knowledge, and perspective, and intuition. Anything that squelches these is bad for business.

Boundaries should be primary when they produce good and not harm. We can and should be intolerant of misalignment with the vision and values, destructive behavior, people who need "managing," and unhealthy consensus. What kind of unity do we need? Unity of direction, values, commitment, and execution. Unity is more than boundaries, but it cannot be maintained in human organizations without clear boundaries.

At its best, leadership is aware of more than the bare-bones potential conflict between freedom and boundaries. We act on two mutually reinforcing ideas: that there is no sustainable freedom without the guidance of reasonable boundaries, and that there are no sustainable boundaries without the guidance of reasonable freedom.

In all things, paradoxical leaders insist both on freedom and on an ever-renewed "best" way. They know that some people won't want freedom and others won't want "the way," and they don't care—because they know that their freedom-lovers need "the way," and that their way-lovers need freedom.

If we hold both in our hands, and exploit the tension between them, we can have freedom that feels safe—and boundaries that feel free.

CHAPTER **14**

INCREASE PRESSURE AND REDUCE STRESS

Hasten slowly.[1]

—*Suetonius*

Great leaders, we are told, "hold people's feet to the fire." They "turn up the heat." They "push people out of their comfort zones." They increase the pressure on people to perform.

At the same time, we know that stressed-out organizations and people are unlikely to perform at a high level. The internal resources to deal with problems and opportunities simply aren't there. People are struggling to stay afloat.

We might wrongly conclude that the only way to increase the pressure to perform is to raise people's stress levels as well, and that the only way to reduce people's stress is to reduce the pressure to perform.

As leaders managing this paradox, we have a simultaneous mission: to relentlessly increase pressure while systematically reducing stress.

INCREASE PRESSURE

Pressure comes from the outside. Because it can make us extremely uncomfortable, we can work very hard to resist and reduce all pressure, even the pressure that drives achievement. Here are some ineffective ways to handle pressure:

• Deny reality—"Things aren't really that bad"; "It's only a temporary dip in sales"; "The market is bound to turn around soon"; "We're due for a break"; "Our customers really can't be expecting that." Reality might be speaking to us very loudly—we should listen.

- Procrastinate—We know we need to change. We're feeling ever-higher levels of anxiety. But there are a million excuses not to change—we haven't studied the situation thoroughly, we don't know all the parameters, we don't have the plans or resources in place, and so on—we really know that we won't be able to dodge the pressure forever, but deferral can seem sweet for a time.
- Focus on the near term—Long-term trends (demographic, customer expectations, product or service viability, etc.) are bearing down on us like a runaway train. We know we need to address them with clear thinking, effective strategy, and serious resource allocation. But there's this other thing we need to take care of first...
- Hope for a miracle—History is replete with stories of leaders facing pressure who, instead of taking action, wait for the saving event. "There's nothing wrong with us that _____ won't fix." Even if a saving event comes, it only saves us for a short time because we haven't addressed the underlying problem.

Building pressure can push us toward renewed excellence even while we're enjoying a lot of success—and even before the current party is over. Jack Welch was right when he said that there are no modest revolutions. Organizations are not transformed without exposure to a lot of pressure. The status quo is too strong, has too many constituents, and is already entrenched.

It takes strong and intelligent leadership to translate all of these voices and languages into effective pressure. If we overstate the case for change, we'll bring too much pressure to bear, and people will resist. If we understate the case for change, we'll bring too little pressure to bear and nothing will happen.

Pressure is a great tool for developing and measuring the maturity, competence, and commitment of an organization or individual. When we apply pressure, we're going to see several things:

- Growth—Pressure makes it impossible to stay in our current condition. We have to change to be able to deal with the pressure—at first to survive, and then to thrive, and then to exploit the opportunities.
- Cracks—Pressure will delineate any cracks in an individual's or group's character. We can see what they are able to do when they're hard-pressed. It lets us know how to assign, develop, and advance them going forward.
- Questions—Pressure makes people ask better questions. "Am I doing something wrong?" "What could I do to make this easier?" "Do I need to change my basic approach to meet this challenge or take advantage of this opportunity?"
- Skills—If we have areas that need development, there's nothing more potent to highlight this than pressure. Someone doing good work under "peaceful" conditions may be wholly inadequate under pressure.
- Tenacity—Pressure lets us see whether people respond with more commitment and determination or less. Do they dig in? Do they drop out? Let's find out what our people are made of. "A man is not finished when he's defeated," noted one U.S. president, "he's finished when he quits."[2]

So pressure is extremely valuable. How should we increase it? There are some very effective ways to increase pressure.

Have high expectations. There is no question that we are likely to get what we expect. In organizations that expect people below the senior leadership team or middle management to be uncommitted, lazy, or incompetent, it is amazing how frequently that is exactly what we find. If we expect people to be committed, energized, and focused, this is what we find. People need high expectations to achieve, but because of their fear of failure, they can push back on those expectations. "Keeping our expectations low protects us from disappointment," writes Gordon Livingston.[3]

Avoid false hopes. There is a big difference between high expectations and false hopes. High expectations will require a stretch, but we really do have a chance of meeting them. We are committing ourselves and our people and our resources to their accomplishment. False hopes, in contrast, are rooted in wishful thinking. Saying, "We want to double our sales in five years," without the necessary thinking and planning and hard work and willingness to face reality and change is a pipe dream.

Focus on, or create, opposition. Few things bring pressure more than a serious opponent. The opposition can be high customer expectations, new pressure from competitors, tight deadlines, required deliverables based on strictly limited resources, or simply "They say" statements (that we can't do it, that nobody can do it, etc.).

Set hard-to-hit, measurable goals. If we want to encourage ingenuity and creativity, few things are as effective.

Introduce healthy comparisons—Something about being compared to others brings out the competitiveness in most people. We don't want to do it in a degrading way, but we can accomplish a lot by asking, "What do they know that we don't?"

Know where to "drill down" and where to ease up. When do we dig into the details? When do we apply the pressure of close scrutiny?

- To ensure nonnegotiable results—If something has to happen or else, we'd better drill down.
- To teach the vision, mission, values, behaviors, strategy, or process—We should constantly test our people on whether or not they "get" these.
- To set an example—We need to show them how to do it "our way" (e.g., how we relate to customers) and how not to do it.

However, it is destructive to efficiency and morale to drill down on details because we don't trust our people, have a need to control, or want to throw our weight around.

Relish a defeat. "The real glory," said American football legend Vince Lombardi, "is being knocked to your knees and then coming back." Instead of sweeping failure under the carpet, we should challenge ourselves to beat that result in every conceivable way going forward.

People do not burn out because they work hard. People burn out because they are misplaced, misused, or mistreated. They burn out when we forget that people are not the same thing as their job, and when they fail to remember that they are much greater than anything they can do.

The pressure to perform, if managed well, is the key to ignition, not burnout.

REDUCE STRESS

Stress comes from the inside, as an internal response to external pressure (real, perceived, or imagined).

Most of the "work–life balance" experts have a simplistic plan. Their basic proposition is usually to reduce the amount of work, and then to equate that with reducing the amount of stress. But what if work is pleasurable and the rest of life is stressful? What if work feels like heaven and home feels like hell? "What we call stress is sometimes stimulating and can bring out the best features in our makeup," said famed Dr. Michael DeBakey, then ninety-six years old, "Work can block out the unpleasant things we have to deal with every day."[4]

Even so, the need to reduce stress in organizations has become paramount. Stress-induced health issues and friction between harried people—these problems have indeed become an epidemic.

Unaddressed stress eats up human beings and also eats up performance in a long, slow process. Performance goes down, creativity disappears, and the thought becomes "How do I get this done?" rather than "How do I create value?" We can become like the many soldiers who no longer think about why they are fighting but only about how they can avoid being killed.

In spite of this reaction, leaders often refuse to reduce stress. There are a number of reasons that they might offer:

- "It's not my problem"—We can take the approach that stress is a personal issue and not a matter of organizational concern. "If they can't take the heat, they should get out of the kitchen."
- "The advantages far outweigh the disadvantages"—A few people may suffer ill effects, but that's a small price to pay for the overall positive effects of people internalizing pressure.
- "It will produce a loss of momentum"—We've finally got the engine moving. Why stop it now? If people are more relaxed, how can results go anywhere but down?
- "These people can take it"—At times, it seems like we are "babying" people. Why don't they just step up to the plate?

This resistance to reducing stress gets compounded when performance is less than acceptable. "I'm supposed to reduce their stress when they're already underperforming? Are you kidding? They need a little *more* stress!"

But reducing high levels of unrelenting stress is, ironically, crucial to high performance. There are several important reasons.

First, stress leaves people with no "margin." Margin—space, slower pace, time for thought, room for fragments of new ideas to materialize, opportunity to sit with a colleague and create something new—is where the future is conceived and born.

Second, stress can and will take a massive toll on human beings and human institutions. Even brilliant, goal-oriented people can collapse under the strain. Team relationships can be reduced to mutual annoyance punctuated by open conflict.

Third, stress turns normal commitments into overcommitments. What would have been reasonable to commit under less stressful times is now unlikely to occur. This is in part because people don't have the time to fully evaluate the nature of the commitment before they make it. It is also because they make the commitment based on their memory of what they used to be able to do, rather than on current realities.

Fourth, stress decimates quality over time. People who used to perform at a superb level are now operating at a very high level. Soon it will be high, and even sooner it will be average. Only when the pace of deterioration picks up does it become apparent that the star performing person or team has lost it.

Given all of this, there have been attempts made to reduce stress that have not gotten the job done:

- Wellness programs—Although there is nothing wrong with these programs in themselves, and they can produce some good, they are terrible substitutes for having an organizational focus on reducing stress.
- Environmental trinkets—Soft music, dress-down Fridays, company-furnished lunch—all are fine ideas, but they can't even dent true, endemic stress.
- Sabbaticals—A sabbatical, from a few days to months, can be a wonderful tool for getting people out of thinking/acting ruts and refreshing their creativity. They are the wrong tool for dealing with an untenable situation. If the person coming out of that kind of situation faces a return to it, the sabbatical won't even last until they return. The stress will begin bearing down as they get close to doomsday.
- Exercise—Although vigorous exercise or physical activity can indeed lower stress, it is insufficient to reduce stress long enough or deeply enough to allow the person to be creative and add maximum value.

There are some very effective ways to approach this critical area of reducing stress:

Focus on the positive. Pressure derives from a call to help meet a challenging goal. Stress comes from a call to avoid mistakes. People and teams respond very differently to positive and negative messages. A focus on scoring touchdowns brings a positive pressure. A focus on not fumbling brings negative stress and, ironically, a greater likelihood of fumbling.

Don't overpromote. People who are good and like what they do are generally promoted until they aren't good and hate what they do. This produces a daily stress that few are capable of handling well.

Don't underpromote. In contrast, people can be so good at their current jobs that the organization won't promote them to something they could be even better at and enjoy even more. Promotion is important because it reduces the stress that derives from feeling unfulfilled.

Place people where they are appreciated. Mike Murdock encourages people to go where they are celebrated, not tolerated. Why have people working for a boss who isn't their biggest cheerleader?

Move people away from working with major annoyances. Warren Buffett reminds us not to work with people or organizations who make our stomachs churn. We should always move people away from the bad attitudes, which are more contagious than the flu. While we're at it, we should also consider firing nasty, demanding, chintzy customers who make it miserable for our people to work for us.

Eliminate the peripheral pressures. Life and work create enough unavoidable pressures. People are under pressure to meet goals, increase sales and margins, serve more people, have higher quality. These are the nonnegotiable pressures, and they are good ones—pressures that produce higher performance. But all of the peripheral pressures—like unnecessary internal presentations, long review chains, arbitrary report deadlines, non-value-added meetings that absorb precious time—are under a leader's control and should be eliminated.

Encourage people to prepare. A lot of stress is generated by procrastinating on a dreaded assignment that becomes more dreaded by the passing day. Simple, early steps of preparation, even if they only amount to a small percentage of the total work, can eliminate the stress that comes from fear of the unknown. One of my publishers requires submission of the first three chapters early in the writing period. An early milestone on any project or assignment can have the same effect.

Become risk and mistake friendly. It is very hard not to build up a lot of stress when every day seems to bring career risks and any mistake can be a fatal one. Paradoxical leaders know that people have to execute better and make more mistakes. They weed out all waste, no matter how small, in part to free up resources to make more mistakes. They are willing to try goofy ideas because they have created some margin to allow for the try. They push for fresh initiatives out on the cutting edge and accept with good grace that some of them just won't work. These leaders eliminate incompetence and forgive mistakes.

Let people have a little time to float between challenging, high-pressure assignments. This type of respite is partly so people can recuperate, and partly so they can operate on a different plane, where thoughts and ideas and innovations that had no room in the midst of the adrenaline rush can now find a home. We need to let a little of this "focused wandering" occur and not assume that people are "off point."

Take actions to reduce your own stress. Remember that your attention is your most valuable and scarcest personal resource, so spend it only where you feel good about the purchase. Ask yourself, "Will this *really* be a place for me to make a unique contribution?" You need to check to make sure you're doing only that which you care about most. When feeling the negative feelings that come from hearing that a certain person is on the phone, ask, "Why am I responding to this?" or "Do I *really* have to do this?" The only answers aren't "yes" and "no." Other options: "maybe," "later," saying "yes" to part of the request, and offering alternatives.

A big part of reducing stress is just to admit your own frailty, which is hard for "Type A" leaders to do but more critical for us than anyone else. As a leader, you'll probably have to create your own margin. If we don't, we'll kill ourselves and take a strong step toward killing our team with unremitting pressure that is coming in part from our own unmanaged stress.

As leaders, it is our responsibility to manage the stress levels in our organizations. We need to be able to say to our people, as writer Jonathan Swift once said, "May you live all the days of your life."

THINKING AND RESPONDING PARADOXICALLY

Great leaders know that they have to turn coal into diamonds—fast. So they step up the pressure and make everyone feel the urgency. But they very deliberately build in stress relief.

We have to stretch our people without stressing them. Human performance evaporates under a long period of unrelieved boredom—too little pressure—and it evaporates under a long period of unrelieved stress—too much pressure. People need to work at something long enough to get good, to develop real competence, but not long enough to get stale, to develop cynicism.

Great leaders manage the pressure and stress levels in their organizations. When they raise the pressure to meet higher expectations, they watch the corresponding levels of stress. They know that the stress levels are going to go up, that this is useful for moving people out of their comfort zones, and that at some point the pressure will increase the stress so much that people will begin to fold.

They know that there are two ways to manage these levels. One is to reduce the pressure. We've increased the pressure to develop new products, and we're now significantly past our designated result of X percent of our sales coming from products introduced in the past Y years. So we don't raise the bar higher, and we may in fact lower it a bit—in part to reduce the stress, in part to give the organization a needed pit stop so we can effectively reenter the race, and in part to allow us to optimize what we've already created. At an appropriate time, we raise the bar and the related pressure again. Changing levels of pressure are more effective than an unvarying one.

Reducing the pressure is definitely the course of action when we've gone too far, when we've raised the bar too high, when we've gotten people not only past their comfort zones but past their competence or experience or talent. We're admitting that we're not all-knowing, and that we weren't sure exactly where to set the bar. But reducing pressure is not the preferred way to reduce stress. To reduce the pressure is to relax the expectations. It's a good way to reduce stress but often a terrible way to run a business.

The second way is to reduce the stress directly, while leaving the pressure alone. We call time-outs. We deliberately design spaces between heart-throbbing assignments, especially for our great performers. We insist on focused sabbaticals, both short (a long lunch, an afternoon, a few days) and long (a week, a month, a quarter), but all with a purpose—to redesign the job and environment when they return. We provide a stress-reducing kind of pressure by moving people to new areas and new projects—stress takes on more power when it's the same material for a long period of time.

We need to manage the pressure/stress levels in a customized way, by person or department. Not every person or team responds to pressure in the same way. One may need time away, another more encouragement, another more hand-holding, and yet another more resources.

Here is a key question: How can we have high expectations and high tolerance at the same time? High expectations make high *performance* possible, and high tolerance makes high *expectations* possible. No one will go out on a high wire if there is no safety net. To ensure high expectations will be met, create a risk-friendly, mistake-friendly environment.

In our firm, for example, one of our cardinal tenets is that we never cancel, miss, or show up late for a client meeting, phone call, or other interaction. The pressure not to do these things is intense. People are expected to make all necessary preparation, take all possible steps, and be tenacious in meeting this expectation. We have left for client meetings in other cities days early to beat the weather. We have finagled and negotiated and paid extra. We have gone to meetings with headaches and knee braces and crutches, and without voices or spare clothes or food. Clients can cancel or be late, but we cannot.

At the same time, we are relentlessly concerned about the well-being of the wonderful people who have chosen to commit to our vision and mission and team. We encourage people not to travel if conditions are poor. We send people home early to make sure they are safe. We nudge people to take mental health days and to attend special midday family events. We bleed with people when they suffer a personal loss. We allow flexible schedules when we can.

We know that people cannot compartmentalize their lives so that problems in one area won't carry over into another, so we do what we can to make everything work coherently for them. We don't want work-life balance, we want work–life *interdependence, whole*–life balance.

If we are leaders who have both someone to report to (and even CEOs have a board of directors or trustees) and direct reports, we have to bring pressure to our team on behalf of the people to whom we report. We have to protect the interests of the organization and its leaders by delivering high-pressure results.

At the same time, we have to reduce the stress of the people who report to us. We have to protect the interests of the organization and its staff by delivering low-stress structures and processes. We have to protect the organization as a whole by constantly pouring on the pressure and continually reducing its destructive edge.

Environments that grow people are concerned more with personal development than career development. "Let's turn up the heat. Let's see what they can do and how their character responds and develops. Let's stay close to provide support and a safety net. Let's make sure we don't leave them out there so far that they fail." Who knows what people can grow into being if we develop them as people rather than channeling them into a "career development" path. We need to develop multifaceted human beings, not single-view "managers-in-waiting."

Great leaders increase pressure, day after day, on issue after issue. And they reduce stress, day after day, person by person, team by team. Their goal is to build teams that can continuously respond to high levels of pressure *because* they have the freedom to do so with low levels of stress.

These leaders know a powerful truth: We need both war rooms and party rooms.

And the rooms should be adjoining.

CHAPTER 15

ELIMINATE IDEAS AND EXPAND CREATIVITY

Those who govern, having much business on their hands, do not generally like to take the trouble of considering and carrying into execution new projects. The best public measures are therefore ... forced by the occasion.[1]

—*Benjamin Franklin*

"Jim, I hear what you're saying about stirring creativity in the whole organization, but won't that cause problems when we get stupid or impractical ideas, don't give feedback on all of the ideas we receive, or decide not to implement many of them?"

I have heard these kinds of comments from hundreds of leaders over the years. If we're afraid of what we'll get, we have created an intense emotional incentive to discourage creativity.

The interesting thing is, expanding creativity doesn't have to produce a flood of bad ideas, require a massive feedback infrastructure, or force leaders into a "thumbs down" mode with their people—*if we approach it properly*. Expanding creativity will only produce all of those unpleasantries if we take the approach that is standard in 99 percent of organizations.

We need a wide array of ideas so we will have a better chance of finding real winners for execution, and we need to keep ourselves from being distracted by good, mediocre, and bad ideas—or the act of processing them.

We need to expand our innovative capabilities dramatically and develop a seamless way to eliminate most ideas those capabilities produce.

ELIMINATE IDEAS

A lot of energy can be spent thinking about and trying to implement stupid, worthless, or low-value-added ideas. To eliminate these organizational distractions is critical.

Unfortunately, the following approaches to eliminating ideas are both widespread and awful.

- Dismiss the case without a hearing—A lot of good ideas can be eliminated simply because they aren't understood.
- Use emotional blitzkrieg—People who can stand up to rigorous intellectual scrutiny of their ideas can often be vulnerable to emotional assault. It can be subtle—a grunt, a frown, making a face, a shaking of the head—but it can be a more effective eliminator than a well-thought-out response.
- Use strict evaluation criteria—Unformed ideas simply can't stand analysis driven by highly developed metrics that were designed for fully functional plans.
- Require extensive reviews and approvals—Some ideas will be eliminated simply because the proponent doesn't want to deal with the "system." Others will be destroyed by politicking, turf disputes, defenders of the status quo, and mindless opposition. Some will die because the journey to implementation is just too long.
- Use mistakes as a death sentence—Mistakes can end or derail the careers of people who might invent our future, bury an idea that simply needs to be rethought or repackaged to work, or simply silence new ideas because they are "too risky." A high tolerance for mistakes—actually, a celebration of mistakes—is crucial to a high-creativity environment.

We want to eliminate ideas without destroying the environment that can produce them. So how can we eliminate ideas without destroying creativity and enthusiasm?

Remember that innovation is directed change. Ideas that are irrelevant to our vision, mission, and strategy are wasteful of time and energy. It's not a matter of discarding ideas as they come in but of having the ideas vetted by each person before they are suggested or implemented. Our people need to be taught to ask, "Will this idea create value for our organization in line with our vision, mission, and strategy?" We need to end the process of people submitting whatever pops into their heads, however inapplicable, and then leaving us with the awful chore of telling them that the ideas are stupid.

Focus all innovation on making our customers' lives and experiences with our organization better. Some ideas make life better for us, with the cost being paid by our customers—inconvenient hours, mystifying procedures and forms, policies that annoy them. We need to say, over and over, "Tell me about new ideas that will serve our customers."

Expect people to be their own eliminators. Why should we have to be the bad guys? Often it's because we've assigned ourselves the role—they can't do it unless we say "yes." We are like watchful sentries, guarding...what? We're protecting our organization from fresh thinking and better results. We need to expect our people to know what makes sense and tell *themselves* "yes" or "no." We'll have to let them be "in the know." If people can't see how their ideas tie in (or don't tie in) to where we are heading, they can't make intelligent decisions about whether those ideas are useful or not. More time educating them up front can save a lot of time—theirs and ours—down the road.

Use an "Innovation Log." Have people log their ideas, for their own tracking and for sharing with others. The more exposure the better. Ideas can feed off each other, and the recognition will spur people to action.

Define outcomes for different kinds of ideas. For maximum creativity, people need to be very clear on where their idea needs to "go" for approval (if required) and implementation. It will take some time to define this and get it right (our experience with clients says nine to fifteen months), but it will make a huge difference.

Create incubator teams that can kill ideas without killing thinking. These teams should be "unsettled"—no long-term membership, lots of rotation and diversity.

Provide timely, directed feedback. If people don't hear back on ideas they can't implement directly, the stream will dry up. Some worry about starting an idea program because "It will lower morale if we don't implement." But this isn't true. People can handle a "no," as long as they understand why. And they have to hear back quickly—we can't leave them wondering what happened to their "baby." To make the feedback useful, we need to tell them such things as what was missing, what didn't fit with other programs, what we couldn't afford, and what we didn't have the talent to deliver.

Define quality in terms of creativity. The definition of "quality" has been reduced in many leaders' minds to a system. At Luman Consultants International, we define quality as "a passionate desire to meet all stakeholder needs through constant innovation in all phases of delivery." Quality is about desire more than about numbers. It should be focused on meeting needs—and that's done by continuous creativity in every part of the process.

Have a plan for the legacy ideas. It isn't just new ideas that need to be eliminated. People need to be free to challenge any current strategy, structure, process, policy, or procedure that presents a strong (or insurmountable) barrier to something new and valuable. We can make it easier for them by providing a forum or mechanism to make the challenge in a straightforward, nonthreatening way.

EXPAND CREATIVITY

I love to ask this question: "How many of you think that creativity and innovation are important for your organization?" Every hand shoots up.

And then I ask follow-up questions: "How many of you are measuring creativity?" (an occasional hand) "How many of you know the number of new ideas you're getting in a year?" (no hands) "What percentage of ideas can get implemented without formal approval?" (confused looks) "How many have innovation as a core value?" (a few hands, mostly technical companies) "How many of you make innovation part of your performance process?" (no hands) "How many reward and recognize all innovation?" (no hands) "What percentage of your bottom line comes from widespread innovation?" (confused looks, some worried looks).

Creativity is often discussed as though it's a fairy tale, some mythical activity reserved only for the slightly deranged genius in his or her ivory tower (or padded cell). But creativity is actually one of the most commonplace things on earth. People are creative from the moment they wake up. They decide when to get up, how to get up, what to wear, what to eat, whether to follow routine or break it, whether to go to work the same way or change it, what to start on when they get to their workplace. They don't need a system to be creative. They simply *are* creative.

So when we talk about "expanding creativity," we're really talking about getting more of what people are already designed to do and then making it more productive.

There are some great ways to expand creativity, but we often rely on these ineffective methods:

- Encourage people to "share their ideas"—There's so much we think we can accomplish with general encouragements, and so little that ever actually gets accomplished.
- Install a suggestion box—There are few things more visible and more useless than a suggestion box. Even if it collects a few good ideas, it will become a symbolic substitute for real widespread innovation. The message is, "If you have a good idea put it in the box," rather than, "If you have a good idea, do something with it."
- Rely on brilliantly designed teams—This can be useful if we're trying to brainstorm a specific topic, problem, or opportunity. These teams are usually limited by topic and time. This approach can probably address less than 10 percent of the actual creative need and potential of our organization.
- Quiz people "off the cuff"—We can believe that creativity is waiting if we simply pop out, "So what do you think about this?" Too often, our people don't have enough information to make a contribution, haven't been developed to think about things in an unstructured way, or work toward an answer they think we'll like.
- Solicit anonymous opinions—This sounds like an answer: Let's ask the troops without the pressure of the hierarchy and career-limiting reactions. But people then have an incentive to share complaints; they don't have an incentive to share good ideas. Also, they'll suspect that someone else will take credit for the idea.

Many leaders have tried these ideas. But they just don't work. We need not so much to tap into creativity as we need to unleash it. So how can we do this?

Establish the right mindset. We have to expect innovation in every area by every person every day. People are intensely creative, but they are also smart, and if they discern that their ideas are not welcome *as a normal operating principle*, they will file them away. If we don't expect very much, we won't get very much.

Get out of the way. This is one of the most important things to do. We don't so much need to generate some sort of "creativity" program as to avoid destroying creativity. We have to get all of the obstacles out of the way so natural creativity can flourish. Some of the biggest obstacles include required approval and implied disapproval.

Create a safe place for dangerous ideas. Most of us like talking about new ideas because that makes us feel like we're making progress. But we hate actually changing in line with those ideas because changing makes us feel bad (and actual change is not cheap). When brave souls actually start pushing for real change, they will be perceived as dangerous. We have to give people incentives and a secure area within which dreaming up ideas for change will not get them punished.

Move people around. The ability to be creative about our work evaporates the longer we do the same thing. Change allows us to apply what we already know in our new circumstances and to apply what we didn't know before in our old circumstances. This seems counterintuitive—sacrificing short-term efficiency for long-term value—but the payoff can come in ways we can't even imagine.

Create forums for ideas and the liberty to implement them fast. Ideas become more robust when exposed to dialogue. We want to hear a lot of "that discussion really told me we were on the right path" and an equal amount of "I never thought about it that way." Forums about projects, opportunities, or problems can almost create something out of nothing. And the ideas will be much more honed and street-ready if those involved know they can implement them *now*.

Get past the irony of having a knowledge economy in which no one has time to think. We have to find ways to make creative "space" for our people—time (and place) to work off-site, long lunches, meeting-free zones, phone call–free blocks, e-mail boxes cut down to size. All too often, thinking time is viewed as laziness or wastefulness.

Have some structure (but not too much). Without a structured focus, it's unlikely that we will get consistent levels of creativity—and we can't expect the absurd: that we will get substantial ideas emanating bottom-up from an organization that intends to do top-down analysis, dissection, ridicule, and rejection of those same ideas.

Measure creativity. Even in universities, which we would expect to be hotbeds of creativity, there is "not a single index that ranks colleges by the extent to which they foster creativity." [2] We have to measure creativity—or better yet, our people have to measure it.

Recognize and reward creativity. Some rewards need to be in reference to people's peers—using our Intranet or bulletin board or meetings to honor original activity—and some need to be in reference to their own sense of accomplishment—making it a component of performance agreements and promotion decisions.

In one sense, expanding creativity is one of the easiest things to do as a leader. In leadership, we often find ourselves encouraging activity that doesn't "come naturally." With creativity, we are simply tapping into something that is part of being human.

THINKING AND RESPONDING PARADOXICALLY

While facilitating the first global conference for a multinational high-tech company in Morocco, I watched as an understandable—but extremely narrow—scene unfolded.

The company had just selected eight core values that would guide it in the new millennium. We broke the attendees (about 100 people) into eight groups to discuss what those values would "look like" in practice.

People from all parts of the organization were blended on teams to discuss each value except one: innovation. The only people who thought they should be on the team to discuss innovation—the only people *everyone* (except me) thought should be on this team—were scientists and engineers who had the specific function of doing research. As so often happens, innovation got put in a box.

In most organizations, there are thousands of untapped ideas that could *add value* (help us play the current game better) or *create value* (help us play a different game). A few organizations have found a way to get an average of ten, twenty, or even fifty ideas from every employee *every year*. Most of us would fall off our chairs if we got two or three. But the vast majority of organizations receive less than one per employee each year. I remember going into a facility with one leader who told me his organization used "suggestion boxes." When we opened the box, which hadn't been touched in months, we found candy wrappers and other trash.

We cannot be successful trying to execute "perfect" ideas selected from the past or from current formal leaders. In many organizations, we expect ideas from the top but not the middle or front line, and yet that is where many of the best ideas reside. In fact, "75% of product-improving and money-saving ideas come from workers who deal with the products and problems every day."[3] We have every incentive to release that creative power for the benefit of our organizations.

To manage this paradox, we have to focus creativity. "It's what I call walking the management tightrope, blending creativity with staying focused," wrote the founder of Paychex.[4] Typically, we encourage people to share their ideas, and if they respond, we have to deal with a flood of suggestions that we cannot implement or even respond to. But this won't do. We have to set the parameters that will allow creativity to flourish.

So we take the time to define, as an organization, what creativity is, the language we will use to discuss ideas at various stages, the standards against which new ideas will be measured, goals for creativity (so many ideas/person/ year), and the process by which ideas will be implemented or approved. Structure actually promotes more creativity. We know what we can't do, which makes everything else possible. "Counterintuitively," two authors write, "standards fuel creativity."[5]

We have to untie people from the corporate "administrivia." In an article on the Ford Mustang's fortieth anniversary, *USA Today* reported that "the inside story is not one of a sharply honed organization coming up with just the thing. It's a tale of rank-and-file perseverance against brass-hat opposition." The Mustang was developed at a record pace "because it happened outside channels, avoiding . . . 'aministrivia.' 'You can do it twice as fast for half the money' when unshackled from corporate procedures, says famous hot-rodder Carroll Shelby."[6]

It is up to our people to generate and eliminate more and more ideas. We expect them to do both. If the four stages of breakthrough thinking are preparation, incubation, illumination, and testing,[7] we expect each person to do them all: to prepare themselves with understanding, to meditate on the idea before sharing it, to work on the idea until it blossoms, and then to test it to see if it's valuable. If we separate these functions into different people or groups, we will generate few good ideas—and then probably eliminate them.

If people generate ideas that don't fit, we assume not that they have bad ideas but that they have undirected ideas. They need to thoroughly understand our vision, mission, strategy, objectives, and goals. "Better profitability in the future depends on innovating in ways that capitalize on the company's strategy—its source of uniqueness," wrote one strategy expert.[8]

Many of the ideas are already out there but have been preemptively eliminated. In one large manufacturing operation with which we worked, revised thinking on creativity generated 120 ideas in the first four months with an annual savings of $3.5 million. Most of the ideas came from people who had been there ten years or more. In other words, "what passes for new at any given time has in fact been around for quite a while. . . . 'The future is already here. It is just not uniformly distributed.'"[9]

To manage this paradox, we've got to find a way to "road rest" ideas quickly, with a reasonable process but without much data. The pipeline will clog up rapidly if ideas can't be pulled out, inspected, and either moved to the next level or purged.

We need to hold people accountable for the results of their creativity. If their job is just to "share ideas," they are devoid of responsibility to make them work. This is another reason to eliminate most or all approvals, which are excellent devices for diffusing responsibility for outcomes. If people know they will be held accountable for implementing ideas that produce tangible results, they will eliminate the chaff and focus solely on the wheat.

We have to grant some trust as well. You have to "trust that creativity will be conducted in a manner consistent with organizational values and other constraints," says one thoughtful professor.[10]

When the next "cycle" of the same problem or opportunity comes around, we need a largely different team if we want to get a fresh look at what is no longer fresh. The original team will be psychologically and emotionally hampered from treating the idea critically, as they have created it and invested themselves in it. They will be tempted to defend the idea. Their work should be honored, but not given tenure.

If we want to reinvent our better selves continually, we will need teams with little vested interest in the status quo. Having a person or two from the earlier team to ensure that the best of the past doesn't get trampled might be wise, but only if they have clear guidance against obstruction and are few enough that they can't defeat the innovative approach.

An early 3M leader wrote, "Every idea should have a chance to prove its worth, and this is true for two reasons: (1) If it is good, we want it; (2) If it is not good, we will have purchased peace of mind when we have proved it impractical."[11]

Creating. Eliminating. Creating. Eliminating. It is a cycle of newness, an unrelenting process of structured growth.

CHAPTER 16

ENCOURAGE COOPERATION AND ENCOURAGE CONFLICT

As conflict—difference—is here in the world, as we cannot avoid it, we should, I think, use it. Instead of condemning it, we should set it to work for us. . . . It is possible to conceive of conflict as not necessarily a wasteful outbreak of incompatibilities but a normal process by which socially valuable differences register themselves for the enrichment of all concerned.[1]

—*Mary Parker Follett*

Because almost everything we do involves other people, cooperation is a practical necessity. In the sciences, extraordinarily open cooperation is encouraged—the voluntary sharing of ideas, research, data, methods, and findings. Many forums are provided, and not sharing is considered a professional discourtesy.

But even in the most mundane organizational transactions, cooperation is necessary. It may be hard to come by, but few question its rightness or its value.

Not so with conflict. Conflict is almost without exception viewed as a negative. There is probably a course being offered somewhere in your city this week on "Managing Conflict in _____ (the Workplace, Your Team, etc.)." But where are the courses on "Discouraging Detrimental Cooperation" and "Managing Unhealthy Consensus?"[2]

Conflict can indeed be disastrous, but so can cooperation. Managing in a world of paradox requires us to avoid putting a halo on cooperation and horns on conflict. Either can be bad, and either can be good.

To be maximally effective, we need to lead organizations that understand and score high on the right kind of cooperation and the right kind of conflict. James Surowiecki observed that "science presents us with the curious paradox of an enterprise that is simultaneously intensely competitive and intensely cooperative."[3]

Not a bad model for any enterprise.

ENCOURAGE COOPERATION

Cooperation is willing collaboration by free individuals in a collective effort that creates more value than it expends.

We preach cooperation better than we practice it. Given hidden agendas, groupthink, hierarchical domination, and most people's fear of conflict, cooperation often provides a very low level of return.

Even in schools, where cooperation is stressed and many projects are done in groups, cooperation is more a source of annoyance than of useful results. Students typically complain about their peers' laziness, conflicting ideas that defy productive solution but beg for compromise, and lower grades than would have been received if they had worked alone. Without serious training in effective cooperation, and an understanding of the necessity of constructive conflict, schools become perfect training grounds for pitiable cooperation.

Here are some very poor ways to "cooperate:"

- Insist on acclamation—A request that everyone "get on board" with an idea with which many have substantial disagreement is a plea for mindless following, not cooperation.
- Act like "team players" —People need to *be* real team players, not just *act* like them. What is usually meant is, "You can say anything as long as it agrees with me (or the team)."
- Knuckle under to dominating authority—There is a huge difference between cooperation and coercion, but many leaders don't even see it.
- Keep our opinions to ourselves—Why would we continue to work for an organization that doesn't want our opinions? A leader in one organization said to me, "I'm amazed at how much they're willing to pay us to do little and say even less." Tough truth is just as valuable as good news—more so, in many cases. The old saying is, "If you can't say anything nice, don't say anything at all." That's a very bad old saying.

Real cooperation is built on substantial agreements about core ideas. When we have vigorous dialogue about central things—vision, mission, values, and the like—and come to solid conclusions that aren't "lowest common denominators," we have the basis for genuine cooperation. We avoid the apparent cooperation that comes from saying "yes" when we mean "no," working on things half-heartedly while pretending to care, and giving lip service to ideas and actions that range in our minds from silly to abhorrent.

If we don't have these core agreements, real cooperation is virtually impossible. Because people know instinctively that they can't disagree about everything and hope to keep their jobs, they will (in the absence of real unity on important issues) substitute fake unity on almost everything.

We can do many things to encourage vibrant, competitive cooperation.

Select worthwhile destinations. In the absence of willing cooperation around the core of our vision, mission, values, behaviors, strategies, and goals, we allow our organizations to fragment and individuals to substitute their own agendas. Genuine cooperation requires agreement on meaning and purpose.

Define cooperation effectively. We need to tell people what we mean—and just as important, what we don't mean—by "cooperation." Use this chapter as your basis of definition.

Spend what it takes to get it. It is very hard to get just the right amount of cooperation. It will deteriorate over time. It will lose its energy, its goal, its method. Real cooperation always tends to give way to the phony kind. Leadership must fight relentlessly to maintain it.

Decimate false ownership. We can't allow or support the creation of silos—places in which power has become a goal rather than a tool. These get solidified into overly defined boundaries around departments and functions, and these unit charters or individual job descriptions become roadblocks to cooperation. Basic human nature completes the picture: "This is mine, not yours."

Penalize victimizers. We should never hire, promote, or keep people who don't value cooperation or who focus on "winning" at the expense of others.

Eliminate bogus or counterproductive competition. We have seen far too many leaders who preach teamwork while praising and rewarding dog-eat-dog internal competition. They have sales competitions that void any sense of cooperation. They have employee awards that recognize one winner and make everyone else losers (a sports-playoff model that works terribly in real life).

Eliminate unprofitable conflict. We all have some people with whom it is hard to get along, with whom personal clashes get in the way of productive harmony. Wherever possible, we need to eliminate these points of conflict rather than spend enormous amounts of energy trying to help people "get along." Shifting people is a lot easier than shifting likes and dislikes.

Reward and recognize it. If we're fortunate enough to have a team deliver real results through intense cooperation, we need to take such good care of them that noncooperation looks stupid.

If we make it a priority, we can encourage a cooperation that moves us toward collective greatness, but we have to remember that cooperation is not the natural result of assigning people to teams. It's a whole lot harder than that.

ENCOURAGE CONFLICT

Conflict is, at its best, the productive clash of free individuals that results in the creation of value. "Conflict at the moment of the appearing and focusing of difference may be a sign of health, a prophecy of progress."[4]

There are several unproductive forms of conflict, of course. We can:

- *Play favorites*—There are few more effective ways to create destructive conflict than to favor one person or group over others. The favored will fight to keep their position, and everyone else will fight to destroy it.
- *Be hypocritical*—There are actually two ways to be hypocritical, and both are designed to produce bad conflict. In the first case, someone says something but doesn't do it (they don't "walk the talk"). But the other kind of hypocrisy in leaders may be even more devastating, because it's so subtle. This is where someone says something but doesn't *believe* it (or mean it). People are smart and will eventually make their own reading of what the internally divided leader really means.
- *Permit trivial disputes*—There is a difference between useful conflict and squabbling. Too little of the conflict that occurs in organizations has any worthwhile point. People who squabble are asking for more responsibility and accountability. We should accommodate them.
- *Allow exhibitions of jealousy or envy*—When someone wants something you have, or at least doesn't want you to have it, it might seem like conflict. In reality, it is just low-life grasping.
- *Let people war over boundary lines*—Many of the "conflicts" in organizations are boundary disputes, either functional (department, division, or business unit) or positional (manager, director, officer). People might die fighting for their claim, but value will almost certainly not be created by this silliness.
- *Reward individuals for team performance*—If we want to promote "lone ranger" behavior and annoy and frustrate teams, there are few ways surer than holding the team accountable for results but rewarding individuals for delivering them. The reverse—rewarding teams for individual results—is bad but not quite as bad, since the people doing the work are at least being rewarded.[5]
- *Permit people to shift and delegate blame*—A lot of supposed conflict comes from allocation of "mistake misery": "It's your fault!" "No it's not, it's yours!" If a small fraction of the mistakes in organizations were quickly owned and used for learning and growth, we would see a huge move toward high performance.

The irony is that people are more likely to have conflict over little things, where the potential value to be gained is small or nonexistent, rather than over big things, where the potential value to be gained is enormous.

Organizations do many things to discourage conflict, in large part because it seems unprofessional and counterproductive and, frankly, distasteful. This is usually because we've had tremendous exposure to the wrong kind of conflict.

First, we can use formal and informal evaluations to critique people who are willing to rouse the rabble. We score them lower on things like "promotes teamwork," "creates a sense of harmony," and "is a team player." Because these evaluations affect their careers, only the very hardy continue to dissent from the prevailing opinion.

Second, we often prize orthodoxy and condemn heresy. Orthodoxy is "the way we do things around here" and includes spoken and unspoken philosophies, written and unwritten rules, and working and worthless traditions. Heresy is anything that varies from the generally accepted norm, and people naturally become defensive when they see it. The only problem is, of course, that sometimes the "heresy" is right.

Third, we tend to classify all conflict the same way. In my book *Fatal Illusions*, I recommended that leaders identify the "Cooperation Illusion" by asking whether their organizations "encourage healthy (i.e., constructive and pointed toward organizational goals) competition and discourage unhealthy (i.e., destructive and pointed away from organizational goals) competition."[6]

Fourth, we frequently try to model our organizations on sports, where internal cooperation is mandatory and conflict is highly controlled. Is it a good idea to look to the world of sports for organizational ideas, or is it a terrible idea? The answer is "yes." It's great if we're using sports for analogies, because sports events happen in small time frames with frequent chances for failure or success. Sports examples encapsulate some ideas well, especially those related to character. But analogies from sports are terrible if we're using them for principles and practices. Professional sports organizations are supermicromanaged, with teams of 45 players having 20 or more coaches (bosses). Most never want, and won't allow, internal conflict. There is no debate on game plans, no matter how awful they are.[7]

So how can we encourage true, value-add conflict?

Honor constructive dissent. Let people know that constructive dissent will always be welcome—and that you can't even *hear* destructive or negative dissent.

Assign conflict responsibilities. Don't assume that a "speak up if you disagree" policy will have any real effect. Deliberately assign dissenters and "devil's advocates" to projects and team meetings.

Create forums for conflict. Dissent is hard enough to come by, but even harder if there is no room for it. Allow time at the end of staff meetings or brainstorming sessions for anyone who has a major disagreement to express it. Require a section at the end of any executive summary or report entitled "Issues with which I have important disagreement." We should "find many ways for people to tell us what we *don't* want to hear."[8]

Reward conflict. Thank people publicly when they disagree openly. Thank them twice as much when they disagree with you. Give financial rewards to anyone whose thorny disagreement saved your bacon.

Stop the presses. When there is no dissenting voice or doubting question, we should pause to reevaluate the project, idea, or solution we're about to put into action. Nothing is that good.

Eliminate false cooperation. We are always leery about hiring anyone who scores too high on "gets along with others." There are only two reasons for this: they agree with us on everything, in which case we don't need them, or they disagree but won't be open about it, in which case we don't need them.

Discourage non-value-added cooperation. Courtesy copies, meeting attendance where no contribution is made or expected, and politeness as a substitute for truth give cooperation a bad name.

THINKING AND RESPONDING PARADOXICALLY

Paradoxical leaders know that they must have high levels of cooperation to succeed, and no less that they must have high levels of conflict to succeed.

What kind of cooperation do we want? The kind that comes from hard-fought dialogue and lengthy negotiation and respectful warfare. In other words, we encourage meaningful cooperation by encouraging meaningful conflict first.

And what kind of conflict do we want? The kind that comes from a desire to add value and to build something collectively and not to let illusions derail us. We want to encourage a powerful cooperation based on a widespread conviction that every significant disagreement has been heard and debated. In other words, we encourage meaningful conflict by pointing toward, and agreeing on, the prize of ultimate cooperation.

We have to assess continually whether we have too much cooperation or too much conflict—or too much of the wrong kind of cooperation and too much of the wrong kind of conflict. We want to cooperate fiercely internally so that we can compete ferociously externally. We can't allow "silo" thinking, individual competitiveness, bogus definitions of loyalty and collaboration, or our reward and recognition systems to destroy teamwork that is both rowdy and synergistic. At the same time, paradoxical leaders manage consensus so it doesn't get out of hand. We let everyone know that cooperation and conflict are *both* the norm. Whatever mix is adding the most value, that's what we're going for. We ensure that we agree on the important things so we can disagree on everything else.

We want internal competition that isn't competition so much as it is *parallel accountability*. Defined results and goals move us toward accountability, but competing with others who have similar results and goals can move us toward that accountability much faster. It will take some energy and time to define this kind of internal competition and to differentiate it from the kind that destroys effective cooperation.

Externally, we also want competition that makes sense, competition that provides a spur to achievement while making a way for productive alliances and partnerships. There is a time for cooperation—so we can later on compete even better in the marketplace, which is the real objective.

Although we generally seek cooperation around our shared vision, mission, values, and behaviors, we need to create forums to introduce needed conflict, even about these core issues. Nothing is perfect, and even near-perfect can change over time. We need to revisit our core periodically to ensure that we are heading in the best direction.

Although we generally seek conflict around our strategy, structure, process, applications, results, and rewards, we need methods to bring our conflicting ideas and convictions into workable harmony. We want people to sing different parts, but we also want them to sing those parts in harmony.

In fact, we need to *insist* on unity and *insist* on diversity. Neither one comes by itself, and neither one comes easily. If we have unity without diversity, we will be highly successful only if we have stumbled on a higher-order, sustainable competitive advantage that will need little adjustment in the foreseeable future. If we have diversity without unity, we will be highly successful only if each person or team is excellent and has the full authority and resources necessary to exploit their ideas. Neither of these situations is very likely to occur in the real world.

It is up to paradoxical leaders to create a unified environment within which diversity can flourish. A "unified environment" is not one in which every movement is orchestrated by formal or informal philosophies, policies, and procedures. Instead, it is one in which individual and collective goals can be achieved.

Managing this paradox requires us to make tolerance a core organizational practice. Healthy cooperation and healthy conflict both require a strong dose of tolerance, since both can only be built on authentic expressions of truth and the truth will often annoy us. And we can't define tolerance as "I'll let you say it as long as it's fairly close to what we already believe" and expect to have any success. Acceptance by "acclamation" always papers over things that would best be brought into the open. We need a tolerance that welcomes and absorbs exceptions to agreements as well as fundamental disagreement. While we need to differentiate between a tolerance for destructiveness and a tolerance for difference, we have to allow our tolerance for difference to extend as far as we can stretch it if we want significant results.

When analyzing a particular situation, the question shouldn't be, "Is there cooperation?" or "Is there conflict?" but, rather,

- Is this cooperation (or conflict) adding value?
- Could changes in how we're cooperating (or having conflict) add even more value?
- Could the introduction of a measure of conflict increase the value?
- Do we need to find some areas in which some easy cooperation would make the remaining conflict more productive (in other words, use agreement wherever it can be legitimately found to clear the decks for focused conflict)?
- Does this cooperation need to be replaced by conflict (or conflict replaced by cooperation)?
- Do the costs of this cooperation (or conflict) outweigh the benefits we're obtaining from it?

U.S. World War II General George Patton "understood that . . . individual action is vital, but that team work also requires subordinating ego to collective goals."[9]

Paradoxical leadership means finding a balance between two truths. We can and should have conflict about how to achieve our goals, but at the end of the day we all have to answer for the results.

CHAPTER 17

NURTURE CUSTOMERS AND FIRE CUSTOMERS

We have no eternal allies and we have no perpetual enemies. Our interests are eternal and perpetual, and these interests it is our duty to follow.[1]

—Lord Palmerston

Customers—whatever we call them—are the lifeblood of any organization.

A customer is a person or group that needs to be served. This means that not-for-profits and government agencies have customers just as genuinely as companies selling products or services for profit do.

We know instinctively that we need to nurture our customers. We don't always do it perfectly or even well, but we know that we should.

We're not so sure about the need to fire customers. Why would we do that? They're sending us regular checks! Even if they are monstrously challenging, it is hard to cut them loose. So we try to make it better. We cajole, we plead, we give in, we give up, we let them run over the top of us.

We should change our mindset from "Any customer is a good customer" to "Any *good* customer is a good customer."

And if we don't do this, how on earth will we have the resources, energy, time, and will to nurture the good ones? Compared to good customers, bad customers cause ten times the pain for every sale.

Nurture the good customers and eject all the rest.

NURTURE CUSTOMERS

It is always the time to take care of our customers, but paradoxical leaders know that they should focus on the ones who have more options and opportunities and needs. In business, these customers are the ones with cash and profitable orders. As Peter Drucker has reminded us, ultimately the only valuable thing in the marketplace is a customer whose check doesn't bounce. For government and not-for-profits, we want to work with people who support our work, who put our services to use and benefit from them.

Over three decades, I have repeatedly seen the following pitiful ways to "nurture" customers:

- Provide "throw-in" product features, quality, or service—There is no doubt that this approach will keep some customers. The giveaway will become transparent to any savvy customer, and they'll just keep coming back for more.
- Give away our know-how—Some customers really don't want us. They just want what we know. They grudgingly agree to buy or contract with us, but only so they can access our intellectual capital.
- Let them run our business—There are few things more frightening than a politician with a mandate or an organization with market dominance. We should all be open to constructive input from a customer. But when that turns into telling us how to manage our organization, they've gone too far.
- Don't speak up when they are out of line—Conflict might cost us money. That's a fact. But not disagreeing will cost us *us*. That's a harder fact.
- Enable their bad behavior—They throw a tantrum and we respond (perhaps even with unfounded guilt). They make a ridiculous demand and we nearly break ourselves trying to meet it. They continually create their own problems and expect us to do what their own people can't or won't do. They treat our people badly, and we apologize for making them mad. They'll probably stick around—what bully would voluntarily give up an available punching bag?

What makes a customer worth nurturing? For any type of organization, a good customer—one worth our best efforts—has some clear and definable characteristics:

- Appreciation of value—good customers don't just know the price and terms, they know the value they are going to get from doing business with you.
- Applied empathy—they know from their own experience how hard it is to succeed with customers and in business and life, and they have the grace to apply that knowledge to their dealings with you.
- A focus on the big picture—they are able to look at your intentions and overall effort and don't let one mistake or misstep define their whole experience with you.
- Respect—in virtually every interaction, you can feel their genuine esteem for you and what you are offering; doing business with them makes you feel like a better person or organization.
- No surprises—they don't regularly surprise you, with things like last-minute demands, built-up concerns, or constantly shifting rules of engagement.

- Partnership orientation—they have trained themselves to think of people and organizations with which they do business as allies; they assume you're on their side until you prove you aren't.
- Humility—they know they can't always be first, demand the most, expect perfection, and critique you for things that they themselves might do. They're willing to take the heat for their own mistakes.

Customers are fallible, so they can fail on any of these. But if they do it consistently, it's time to put them on probation.

So let's say we've got a few customers worth nurturing. If we're really serious about being customer-centric, there are a number of effective ways to care for them.

Ask the question. We need to ask, "Within the bounds of sensible business, what could we do to consistently serve you and let you know how important you are?" Otherwise, some of what we try might seem annoying, as when hotel front desks call us before we've put down our bags or taken off our jackets to find out if everything is fine (it probably was until they called).

Understand their entire experience. What are they trying to do that requires our product or service? What do they really value? Until we know how we fit into their universe, it's impossible to nurture them well. "Few companies have bothered to look carefully at the broad context in which customers select, buy, and use products and services," wrote one expert. "They've been so focused on fine-tuning their own offerings that they've failed to see how those products and services fit into the real lives of their customers."[2]

Involve them in changes. We're going to enhance and recreate our offering over time. Involving customers in changes is an outstanding way to show them that we care and value their input. This might include giving them advance notice and asking for prerelease testing, product-development input, and marketing advice. The more we can help them feel like they are "part of us" the better.

Help them maximize their own opportunities and minimize their meltdowns. We don't want to give away our know-how, but we do want to give away our wisdom. If we've been around very long, we've learned some things watching and working with other customers. When we see a customer about to miss an opportunity or about to take a step off the ledge, we can bring that hard-earned insight to their rescue.

Find ways to become even more indispensable. The day will never come when our customers no longer have needs or problems. One of our clients likes to use quotes when talking to staff or outsiders, so we supply those quotes gladly. What can we do so our customers, here and there, will find themselves asking, "How on earth could we get along without them?"

Assign people to customers to make sure nothing is taken for granted. In our practice, we have "client care" people whose primary goal is to find the flaws fast.

Customer service isn't listed above because customer service is table stakes. Everyone has been talking for decades about the "age of the customer" and "customer focus" and "customer delight." The few organizations that actually put this into practice won't find it a crowded field.

FIRE CUSTOMERS

We've got to fire some organizations that are sending us money. A bad customer—one worth firing—has a clearly defined set of characteristics:

- Reality impairment—One of my favorite newspaper story summaries was on the front page of the *Wall Street Journal*: "GM and Ford saw sales decline 5% last month, blaming economic factors. Japanese auto makers reported a surge in sales." [3] Isn't that delicious? Apparently, GM and Ford are operating in a different world economy than the Japanese auto makers. When we are dealing with customers with SRIS (Severe Reality Impairment Syndrome),[4] we do so at our peril. Whatever it is that has shrouded them in a cloud of illusion,[5] we can be assured that it will infect our relationship with them sooner or later.
- Scope creep—Bad customers are always looking for more than they bargained for; they actually want what they *didn't* bargain for. They'll agree that specifications or services should be reduced to get a lower price and then push at the edges to get these things increased at no cost.
- Blame delegation—They will never take responsibility for any portion of their dissatisfaction (e.g., misuse of the product, bogus expectations, internal sabotage). It's always our fault.
- Penny wisdom—They aren't frugal, they're cheap. Whether they see the value or not, they'll never admit it and will whine about what we're charging (even if "charging" is requiring that they fill out a form to access free services).
- Unrealistic demands—If we offer it in ten days, they'll want it in five; if we can put someone on a plane on Thursday they'll want them on Tuesday. They always ask but never offer anything in return. Everyone has legitimate crises. They have illegitimate calamities, usually of their own making.
- Win/lose mindset—Everything with them is a power play. They only feel like it's a good transaction if we feel pillaged.
- Entitlement mentality—They think we "owe them." People with this attitude cannot be satisfied.
- Invincible dissatisfaction—No matter the level of quality we bring to them, they will never be happy with it.
- Arrogance—They know they're better than us, and we'll feel their condescension in every transaction.
- Abusiveness toward our people—Even if someone has made a mistake, disrespect should never be an option.

If we see these things, we should run for the hills. And yet, there are some terrible ways to fire customers:

- Take them for granted—They used to love us, but they can't remember why. Customer churn is another name for lousy imagination.
- Forget to renew and create relationships—People change. Sometimes an individual changes and doesn't see the world the same way. Other times, the person is replaced by someone else.
- Change our offering without changing our relationship—Not everyone wants "new improved" products or services, but everyone wants tried-and-true relationships and processes. The customer defines what makes it hard to do business with us.
- Use the wrong numbers—We've seen organizations perform market segmentation studies and deliberately turn their backs on some good midterm and long-term bets. Deciding not to sell to Bill Gates when he was in a garage without any numbers would have been an incredibly bad plan. Most of the growth and new employment and future are not being invented by the "obvious" good (i.e., big) customers.
- Fire bad customers badly—Even when we know they need to go, there are some very bad ways to go about it. Leaving them without sufficient notice, fulfilling the letter but not the spirit of our commitment, and choosing poor words can all come back to harm us later can cost us business about which we will never even be aware.

Paradoxical leaders make a priority out of cleaning out the Rolodex. At Luman Consultants International, we take steps to fire them in our "up front" contact. On our Web site, we have a "Contact Us" button. But we also have a "Don't Call Us If…" button, where we encourage them to leave us happily unaware of their existence they're a bad customer. We tell them not to contact us if:

- They want someone to give their people a "rah-rah" motivational speech but have no intention of making the necessary changes to build a passionate organization.
- They want confirmation of what they are already doing more than insight into what they could be doing better or differently.
- They expect us to give them solutions without allowing us the freedom and access to gain the knowledge of their organization that will allow us to prepare an accurate diagnosis and prescription.
- They think that change, including leadership and cultural change, is easy.

We've got to get rid of bad customers. There are some important methods for firing bad customers.

Fire them before you even know they exist. Try to find ways to let bad customers self-select out of doing business with you. For you, this will be a very healthy natural selection and survival of the fittest.

Distinguish between excellence and grumpiness. Just because a customer is "nitpicky" doesn't mean they are "excellent." In fact, excellent customers don't want to pay for tweaking worthless details. Nitpicking can be driven by a host of bad causes—rigid bureaucracy, overloaded staff, desire to avoid taking any risk, or just plain meanness.

Don't let good customer contacts seduce us into bad customer relationships. We may run into good people or departments inside bad organizations that are our customers, but we do business with them at our peril. Their commitments may not be honored, and if they've got any character they won't be able to stay there in the long run anyway. We'll end up dealing with what bad customers have in abundance—people who have been steeped in their bad ways.

Use them as testing grounds. The customer we really don't care about keeping can be the perfect customer on which to road-test new products or services. But we must still act with morality: we still need to offer value and not let our drive for excellence falter; we still need to give them more than they deserve. Acting ethically even has a practical benefit: we avoid creating any bad marketplace noise.

Leave the door open if they stop being bad. Customers can change, often with a change in leadership. Just because we can't work with them now should be no "final statement" on our ability to work for them in a different future.

Firing customers is an underdeveloped skill almost everywhere. We can do it right and save the best of who we are for the people who deserve us.

THINKING AND RESPONDING PARADOXICALLY

We've got to fire the bad customers so we'll have the time, energy, and resources to nurture the good ones.

Bad customers always soak up more of everything than average-to-good customers. They complain, they request, they demand, they insist, they nitpick, they wear us out for a handful of change. They will hold out just enough opportunity, just enough business, just enough interest, to keep us on the hook. We might be able to develop five or ten current customers or prospects for every bad customer littering our business.

One CEO said that firing a draining, miserable client opened up resources to land new clients and ended up "showing me that not only had we done the right thing by ridding our agency of such a negative influence, but we'd further opened ourselves up to attracting and retaining the right kind of client...[I can't] let any customer's demands take control of my business."[6] It's hard to let go of a customer—and the bigger they are, the harder it is—but it is the only sane way to run an organization of possibility and creativity.

We should set up criteria against which customers are regularly evaluated. We probably do that with our employees—why wouldn't we do it with our customers? A good place to start is with the "bad customer characteristics" list earlier in this chapter. Let everyone who has contact with them, or knowledge of them, rate your customers on these criteria on a 1–10 scale (with "10" being "exceedingly ugly"). An average north of 60 should make us break out the pink slip. Anything north of 70 should make us sign it.

Of course, we nurture all customers initially, in part to give us a chance to keep them but also so we can find out who to fire. Who takes advantage of our graciousness and generosity? Who has an entitlement mentality? Who always asks but never gives? We won't find out if we don't offer everyone initial nurturing.

The most natural response in the world to a new customer is elation. We did it! We won! But we might have just won the customer who is going to wreck us. Balancing our joy with a reminder could be smart business. "We're glad we've got them; let's remember we may have to fire them." Let's see how they look in six months.

Once we really start taking care of good customers—going above and beyond what we have offered or that they have experienced before—the thought of offering that attention to losers will make us sick. We will start to get a sense that "these people aren't worthy of our best efforts."

We need, as many organizations do, to ask our customers what they think of us and what we do. We should listen to their answers in part to determine what we should change. But if they want us to become "not us" to meet their demands, we need to lose them.

Gap analysis is important here. Customer surveys are a wonderful way to identify dreadful customers. We certainly want to be open to the individual customer who is insightful, brave, and thoughtful enough to give us a criticism that no one else mentions. But we need to have the other view in mind as well: the possibility of a customer who sees our gold and calls it dirt.

The 80/20 rule seems to operate in the customer realm. Many organizations spend 80 percent of their energies on the 20 percent of their customers who range from poor to awful.

We need to change the model. We need to spend 80 percent of our energies on the 80 percent of our customers who are good and worthy of nurturing, and we need to spend the other 20 percent there, too.

CHAPTER 18

BENCHMARK COMPETITORS AND IGNORE WHAT THEY'RE DOING

The trouble with the rat race is that even if you win, you're still a rat.[1]

—Lily Tomlin

A whole world of research and consulting has been built around "benchmarking" and "best practices." Some organizations look to these methods to keep them at the forefront of their industries, whereas others merely seek to be "fast followers." A rare few survey the landscape to see what everyone else is doing so they can do something entirely different.

No one, it seems, doubts the value of copying. Not even when the small voices at the back of our minds say, "You can't mimic your way to greatness."

At the same time, most of the really great success stories have a common theme: A person or organization throws out the current paradigm, "breaks the mold," "cuts a new path through the forest," makes a new way. There is a sense of excitement, of creativity, of individuality, of thumbing the nose at the hacks and plodders. These are the heroic stories that we love to read and hear, even while we focus on benchmarking and best practices.

No one, it seems, doubts the value of taking a different road. Not even when the small voices at the back of our minds say, "You can't win by reinventing the wheel."

So here we have it: A whole model of organizational practice that tells us to find out what others are doing and do it, and a whole model of organizational heroism that tells us to ignore what others are doing and do something different.

Which is it?

BENCHMARK COMPETITORS

A benchmark is a "surveyor's mark cut in a wall, pillar, building, etc., used as a reference point in measuring altitudes," a "standard or point of reference."[2]

This means that we don't benchmark theories or ideas or academic notions. We benchmark reality, what someone is already doing. There are a lot of things we can do that look like benchmarking but are really something quite different:

- Copy out of context—Many practices make sense in the situation in which they are found, but pulled loose from their moorings, they can be useless.
- Provide a vision without an infrastructure—People look at organizations that are "best in class," appreciate the organization's blood-stirring vision, and then try to deliver a similar vision to their own organizations without the well-designed supporting infrastructure that has evolved over time in the original setting.
- Duplicate at the wrong scale—When we see huge differences between our organizations and others, we can reduce what we've learned to a scale that doesn't "upset" our current way of doing business. To ease the pain, we can diminish a potential change into a linear extension of what we're already doing.
- Copy irrelevant features—It's all too easy to copy items that are not important to our market, or around which we have no core excellency (or even competency).

There are, however, some steps we can take to ensure that whatever benchmarking we do will have strongly positive results that far outweigh the costs of obtaining and implementing them.

Identify what our critical success factors are, so we know what's worth benchmarking. It is too easy to benchmark against relative trivialities (such as motivational schemes, small ways of rewarding, recognition programs) rather than the real drivers of high-performance cultures (such as powersharing, genuine authority, respect). We have to know what factors are important to our customers and other stakeholders, so we know where to start measuring. If an activity has little value to the marketplace, it should have little value for us.

Benchmark the underlying principles. The form of the practice we're reviewing can be misleading and can even camouflage the principle. We need to look for the core principles in the organizations we are reviewing rather than merely benchmarking their various practices.

Get out of our industry grouping. The best ideas often come from organizations in other industries that are dealing with the same core issue. Whole consultancies have grown up like bees moving from one flower to the next in the same field. They see an idea in industry organization A and pass it along (for a nice fee) to industry organization B. There is nothing inherently wrong with this process, and some value can certainly be gained, but passing the same idea around to everyone in the field is unlikely to allow any of the organizations to excel in comparison to their competitors. If it's a good idea, the best we can hope for is that the performance of the whole industry improves. There is a certain irony here: that benchmarking, so often undertaken to increase competitiveness and excellence, can lead to lower competitiveness and excellence because we've simply copied what our competitors are doing.

Benchmark the little guys. It's easy to fall into reviewing only "peers." "We're a billion-dollar operation—why would we look at that dinky outfit?" Because: they know what they're doing, they're creative, they have to try different things because they're small, they have nothing to defend, and our own peers all look alike. Besides, we'll trade places if we don't.

Only benchmark what we intend to beat. We need to put the resources behind the process so that we can do better than what we find. Novelist Ernest Hemingway believed that there was no value in writing what had been written before unless he could do it better. Because the organization being copied has already been practicing the approach, it's unlikely that we will beat it without expending significantly more resources than they do.

Focus more on how we contrast with, rather than how we compare with, our competition. Gaps are often more exploitable than similarities. Where are the gaps that we have the wherewithal to exploit? Where are the gaps that competitors could use to even the playing field or destroy our current competitive advantage?

Establish our own benchmarking metrics. This means setting metrics on areas that are important to measure but that few people measure, like organization-wide creativity or level of knowledge-sharing. If we don't find anyone using our measures or able to give us data related to our measures, we may have a prime differentiator. If we're measuring what other people are already measuring, we have to find a new way to measure it—to find a nuance in performance capability, something fresh that we can attack.

Start our benchmarking with ourselves. Great wisdom is often lying around untapped inside of most organizations. We have built a consulting practice around tapping into that expertise as well as bringing our own expertise to organizations. Why benchmark enemies when we have wise friends standing so close?

Benchmarking holds out to us both promises and deceptions. If we can follow the principles above, we have a chance to receive the promises.

IGNORE WHAT THEY'RE DOING

Why would we want to ignore what others, especially our competitors, are doing?[3] For one thing, it takes a lot of energy and resources to find out what they're *really* doing. We can get glimpses from annual reports and industry scuttlebutt and magazine articles, but we're not likely to intelligently benchmark off that. Instead, we'll have to root around and dig down and ask a lot of questions. Ignoring others is a lot cheaper than benchmarking them superficially and is a lot less likely to cause us harm.

We also don't really know what results they are getting from whatever we're benchmarking, unless they really open up their books and let us become "them." Making the connection between the action and results is often a very tenuous process. What they aren't telling us or showing the world might be the critical ingredient that makes the whole process work.

What they're doing can also be a distraction. It can prevent us from focusing on our own good ideas and unique talents. We can try to be like them when we'd do much better if we tried to be more like us. In one example, Intel barred AMD from emulating a key new product and resisted sharing information. "It was almost as though Intel closed doors for us that allowed us to find new ways to compete with them," said an AMD executive, pointing the way to the power of ignorance. AMD's inability to benchmark forced it to take steps that caused Intel to benchmark them.[4]

We probably don't have the people or infrastructure to incorporate productively most of what we might learn anyway. Just because we know it doesn't mean we can do it. Benchmarking can cause discontent without a means of satisfying it.

So we might just decide that a little ignoring might go a long way. But we can ignore what others are doing for a host of terrible reasons:

- Arrogance—Most organizations are locked into the "this is the way we do things around here" mindset, which is codified in their structure and systems and policies and procedures. There's no reason to benchmark if you're already better (only in your own mind, of course) than everyone else.
- Limited field of view—As I write this, a giant cable operator has just announced "aggressive rollout plans" to enter the phone business via the Internet.[5] Why weren't the telecom companies paying attention to the threat provided to their core business by the cable companies? If we don't expand our field of view, small pieces of market share over which we're grappling with traditional competitors can be pulled out of our hands by strangers in a moment.
- Limited ambitions—We might not do enough to compete on new ground relevant to our excellencies. Telecom companies have been moving into the cable companies' turf (high-speed Internet business, television programming), which are natural areas of extension for them, but not soon enough to have made the investments in infrastructure to allow them to compete. "Telephone companies must still invest billions to be able to offer television over their networks."[6]
- Groupthink—If we are all thinking about the important issues in exactly the same way, it can give a sense of rightness, security, and durability that is out of all connection with reality. It is easy to ignore anything that is never a subject of thought or conversation.

So we want to ignore our competitors, but we want to ignore competitors in a smart way. There are some key things to keep in mind if we are going to effectively ignore what others are doing.

Don't fall for seductive comments. We should be on alert when we hear things like, "No one has ever tried that in our industry before," "Wait until you hear what XYZ company is doing," and "I think we've found the key." Perhaps no one has tried it because no one has ever broken out of the industry-constructed box. Or it may be that trying this magic is really stupid.

Set our own standards and targets for high performance, regardless of what our competition is doing. If an organization is high-performing, it

- Answers the four big questions well — The organization defines and revisits the vision question (why are we here?), the mission question (what will we do to achieve our vision?), the strategy question (how will we execute and deliver results), and the values/behaviors question (how will we act and interact to best deliver results?).
- Faces reality — The organization recognizes the trap of reality-impairment and develops methods and mechanisms to force it to face reality, define what it means, work to align with it, and assist in changing the reality over time.
- Produces intelligent growth over time — The organization delivers growth that is profitable, organically driven, differentiated, and sustainable.[7]
- Squeezes costs and expands the middle — The organization grows its gross margins and earnings, even in times of flattening or declining sales, by attacking both variable and fixed costs. It is a process cost-*reducer* rather than an event cost-*cutter*.
- Delivers consistently high levels of quality and service over a long period of time — The organization defines quality and service as *mindsets* rather than as systems or methods.
- Attracts, develops, promotes, and inspires "Winners and Believers" — The organization invites people to invest, powershares with them, ignites their creativity, puts them to work on its best opportunities rather than its worst problems, and creates an environment in which their passion can flourish.
- Changes before it has to — The organization takes the initiative to change ahead of the curve rather than waiting for forces or events to force it to change.

Know that we can't beat something with nothing. We have to set our own objectives to stretch us beyond anything anyone is currently doing. Instead of first benchmarking the competition so we can see how to get ahead of them a bit, we can establish goals that force us far beyond the current standards and then benchmark the competition to see how to do different facets of our plan better. Benchmarking then becomes a secondary, rather than a primary, method of improvement.

Build benchmarking into our people. Instead of forced ranking of people against each other, we could negotiate individual performance agreements with them that establish "stretch" goals. We could then encourage them to "benchmark" each other for ways to improve their performance and achieve their objectives. Benchmarking becomes a tool for improvement rather than a brutal way to compare. After all, if our best performers are underachieving — not in comparison with their *peers* but in comparison with their *possibilities* — forced ranking doesn't have much value anyway. In this way, benchmarking becomes an organization-wide mindset that touches everyone.

Remember that benchmarking has inherent limitations. We can only copy what someone is already doing, which is a pretty narrow field of vision. One reviewer summarized a recent book this way: The "best managers aren't alchemists, they're copycats. Smart leaders should skip the strategizing and hold up their best teams and workgroups as templates for the rest of the staff." The reviewer noted that this approach has "one primary flaw: Companies can only be as good as their best existing workgroup."[8]

Ignore things that are important, but not most important. One strategy expert "reached the conclusion that while quality and cost were important, time itself— or the ability to organize a factory or a business so as to get more done in less time—was the killer app."[9]

Ignore what is different but not pushing the bar. Other organizations might be doing fifty things different from what we do, but only one or two of them might have a value-adding effect on our organization. We have to exclude the variables that don't matter.

Ignorance might not be bliss—but some ignorance is a very valuable commodity indeed.

THINKING AND RESPONDING PARADOXICALLY

We have to set our sights not on being as good as or better than others but, rather, on being the best we can possibly be. We define our own core excellencies and competencies, our own standards of performance, and our own critical success factors. We work as hard as we can to develop an organization not quite like any other—one that puts the "unique" back into "unique value proposition."

We ignore what others are doing so we can learn what's important, what's worth benchmarking later. Let's find out what will arise from our own gestalt before we start investigating the "magic" of others.

We should focus on innovation first and following second. We ignore competitors so we can create something worthy of benchmarking expenditures. We want to encourage our people to innovate, rather than simply compare, on strategies, goals, processes, and methods.

Only then do we look around. We look inside our industry, outside our industry. We look in places that even seem silly to look. How long should we look? Until we can see.

- If we see others doing something like what we are doing, that scares us. If we can't do something entirely different in kind, we at least try to do it at entirely different in degree. We benchmark so that, going forward, we can ignore what everyone seems to be doing.

- If we see the competition doing something different, we need to evaluate it. First, does it matter? Is what they're doing really adding or creating value? Second, will it matter to us and work for us? Will it work in the same way? To the same level? Third, do we have the capability and capacity to incorporate it? Will it reinforce what we're doing or distract from it? And fourth, is the likely return worth the cost? If not, is there another way to negate their competitive advantage without adopting it? We may still need to ignore what we've benchmarked.
- If we see ourselves doing something that no one else seems to be doing, we've got two steps. First, we ask "why?" If it's because we're off on a tangent, heading down a dead end, we need to stop—cut our losses, write off the sunk costs, reject path dependency. If it's because we've found a new path, we need to keep going even faster—redefine our strategy, pour in more resources, put our best people on it. We've benchmarked and found the competition different, perhaps wanting. It's time to ignore them.

When we look around, we do so to learn and not to tout our own performance. We believe that excellence doesn't come from beating others but, rather, from comparing ourselves to where we need and want to be in a year, two years, five years—and we don't allow ourselves to feel better about our poor performance because it's better than our competitors (or at least no worse).

We can do reverse benchmarking, becoming "them" so we can see our vulnerabilities in a new way. "When you tell someone to put themselves in the shoes of somebody else and ask them what it would take to be successful against the company they're in now, the gloves come off," said one market expert. "Then you have some really unique ideas."[10]

Are we going to try to win by looking over our shoulders? Or are we going to win by setting our sights on the prize, by running the best race that we are capable of running? We can't do both. We can try to copy our way to greatness, always worried about what others are doing, trying to learn quickly what they're already doing and then somehow doing it better. Or we can select our path to greatness, always noticing the gaps between us and others, trying to learn how we can exploit the best of those opportunities so that our performance will be different in kind and not just in degree.

In the last analysis, a leader managing this paradox has a powerful mantra: We will learn from everyone, but imitate nobody.

CHAPTER 19

REDUCE COSTS AND INCREASE SPENDING

Money is of no value; it cannot spend itself. All depends on the skill of the spender.[1]

—*Ralph Waldo Emerson*

It's all about the money.

In organizations, a great many of the really serious conversations have money at the center. We want more—for ourselves, for our teams, for our ideas, for our projects, for our entire organizations. And because we know there are limits to what is available, we can at least tacitly want the other guy to have less.

Money tells us where the corporate pressure is—more here, so allocate more money, less here, so strip it away. The difference of 1 percent in a raise is critical, if given to the right person, and 10 percent more to the wrong project or product can drain the life out of our organizations.

Increasing spending is often considered bad, but it can be the very best thing to do. Reducing costs is often considered good, but it can be the very worst thing to do. So is increasing spending good or bad? Is reducing costs good or bad?

Absolutely.

REDUCE COSTS

Reducing costs is an ongoing challenge for managers and is especially critical at certain times or in certain situations. However, as we will see, reducing costs requires an entirely different mindset than cutting costs does.

Cost-reduction may seem like a universal good, but here are some really poor ways to reduce costs:

- Make it a major focus of mergers and acquisitions—In far too many mergers and acquisitions, regardless of talk about "synergies" and "market opportunities," the only significantly discernible long-term gain is through the costs (primarily people) that can be eliminated because of redundancy or excess capacity. This approach has many problems, not the least of which is an intense early misfocus on eliminating overlap rather than on expanding opportunity and market penetration.
- Cut people and development expenditures—It is no coincidence that employee commitment to a long-term relationship has generally disappeared at the same time that so many organizations have begun to define "reducing costs" as "eliminating large numbers of human beings." This approach is especially insane in a knowledge-based and customer-oriented economic world, in which the quality of the investment our people make can far exceed the cost of salary.
- Use budgets as the primary tool—Budgets are excellent for sending messages, setting the tone, and establishing guidelines for the use of scarce resources, but they are designed to limit costs, not reduce them. In budgets, we are looking at line items, not all of the hidden costs in those line items, which only the people on the ground can reduce.
- Launch cost-cutting "initiatives"—Costs aren't debris that can be cleaned away once and for all. Costs are weeds that need to be attacked consistently and continuously. The problem with treating cost-reduction as a cost-cutting event is that the costs just keep coming back. "Never think you've seen the last of anything," warns the old proverb.
- Cut the future to bail out the present—Stripping resources from the future to shore up a shaky present can never make us great. The future is "out there," hard to see, not pressing, murky. The problem is, of course, that the current shaky situation will always be with us, as we aren't doing anything to redesign the future.

There are some times or situations that demand a focus on reducing costs: first, whenever there is a major downturn in the economy, our market, or our major customers; second, whenever we are consolidating organizations and there is significant excess capacity to meet the combined need; and third, whenever we find ourselves in a turnaround situation and the organization is facing its own demise.

But these are exceptional circumstances, rather than the ongoing opportunity to maximize returns through lowering costs. The typical cost-cutting approach is reactive. It misses some of the best reasons to reduce costs: to provide funds for embryonic ideas that may *be* our business in ten years, for products or services needing a push to move into high gear, for making incentives for our best people and teams, and for buying ideas or organizations that will increase our competitiveness.

We don't really buy the future with increased revenues. We buy it with increased margins. At most, we want the costs to go up in the same proportion as the revenues. But our real desire should be to reduce costs as a percentage of revenues—to increase our margins.

So what are some effective ways to reduce costs?

Get out of the mindset of "cost cutting." Typically, we go along, accreting costs on a daily, project, or program basis, until the costs get large enough to get our attention (or something dramatic happens to draw our attention to costs in general). There is a huge difference in perspective between "cost cutting" and "cost reducing." Cost cutting happens when costs are large or revenues are small, whereas cost reducing happens all the time in every area—regardless of whether the existing margins are very good or very bad.

Treat costs like weeds. They grow and thrive more through inattention than through deliberate waste. And we have to know what are not really costs in the true sense of that term. For example, we need to remember that people aren't costs, regardless of the completely inaccurate way they are allocated by modern accounting systems (if by "modern" we mean "still valued on the same side of the ledger that they were when double-entry bookkeeping was invented in the Middle Ages, when most workers were valued at essentially nothing").

Define "cost reduction" more robustly. We can assume people are stupid and only work in absolute dollar terms—"We're spending 5X, and we need you to take that to 4X." But that is a static, short-term approach in a dynamic, long-term universe. Better to define "cost reduction" as a reduction in the *rate* of spending—"We're spending 5X at a 10Y sales level, and we need you to hold that to 8X, not 10X, at a 20Y sales level." They'll be spending more but proportionately less if we get them the numbers and parameters.

Use escalating margin targets. If we target higher margin percentages (not absolute dollars), the only way to get there is to increase spending at a slower rate than we are increasing revenues. Something has to be taken out of the way we do business, out of the cost of servicing those revenues, for that to happen.

Enlist everyone's best efforts in continuously reducing costs. If it is just the job of formal leaders, we're only going to be able to reduce costs in big chunks or in sporadic "cost-cutting initiatives." We should include effective, ongoing cost reduction as a key element of all performance agreements.

Ask ourselves how we can reduce costs without reducing morale. Without help, it is easy for people to view cost-cutting as retreat—backing off on products, services, projects, programs, and initiatives. How can we make this a whole-team effort, rather than something that management is doing to staff? How can we position this as creating opportunity for the future? What incentives can we offer for cost reduction?

In mergers and acquisitions or turnaround situations, focus first on the potential—the opportunities, the growth areas, the possibilities—rather than the downside—the excess costs, the waste, the overlaps. We need to get to those costs quickly, of course. Just not first. If this is done first it sends the wrong message—that we are more focused on eliminating errors than scoring runs.

INCREASE SPENDING

It's hard to make money without spending some. It's hard to make a lot without spending a lot. Spending more in the right places is one of the most important management functions, and yet we can be too cautious or, if we're not careful, fritter it away.

Increasing spending is actually very easy. It can happen all by itself, simply if no one is watching. Increasing spending *effectively* is very, very difficult. Here are some really poor ways to increase spending:

- Pay for pulse—We can find ourselves paying people (and continually paying them more) because they are there—what one authority called "pay for pulse."[2] To be effective, all compensation must be linked to performance. Often, the bigger the organization and the more complex the compensation system, the more is paid for identical work being done elsewhere and the less the compensation is connected to performance.
- Go with the flow—When something is "hot," the easiest action to take is to continue pouring in the dollars. This is bad business if the product or service is nearing the declining phase of its life cycle. These additional funds could be used to prepare or launch the next-generation product or service.
- Act generically—We want 10 percent growth, and our margins are fine, so we approve an increase in spending across the board of 10 percent. This approach appears even-handed and creates little internal conflict, but it is likely to fail (or at least reduce growth) unless everything we're spending money on contributes equally to our growth.
- Ignore the facts—At times, our emotions and enthusiasms and interests can push us in directions that make little sense. We may have to make spending decisions without all of the facts, but that is very different than making spending decisions in spite of the facts (whether we've chosen to ignore them or simply not access them).
- Pay for the future that may not come—There is no question that we have to spend now to prepare well for the future, but we can go beyond this to assuming the future is a "done deal" and spending accordingly. We hire the staff to launch a new product that hasn't even been road tested. We invest in a new design when we don't know if it even meets a real need. There is a large difference between *planning* for the future and *assuming* the future.

However, are there ways to increase spending that can be turned to pure advantage? Yes, but it requires intelligence and discipline. How do we do this?

Tie every increase in spending to results. We have to get away from the "features" of the increase (e.g., we'll have ten new computer stations, five new CNC machines, ten more points of contact with customers) and drill down on the "benefits" (e.g., we'll increase sales per employee by X, we'll serve 500 more customers with average annual sales of Y, we'll increase throughput by 25 percent). This can weed out a lot of nonsense and allow us to evaluate spending after the fact.

Center our results-based spending on critical success factors. We're going to spend X dollars to achieve this result, but how should X be allocated to ensure our success? This is where so much of budgeting breaks down. We allocate the right amount of money to an item, but the money gets misspent. What are the few factors that will move us relentlessly toward our goals? Everything else needs to be starved.

Tie an increase in spending to widespread innovation. This certainly includes research and development, product development, and bench testing, but this isn't even a beginning. How can we increase spending in such a way that it encourages innovation by every employee in every area every day? The spending could, for example, take the form of more staff to cover the routine work so that each employee has some time to think and not just to do.

Tie an increase in spending to satisfying customer needs at a higher level than we—and our competitors—are currently achieving. Money spent on what customers don't need or value is a target for decrease, not continuation. Money spent on what customers need and would value if we offered it is a formula for profitable work and growth.

Connect money to time. Increases in spending often do not have the same effect if made at different times. At what point in this effort can we get the biggest return for these fixed dollars we are willing to spend? Should we allocate 10X to this project but only release 5X until we see Y results? Would this be better spent after we know Z? Not-for-profits are notoriously hand-to-mouth organizations, where all money that comes in is instantly allocated. The money may be there now, but that doesn't mean the opportunity is. Waiting can at times maximize the value of expenditure.

Avoid simplistic extrapolations. If we have one hundred people to serve one thousand customers, we shouldn't accept the straightforward argument that with two hundred people we could serve two thousand customers. Why can't we serve twice as many people with a staff that only grows by 50 percent? What changes can we make in structure or process to serve the two thousand people with the current staff? Extrapolations of budgets are among the most common (and dumbest) activities in far too many organizations.

If an increase in spending isn't tied closely to the above points, we should be on the other side of the paradox. We should reduce costs.

THINKING AND RESPONDING PARADOXICALLY

Poor leaders do across-the-board spending increases and across-the-board spending cuts. Great leaders reduce costs a lot in some areas so they can increase spending a lot in others. They stretch opportunities here by shrinking capacities there. They push resources at great opportunities but also realize that those additional resources come from stripping something else.

We may want to spend now to save later. In the last few years, many of the Asian automakers have invested vast sums that have led to vast cost reductions for both themselves and their customers. Their increases in spending have lowered operating costs and improved operations, safety, and quality, so resale values hold at remarkably high levels. Because they make cars so well, they can charge proportionately even more than their increased costs. And their customers have lowered costs whether buying or leasing, thanks to high trade-in or residual values.

In fact, there are several paradoxical ties between increasing spending and reducing costs.

- Increasing spending to reduce costs—There are times when spending X dollars on a process redesign or new equipment or just the right people can save 2X or 3X on future expenditures.
- Reducing costs to increase spending—We can get funds for a new product or service or acquisition from investors or creditors, or we can get it from our own internal ingenuity. For example, we tell people, "You have the approval to go ahead with that idea, but you'll need to furnish your own funding out of cost reductions on other programs." Now we'll find out just how hot that new idea is.
- Increasing costs to reduce spending—We can make the cost of doing business so high that it forces a reduction in the expenditure. For example, we can raise the rates for scarce shared services so business units cut back on their demands. We have to be careful not to do this badly, by spending huge dollars to save few dollars (e.g., adding additional accounting staff for 10X dollars to watchdog expense reports and save X dollars). We might also allocate more fixed costs to a business unit or project and force variable costs down by holding total allowable cost constant.
- Reducing spending to increase costs—Here, we reduce approval for *spending* on shared services to increase the costs of a business unit, which will now have to do extraneous work themselves, do it outside, or stop doing it. We usually do this badly, reducing spending in ways that cause huge increases in "invisible" costs for necessary activities (e.g., refusing to buy inexpensive printers for individuals and not figuring the increased cost of our people walking to a common printer—waiting in line, talking to others, and losing focus).
- Reducing costs to reduce spending—The question here is, "How could reducing costs in this area help us to reduce spending in a different area?" This is the search for collateral savings.

We have to remember that these two activities—increasing spending and reducing costs—are symbolic of management's intentions. Just as money is the language of the economy, so money allocation by management becomes the language of the organization. An increase in spending is seen as a statement about the growing importance of a program.

We need to tie cost reduction to the spending increases that will build—and perhaps even save—our future. Cost reduction in a vacuum is a bland, boring, even depressing choice. Cost reduction tied to the future fuels passion: "Team, it looks to me that if we can shave 15 percent off our market launch costs on product X, we'll be able to get product Y into our customers' hands two quarters ahead of schedule." We have to remember that people are by nature much more passionate about building than demolition—unless we're demolishing the present to build an attractive future.

In all of this, we have to remember to manage the "invisible" spending and costs. If we waste just 10 percent of an employee's time because we don't want to spend $5,000 on a piece of equipment they need (but right now have to "make do"), and the person is making $50,000 a year, we could pay for that equipment in just one year. But most organizations don't do the math—they reduce the obvious costs and remain oblivious to the hidden ones that may be greater.

We want to think bigger than we are, so we can increase our influence and grow our top-line revenues in a solid way. We don't want to fall into the trap of wanting to grow but spending too little to make it happen. We want to think and act like an $X-sized organization, with very big (but achievable) goals. Everyone on our teams can think this way, not just senior leadership or marketing or sales.

In addition, we want to think small—even smaller than we're going to be in the next quarter or two—so we can increase our profitability and grow our bottom-line revenues in a solid way. We don't want to fall into the trap of thinking we are bigger than we really are and spending our time and money accordingly. We want to think small so we can conserve the resources we have for the really important things. And we need everyone on our team to think this way, not just senior leadership or operations or purchasing.

At Luman Consultants International, we use and recommend an operating value: smart frugal. Smart frugal means we are always looking for ways to spend money if that's smart and are always looking for ways to reduce costs it that's smart. Every person in our organization can relate to being "smart frugal," and we recommend it to you.

CHAPTER 20

MOVE FASTER AND TAKE MORE TIME

Speed is good only when wisdom leads the way.[1]

"Must go faster," said the scientist played by Jeff Goldblum in *Jurassic Park*, as dinosaurs chased him. For leaders today, that's what we hear in our heads: *Must go faster!* The dinosaurs are coming. We can hear the footsteps.

First to market. Fast follower. Should we run hard to get out in front, or run hard to catch up? The answer is probably "yes." Everyone's expectations of speed and delivery and service have grown relentlessly in recent years, and no matter where we are in the competitive landscape, it can seem like we're losing ground. We can go from being ahead to being behind, even while we're running flat out.

However, in the twenty-first century, speed also kills.

Mistakes seem every more costly. New designs and products that are rushed to market can cost us dearly and wreck our brand. New services that haven't been road-tested and that are deficient in meeting needs or delivering quality can stop us cold.

We sense that we need to slow the game down. We need time to dissect what we're doing or about to do and ensure that we're taking a reasonable risk, a risk that has been reduced to a very low and manageable level.

MOVE FASTER

Often, we simply need to move faster. Baseball legend Satchel Paige warned us not to look over our shoulders: something might be gaining on us.

But there are a whole lot of bad ways to move faster.

- Give margin-less deadlines—There is a school of thought that the best work is done when people are under time pressure. This is not a first-rate school. No matter now noble the intentions to do excellent work, the goal in people's minds will be to hit the deadline.

- Eliminate the pilot—Taking six months to test a product or service before we roll it out can seem like a waste of resources. But that is nothing like the waste of resources spent fixing it.
- Make quick people decisions—Interviews, research, and analyzing candidates for hire or promotion take time. Why don't we get somebody in that role? Why don't we try them out so we can move ahead? Because they might be the dead weight that sets us back a year.
- Minimize market research—We know we have a great offering. Why do we need to waste a lot of time doodling with customers and potential customers? Why can't we roll it out and then tweak it? Because customers have their own idea of what a "great offering" is, and tweaking is more expensive than asking.
- Put meditative processes on a fixed schedule—Some of the most important processes and documents—vision, mission, values—need time to mature. We certainly need to finish these, but simply declaring them to be "done" because we have something "acceptable" by the due date is self-delusion.

Speed isn't always our friend. If we go faster where we shouldn't, we're going to have a collision.

If we want to manage the power of this paradox, however, there are many ways in which the typical organization "must go faster."

Ask speed-clarifying questions. Regardless of the activity, a negative answer to any of the following questions is a strong indicator that we need to finish whatever we're working on at a much faster clip:

- Is this worth substantial planning, debating, or review?
- Will this influence our vision, mission, values, or behaviors?
- Will this substantially alter our offering?
- Is there a significant financial implication or downside risk?
- Is impeccable quality really required?
- Will this lock us into paths that will be difficult to alter as needed?

Make strategy a change-management process. How can any organization afford to take months or quarters to develop its strategic plan? What happens in the 180 days while this plan is being developed, haggled over, and approved? What opportunities will we miss? What raging fires will burn around us while we fiddle?

Flexify the structure. The very word "structure" implies to most people something rigid and enduring. And that's the problem. We pull the word from its use in architecture or engineering, when a much better source in today's organizations would be biology. Form follows function, changing as required by the environment (the demands of the marketplace, the morphing needs and expectations of customers, our shifting position in the competitive landscape). An organization chart is nearly incapable of defining "structure" in any meaningful, value-adding way—but it is quite capable of locking us in to waste and destruction of value.

Derigidify processes. For quite a number of years, the practice has been to overlay the flux that is a modern organization with immutable processes—TQM, Six Sigma, Supply Chain Management. Once these processes are entrenched, they have the force of law: "This is how we do things around here." This is especially so when we've been "certified" and have a lot of specialists who are "certified" in the "certified" activity. But who cares if we are doing things efficiently or well if we're the wrong things?

Discard processes. We have to learn how to drain a useful new process of most of its value and then make it yesterday's news. Getting the last increment of value will not be worth the stultifying effect of King Process. Great success does not come from focusing on doing lesser things really well or from using an aging process to meet fresh challenges.

Push people out of comfort zones. The natural bent of most people is to find an area and gain understanding, then confidence, then results—and then get comfortable. We need to move them *after* understanding and confidence and 80 percent of the results and *before* "comfortable" and the last 20 percent of the results. The next results will probably come more easily and effectively to the next fresh person in the role anyway.

Put losers and doubters on the fast track—out. There are a lot of reasons that we delay making good termination decisions. We've spent a lot of time finding people, hiring them, orienting them, developing them, coaching them, counseling them. Our customers know them. Termination will tear up the team. We have a better shot at fixing a competence problem than a character problem. But the odds on either one are not very good.

Streamline customer access. The last place any sane leader would want to go slowly is with customers, yet we can use rational processes to do just that. Most automated phone systems, for example, are perfectly designed to make our customers hate us and potential customers to hang up. Referrals to other places ("May I connect you with the department that handles that?") are death to any hard-charging customer (often the ones who have the money and are ready to spend it now). Executive assistants and other "gatekeepers" can keep us from hearing the truth or connecting with new business. Making customers happy fast is the right answer.

TAKE MORE TIME

Often, we simply need to take more time. We don't find a return on many ideas and decisions until they've rolled around in our heads or organizations for a while. Time "saved" here can lower the quality, diminish the value, and force us to spend a lot more time later to make it right.

But taking more time is not the answer to every question. There are some very poor ways to take more time.

- *Procrastinate*—We aren't smart enough to know how much time it will take to finish. Other things surprise our schedule. The thing we needed to know or have isn't available on the shorter notice. We have no time to make it "fine." And the pressure will eat away at us while we wait.
- *Use the "pocket veto"*—Like a political leader who doesn't want the flak for saying "no" to a piece of legislation, we can avoid the confrontation by simply "sitting on it." But this isn't useful time. The organization isn't moving ahead. People are still waiting and wondering and not developing other ideas.
- *Require or allow elaborate reviews*—Reviews, especially in a "daisy chain" where one occurs after the other, are incredibly time-consuming and seldom have any significant value. The occasional "catch" is usually more than offset by the massive time expenditure and lost opportunities.
- *Be reactive*—We can choose to wait—for direction, for permission, for the customer to call, for the saving event, for the horrible person to quit, for the team to become productive—but the wait might kill us. Being proactive is almost always the better course.
- *Let problems "work themselves out"*—The only problem with this is that problems almost never work themselves out. They do often get worse with time. These are slow death, death by a thousand cuts.

In contrast, there are some "must-do" activities that will help us make sure we are taking more time where it can add significant value.

Ask speed-reducing questions. Regardless of the activity, a negative answer to any of these questions is a strong indicator that we need to slow this juggernaut down:

- Do we have a high degree of certainty that this will advance our vision and mission?
- Have we brainstormed this long enough to ensure that it is a "better-than-all-alternatives" direction to add maximum value?
- Have we exposed all of the potential pitfalls, discussed the possible unexpected consequences, and given every legitimate naysayer a day in court?
- Have we involved a sufficiently large proportion of the team in a sufficiently large way to secure their commitment during implementation and refinement?
- Have we built "rest stops" into the schedule at which we can reflect and revise?
- Have we done sufficient planning, and do we have the resources and infrastructure, to deliver the required quality?

Align around vision and mission. Where are we going in the next ten years? What are the main things we will need to do to get us to there from here? These are huge questions that often get shorted in the rush to develop strategies and plans and tactics. But if we get the main direction wrong, what good will all of our short-term scurrying do? If a manned mission to Mars starts with a quarter of a degree trajectory error, where will it end up? What's next after Mars?

Ensure coherent and effective values and behaviors. Most organizations have an eclectic mix of random and designed values and behaviors. Some work against each other: "We want to be creative and flexible" is trumped by "We always follow the rules around here." Even organizations with strong cultures will face inevitable dilution over time as a result of turnover and growth. We have to take the time to ensure that cultural dysfunctions are not eroding our plans.

Find people very slowly. Very few people like to recruit and hire, but this is where the game—in both the near and distant future—will be won or lost. A cheap mechanical process—lining up job descriptions and resumes, asking about work history or career goals—is almost guaranteed to produce suboptimal results. Why do we keep doing this? Because "we've got to get someone in here fast."

Develop substantial ways to keep people. The "quick and dirty" approach to retention and motivation is compensation—it is tactile and measurable and plays to the prevailing sense that greed is our best chance. But keeping passionate people, and keeping them passionate, takes more than that, and thinking about it in a nuanced way takes a lot more focus and time.

Compensate people thoughtfully. Even with compensation decisions, taking more time can work wonders. Compensation is only meaningful as a performance driver if we ensure that rewards follow results. In our experience, compensation policy is almost a universal failure, with compensation disconnected from performance, often rewarding suboptimal performance, counterproductive action, or mere existence.

Determine the right business measurements. We all know that "what gets measured gets done." But what if what gets done isn't worth measuring? It takes a lot of time and thought and dialogue to come up with metrics that actually gauge high performance and that people can actually perform.

Handle customer problems well. Only in a Scott Adams *Dilbert* world would we make upset customers hobble painfully through a mind-numbing process that inflicts further pain. Every step of a customer-service operation needs to answer the question, "What can we do at this point to make things right?" There is always an answer if we take the time to look for it.

Some of the best things in life are slow—a day at the beach, a fine dinner, a good book, a lazy conversation with an old friend. An organization that knows when to take more time will also be among the best.

THINKING AND RESPONDING PARADOXICALLY

As legendary coach and motivator John Wooden reminded us, we should be quick but not hurry. "With all deliberate speed," the majority opinion in a landmark U.S. Supreme Court case ordered.

One of the ironies of this paradox is that we often need to move faster now so we can take more time later. In critical-path scheduling, the "float" or "slack" built up in the early part of a schedule can be deployed effectively against critical items that require more time later on. It can be very tedious work indeed to try to get an initiative off the ground, no matter how simple or needed it might be. If we're not careful, we linger in those stages when we should be moving faster.

Conversely, we often need to take more time now so we can move faster later. This is certainly true in planning, where an ounce of prevention is worth a pound of cure. It can be very tedious work to slow an initiative down, no matter how poorly thought out or mediocre it might be. If we're not careful, we can speed through important tasks in the present when we should be moving slower.

This paradox forces us to give up a simplistic notion of "speed." "Speed" doesn't mean "moving fast;" "speed" is a term that encompasses all velocities. We're worried about speed when we're driving on the open highway, and we're worried about speed when we're driving in a school zone. When we're driving, the truly important issue about speed is to make sure we are going the right speed for the circumstances.

So it is with organizations and programs and projects and plans. The key is not just to go fast but to know when to go fast and when to go slowly—to go *only* as fast as circumstances allow.

We have to take time to study a process, but when the time comes for a decision, make it fast and move on, making corrections later. We don't let analysis paralysis turn into decision paralysis. We are ready for it to come back to us for further thought, more study, and revisions.

In an automotive race, it is very easy to conclude that the mission is to "go fast." But how many times has the person with a really fast car, perhaps the fastest car in the race, ended up losing? The real key to success is what happens when the car isn't going fast—in fact, when it isn't going at all. The pit is where success is ensured or failure earned. A minor error here—not checking everything, pushing through the protocol a little too fast, adding a defective component, making a deficient adjustment—can produce a major error out on the track.

It would be a mistake to conclude that the "slow" times—the times in the pit stop—are *really* slow or have no deadlines. The pressure is intense in that pit, to get everything right. But its essence is to give the car its rest *really fast*. This is important to the success of a break or meditative time—it has to have a structure and a deadline. A pit stop is not an excuse to lose momentum. Quite the contrary: it's another place where momentum should be gained.

So how will we know when we should move faster or slower? Starbucks has wrestled with this. "Despite the need for speed, Starbucks executives . . . are sensitive to being lumped in with fast-food outlets. . . . 'It's a real trade-off—to move quickly, and not be rushed.' "[2]

We have to set tight but reasonable deadlines. People don't always work better if they have more time, but they often do work worse. We need to use really challenging targets to force speed and creativity and streamlining and frugality. At the same time, these targets shouldn't force panic or even frantic behavior.

We know that it's time to move faster when we cannot plausibly connect what we are working on (or debating) to the creation of value. This would include most of the reviews of organizational structure, most arguments over budget details, most fine-tunings of policies and procedures, most wordsmithing of documents and memos, and most repetitions of information or recommendations as they work their way laboriously up the organization.

But we also have to give everyone the right to say, "Slow down" whenever they see massive danger or opportunity. We need to have speed-evaluation teams at strategic locations or points in any critical process.

We need to be deliberate. "Deliberate" doesn't mean "slow" but, rather, "intentional; fully considered; not impulsive." We can be slow while being intentional and fully considered and not impulsive, and we can be fast while being intentional and fully considered and not impulsive. Fast is no excuse for sloppy thinking or deciding or acting, and slow is no excuse for plodding thinking or deciding or acting.

We need to recognize that most revolutionary ideas have been incubated for a very long time. We want to be quick to throw out a current approach that is not delivering high performance, and slow to settle on its replacement. "[W. L.] Gore is shockingly impatient with the status quo but patient about the time—often years, sometimes decades—it takes to develop revolutionary products and bring them to market."[3]

We should make it faster for customers to get their problems and needs to us, and we should address those problems or needs slowly enough to achieve freshness and creativity and at least a bit of customization. It should take no time at all—and no pain—for their issues to find their way to decision-makers. Once there, we solve those issues with care and precision. We have to handle customer problems with incredible speed *and* incredible thoughtfulness.

One of the big questions in many industries is, "Is our product or service being turned into a commodity?" Our answer should be, "Even if it isn't, *we* should be turning it into a commodity." We should want to make our products or services more cost-effective for our customers as we streamline the order and delivery channels and take worthless steps out of the entire process. "Dell—the company and the founder—*likes* the commodity business," wrote Michael Treacy. "Dell plans to go right on commoditizing the computer industry, piece by piece, while it keeps growing faster than anyone expects."[4]

And our answer to this big question should also be, "Let's fight hard to make sure that no one else turns us into a commodity."

We used to do pen-and-paper surveys for our clients, and it was a tedious and expensive process to enter and check the data. We wanted to turn that service into a commodity, and we did so with on-line surveys that needed no data entry or checking. At the same time, we dreaded the thought of a commodity survey and didn't believe that this would be effective in identifying the unique problems facing every organization. So we have added a customizing capability to our commodity surveys, both in the content and in the reporting of the findings. This produces a process that is more cost-effective for our clients even as it allows us to do a higher level of work.

This paradox can bring us face-to-face with the question of growth. Should we grow fast or slow? Through acquisition or organically? The answer, of course, is "yes." There is no one right way, but rather a rhythm—long periods of organic growth, slow and steady, preparing the organization to intelligently absorb the fast growth of an acquisition. And then, when we get past the period of hype that surrounds every buy, we take the new whole and move back to the slow and steady of organic growth. We should look for the acquisitions that put a nice exclamation on our organic growth and at the same time that can be grown organically after we add them on.

We've been told that "time is the great healer," and also that "time is the great destroyer." Which is it? Both, of course. Time heals—*if* we take the right amount, and *if* we do the right things with the time. And time destroys—*if* we move too fast and *if* we move too slow. We learn from this paradox that in the final analysis, time does nothing. It is only what we do with the time.

The philosophy of a successful basketball coach was described as "patiently aggressive,"[5] a beautiful paradox that could be mistaken for an oxymoron. It won a championship.

But we want more. It's easier to be aggressive than to be patient. "Better is a patient person than a warrior," we're told in an old proverb.[6] We have to keep a steady hand on the wheel and a watchful eye on the road as we push the car into the curve, but we know there are dangers out there—crashes and debris and competitors who do crazy things. We do indeed want to be patiently aggressive, and aggressively patient.

CHAPTER 21

BE CONSISTENT AND CHANGE EVERYTHING

Who is the really consistent man? The man who changes. Since change is the law of his being, he cannot be consistent if he stick in a rut.[1]

—*Mark Twain*

Consistency requires gradual change.

The real world requires radical change.

Once we think of it this way, we see that we have a problem. Consistency over time is crucial to delivering dependable results and to building a durable culture. And yet, changing on a dime is also crucial to delivering dependable results and building a durable culture.

As it turns out, successful organizational change has five overarching requirements:

1. The type of change must be aligned with the true need.
2. The size of the initiative must be scaled to the size of the needed change.
3. The change must begin at the right place.
4. The approach selected must have the potential to overcome resistance and the *good forces of consistency*, creating the momentum to carry the organization through the inevitable pain of change.
5. The change must be anchored to something that isn't changing.

Usually we worry that the change is too "big," that we're attacking a small problem with an oversized weapon. Given our aversion to large changes and our capacity for self-delusion about the magnitude of problems, we select incremental change when radical change is called for. Although it is possible to make radical change when incremental change is all that is called for, human nature makes this an less likely scenario.

The size of the initiative is all too often misscaled. We tend to expend just enough resources to get somewhere near the mark without hitting it. There are a hundred distractions that can absorb limited resources. We might have enough if we spend them on the right things and avoid spending them on teambuilding off-sites and on trite books and trinkets.

We can easily err by starting with the more "tangible" areas like structure and processes. We want to change things that we can get our hands on, where we can move boxes around and change "roles and responsibilities." We can see the changes happening.

But these are not only poor places to start; unfortunately, they are almost always the *worst* places to start. Such changes give the illusion of progress because we are moving the pieces around on the board, but they leave the great opportunities for creating value untouched. The result is often an organization that looks different without actually being different.

Resistance that will surely surface—from personalities who hate change (or you), from parties whose power is rooted in the status quo, from people who think the idea is stupid, from departments that will lose funding, from leaders who are "uncomfortable" with the direction. And some resistance is from those who reasonably question whether the new is really better than the old. We'd better plan for all of this resistance.

Even if we select the right type and size of change, start it in the right place, and have a plan to overcome resistance, we can still lose if we don't tether the change to the unchanging. Somewhere, there has to be something consistent that the proposed change can't touch.

Peter Drucker tells us that "the tension between the need for continuity and the need for innovation and change was central to society and civilization."[2] We need to manage this tension. We need to change, but we need to be consistent. How?

BE CONSISTENT

Most of us know instinctively that if we keep jumping around from one offering or process to another that we have little chance of being successful. We see that being consistent over time can give us a focus and power unavailable to the "fad-of-the-month" club.

But we can practice consistency very badly. Some damaging ways to be consistent are:

- Stick with obviously failing approaches—Persistence is a wonderful trait, but persistence in failing plans can cripple organizations and trash careers. It is a fine line between "he is a rock" and "he is a rock head."
- Make no exceptions—Essayist Ralph Waldo Emerson taught us that "a foolish consistency is the hobgoblin of little minds." I've seen senior leaders tell

various departments, "You're the police." Unless we're expecting homicides, having rule-loving enforcers patrolling the halls is not likely to take us to excellence.

- Define "uncomfortable" as "inconsistent"—We can stop people from moving in healthy new directions by challenging those paths as "inconsistent." One is reminded of the exchange between two characters in the classic comedy "What's Up Doc?": "You're so . . . different," says the Ryan O'Neal character. "From now on, I'll try to be the same . . . as people who aren't different," answers the Barbra Streisand character.
- Use the same solution for different problems—It is so hard to find things that work, we are naturally tempted to apply them to everything. Consistent approaches to divergent problems will lead to an array of suboptimal solutions.
- Assume that everyone has the same drivers—People are so complex that *nobody* has the same drivers. There are common motivational elements, of course, but the mix of ingredients and quantities is going to be unique for each person. Consistency is disastrous if widespread passion is our goal.

Remaining unchanged in circumstances that demand change is the kind of consistency that can destroy us.

A relentless organizational focus on consistency can rob it of its ability to change and advance. Even potentially useful ideas like ISO management standards can lock us into stagnation, and while protecting us from defects can protect us from progress. The *Total Quality Management* journal reported that "ISO 9000 certification has a very limited impact on financial performance [and] this effect dissipates quickly over time . . . The problem is," one leader noted, "it can help drive a company to a plateau level of performance, but it will keep it at that level and, in fact, stifle improvement."[3] Other critics say that "process management helps improve existing products and routines, but can hinder a company's ability to innovate."[4]

If we want to be effectively consistent, what do we need to do?

Remind people of the value of consistency. What are the positive attributes of consistency?

- We don't have to spend time on learning and development.
- We've simplified orientation to "do it the XYZ way."
- We've minimized mistakes.
- We can guarantee, for some period, a certain level of quality and performance.
- We can easily identify and eliminate eccentric behavior that is destructive.

Define consistency well. For most people, being consistent is "not changing." The problem is, of course, that the world around us keeps changing. So being consistent can't realistically be defined as "not changing," but it does imply "changing deliberately and cautiously."

Treat "consistency" as "tightly managed change." We can implement consistency as steady, evolutionary change. Continuous improvement—*Kaizen*, the

Japanese call it. Taking a good product and making it a little better. Adding value to an existing offering. Playing chess, where you can think five or ten moves ahead. Renovational change.

Evaluate the results of consistency. Is our consistency delivering value? Is the value we're getting as great as what we could get by changing? If not, does that greater potential value justify the cost to get it?

Find consistency leaders. This kind of consistency—the steady management of evolutionary change—needs leaders and process. Some people are by nature this kind of leader, and they can be identified and nurtured. Consistent leaders don't always have the same goals as time goes by, but their goals are consistently and clearly laid out and repeated until the organization understands them. They change nothing without good reason, but they consistently prepare the organization for needed change. They need to have an equal voice with "real change leaders."

Support real consistency leaders. It's easy to look at these people as obstructionists and roadblocks, but they are as important as real change leaders. "So the conservative who resists change is as valuable as the radical who proposes it," wrote historians Will and Ariel Durant, "perhaps as much more valuable as roots are more vital than grafts."[5]

There is no doubt that consistency has value. Our stakeholders can rely on us. But our consistency needs to be cutting-edge.

CHANGE EVERYTHING

In the face of a globalized postindustrial economy, everything seems up for grabs. Relentlessly sticking with anything can seem dangerous, even foolhardy. We must be nimble, ready to cast aside even our most valuable approaches if they begin to seem irrelevant.

But we can change ourselves very, very badly. We can do this if we

- Change our core identity—Whatever we are is relatively plain to our stakeholders. When we start tampering with what makes us "us," the change goes beyond being disorienting to being destructive.
- Change too many variables at the same time—scientists figured out a long time ago that they can't learn much from an experiment if multiple changes are made concurrently. Likewise, leaders who change everything don't know what caused the change. Was it the refreshed culture? The new leadership? The exciting strategy? The well-received process? The revised rewards? At Luman Consultants International, we always insist that clients tell us about any other initiatives that they have in wrap-up mode, kick-off mode, or contemplation.
- Change without metrics—If we don't establish a "control," how will we know if the change worked? Changes aren't good because they are implemented successfully. Changes are good because they produce results.

- View change as inherently good—Change sometimes gets a free ride. "What we're doing isn't working, so let's try something new." But we are just as likely to change to something worse.
- Don't build a passion for the change—Real change is incredibly hard to come by. It takes an astounding amount of passion to move the mountain an inch.

We can open our organization up for breathtaking change if we take some steps to do it. Just saying, "we're open to change" won't get the job done. We need to use effective approaches.

Define what can't be changed. Most organizations are very fuzzy about what is sacred and what is not. Things that should be sacred, such as core values, are freely ignored or violated, whereas things that shouldn't be, like political turf, are considered hallowed ground. If we define what can't be changed, we leave everything else open to it.

Treat "change everything" as "loosely managed change." We also need revolutionary change. Continuous reinvention. Taking a good product and making it obsolete it before the market does. Working counterintuitively. Creating value through a new offering. Playing billiards, where you can plan the next shot but can't finalize it until the balls stop rolling. Transformational change.

Avoid overemphasizing structure or process. Structure and process are ways to consistent results and high quality—and they are ways to the graveyard. We simply can't afford to make what "is" too secure. We need to say, "This is the way it is and has to be . . . until we find a better way."

Recognize and war against the enemies of serious change. Transformational change has some serious enemies that must be defeated.

- Resistance to reality—One of the hardest things for humans to do is to admit the magnitude of a problem they are facing. We are all, to one degree or another, reality-impaired. We substitute wishful thinking for careful analysis and rename it "hope." We don't want to admit that our thoughts and plans and actions have core flaws. Even if we pay a consultant a lot of money to tell us the bad news, we'd rather write off the expenditure than take the medicine.
- Prior success—The organizations that are usually the most resistant to revolutionary change are the ones that have been extremely successful with a current model or strategy for a very long period of time. "Successful people are, by definition, good at what they do," notes Intel's Andy Grove. "It's not surprising that they continue to implement the same strategic and tactical moves that worked for them during the course of their careers. But such a repetitive approach leads to inertia."[6]
- Prior experience—Maybe you went through a large-scale change in an earlier job and it was ugly. It produced lots of paper but no profits. *No more of that, thanks*, you think. One writer said that "disillusionment is a major barrier to change, since people cannot be expected to take emotional risks in pursuit of goals they think impossible."[7]

- Current problems—How can we think about what we want to be in three years if we die next quarter? The problem, of course, is that if we don't think now about these problems that are a year or more out, when that time gets here it will just transform itself into another miserable quarter.
- Entrenched interests—Radical change always disturbs people. Entrenched interests can even include our own. It can be very hard to give up on one of our own ideas—it's hard to admit the baby is ugly when it's your baby.
- Evolutionary change—Yes, incremental change can be the enemy of radical change. If you want to grow at a 10 percent clip and you've been stuck at 3 percent for several years, it can be tempting to say, "we'll just push ourselves, work harder and smarter, and we'll get to ten percent," not realizing that with the current design there is a wall at 4 percent. We have seen many well-meaning organizations focus on evolutionary change to avoid needed (but dreaded) revolutionary change.
- Pain—Radical change is having surgery rather than taking medication. However much it's needed, it's a lot more painful than taking a pill.

Establish the right mindset. Great organizations don't try to survive change—or even thrive during change—but, rather, try to exploit change. Change is viewed, first and foremost, as opportunity. We might mess it up, but not because we aren't trying to make the most of it.

Build a championship change team. We have to put structures in place that actually prepare us to exploit the opportunity without adding another burden to an already stretched organization. Change needs passion. Any approach that does not include the involvement and commitment of most of the team is unlikely to give us a good enough payback for the agony of change.

Transform the negatives of change. Of course change will cause stress and confusion and insecurity. How can we convert the stress to positive energy and action, the confusion to an opportunity to learn, and the insecurity into a challenge to grow?

Start the change now. The bigger the change, the more it seems we should talk about it and analyze it. But that keeps us from learning how to do it and allows the fear and forces of resistance to grow in power. The best way to defuse the argument, "Should we change?" is to start actually changing.

Changing everything is harder than it looks. It's even harder than our worst-case-scenario assessments of it. Given human nature, it's a mountain. But there's gold somewhere in that mass.

THINKING AND RESPONDING PARADOXICALLY

Peter Drucker reminds us that "Precisely because change is a constant, the foundations have to be extra strong. The more an institution is organized to be a real change leader, the more it will need to establish continuity internally and externally, the more it will need to balance rapid change and continuity."[8]

People need something fixed to hold onto before they can throw themselves into a change initiative. Widespread change is possible and effective because we first define what will not be changed. If change is needed, we need something that is "fixed" about our organization before we will have the context and willingness and stamina to change the many things that are "variable." At Luman Consultants International we call this "fixed" portion "VMVB" (for Vision, Mission, Values, and Behaviors). Having these written down, even on beautiful plaques, does not fulfill the need unless they are actually being lived inside the organization. If we agree on the core, we can disagree on everything else without that disagreement feeling like betrayal.

In the twenty-first century, the need for regular and continual reinvention should be obvious. But the first question we need to ask may not be so obvious: How can we reinvent ourselves if we don't know who we are in the first place? We desperately need an effective discovery process to determine whether change is needed and what it needs to look like. Perception is not reality. Consistency may actually be our best course. "Managers need stakes in the ground to guide change," noted several experts.[9]

There are two elements that are critical for successful change. Without these, there can be no effective change:

1. Recognition—We have to recognize where we need to be, where we are now, and the type and magnitude of the difference between these locations. Is evolutionary change sufficient? If so, let's not tear up our organization. Is revolutionary change required? If so, let's not tune up our organization.
2. Resources—"Dig a well before you are thirsty," teaches an old Chinese proverb. We have to allocate resources to make needed changes, often before we know what those changes actually look like. We have to pull resources out of current usage and set them aside to make the change we can't identify but know is coming. In many situations, organizations die because they recognize the need for change after they've passed the point of being able to fund it.

Managing this paradox drives us toward *consistent change*. We need to build change mechanisms, consistent structures, and processes. This might include such things as a consistently composed "Sustaining Team" for the change and a related "Sustaining Process." Nothing flourishes over time without consistent attention. "The only way in which an institution . . . can maintain *continuity* is by building systematic, organized innovation into its very structure," notes Peter Drucker.[10]

Consistency can become our enemy. There may be some competitor out there like General George S. Patton, who once said, "I have studied the enemy all my life. I have read the memoirs of his generals and his leaders. I have even read his philosophers and listened to his music. I have studied in detail the account of every damned one of his battles. I know exactly how he will react under any given set of circumstances. And he hasn't the slightest idea of when I'm going to whip the hell out of him."[11] Our competitors know how we're going to react if we're too consistent. We are predictable, and our consistency makes us an easy target.

When we are not able to give substantial answers to three important questions, consistency has become the enemy.

1. Where are we going? If we don't answer this question effectively—if we don't make a real and ongoing "case for change"—we not only are losing a large percentage of our support but are actually feeding the underground resistance movement.
2. What will we do to get where we're going? What must we do to achieve the vision for the change? What isn't working and needs to be terminated?
3. How will we go about delivering results? This question has two parts, a technical component and a cultural component. On the technical side, we need to ensure that our on-the-ground tactics are really producing the change. On the cultural side, we need to align the goals of the change closely with the behaviors of the people and organization. If our new approach requires flexibility but we have an unwritten norm that "we always follow the rules around here," we are kidding ourselves about the likely success of the initiative.

During change, people fall into one of four categories:

- Visionaries—These are the people who "get it," who understand the "why," throw themselves into the "what," and take strong leadership of the "how." These are people who are willing to change everything.
- Supporters—They agree with what we are proposing and will support it if the cost isn't too high but are cautious about their involvement and willingness to defend the process. They are willing to change some things but don't want to let go of others. We need them to provide consistency to the "change everything" visionaries.
- Skeptics—These people are torn down the middle. They want to exploit the change and make the organization stronger, but they've seen it all before and have as many questions and doubts as they have hopes and dreams. They say, "I'm not sure about this, but I'm willing to listen and learn, and if my questions begin to get answered, I'll be ready for the revolution." They are strong forces for consistency and possible forces for resistance.
- Cynics—This is the group that says, "I'm sure this won't work, no matter what you say or what we do." They may or may not actively oppose the initiative, but their attitude will be like a dead weight on the fragile change. This group is tough to convince, but most can be isolated and a few—the ones who were idealists until they got burned too many times—can be pulled back from the grave. They might become the strongest evangelists for the new order. Cynics

are the leaders of the resistance. They don't like the current order so much as they dislike the new.

"Knowing what to change and what not to change will be another important challenge in this turbulent era," write Larry Bossidy and Ram Charan.[12] A consistent approach to change allows us to say, "We're stable—so bring it on." Knowing what kind of change—evolutionary, "consistent" change or revolutionary "change everything" change—parallels this challenge in importance.

VICTORY WITH PARADOX

CHAPTER 22

APPLYING THE PARADOX PRINCIPLE TO CREATE LASTING IMPACT AND WIDESPREAD WEALTH

Only the paradox comes anywhere near to comprehending the fullness of life.[1]

—*Carl Jung*

Only well-managed paradox comes anywhere near creating durable influence or maximum wealth for all.

We've tried to show you in this book how to put paradox to work for your organization. "The paradox is the source of the thinker's passion," wrote Danish philosopher Søren Kierkegaard; "the thinker without a paradox is like a lover without feeling: a paltry mediocrity."[2]

In the long run, the organization without the ability to manage paradox will have to settle for paltry mediocrity. This will be especially true as more and more organizations find a way of combining these "furious opposites"[3] into a third way that produces a lasting effect on organizations and widespread wealth for all stakeholders.

CAN WE DO IT?

One leader recently declared, "We don't think ourselves into a new way of acting, we act ourselves into a new way of thinking."[4] This is a classic example of either–or logic—we can *either* think ourselves into acting *or* act ourselves into thinking. The fact is, if we want to create lasting influence and widespread wealth, we'd better do both.

To get these principles out in front of our people, we will first change the way we talk. We won't let a statement like, "we need more cooperation here," go forward without its twin, "and we need more conflict here." We won't let "we need to be more consistent" take a step without its partner, "and we need to evaluate everything to see what we should change."

Then we need to learn *by* doing and *from* doing and let our actions inform our thinking about paradox. As we encourage our people—no, *expect* our people—to take more risks, we will learn more about the kinds of risk we need to eliminate. As we increase freedom, the boundaries that need to be clarified will come into sharp relief.

We can spend our leadership on business as usual, or we can spend it on building an organization with unique powers of thought and action. "Life is like a coin," wrote Miguel de Cervantes. "You can spend it any way you wish, but you can only spend it once."[5]

We need some robust conversation about each of the twenty paradoxes. Even if our teams are composed of average performers, we can manage paradox to produce effect and wealth, and we will beat teams composed of excellent performers who choose to live in an either–or world.

WHAT'S THE GOAL?

The truth is, managing—or mismanaging—paradoxes is not optional. We're doing this all the time. The only question is, are we doing it well or are we doing it badly?

The goal of our efforts at managing paradox is to move toward higher and longer-lasting performance. Over the past several decades, we at Luman Consultants International have come to a fairly crisp description of high-performance organizations. Despite their unique qualities, they practice these Ten Key Elements all of which are informed and enhanced by the effective management of the 20 Power Paradoxes:

1. Building around shared vision and values and mutual trust
2. Placing a premium on truth
3. Aligning organizational and personal goals
4. Expecting innovation from every person every day
5. Involving people in the creation of value
6. Communicating lavishly and sparingly
7. Focusing on possibilities rather than limitations
8. Creating a safe place for personal risk
9. Challenging people with high expectations
10. Learning and teaching relentlessly

High-performance organizations gain the most return for the energy, resources, and time invested. They take actions that have the most beneficial outcomes. They are aligned around a common vision and focused on core excellencies. They have the right people in the right place at the right time, doing the right things to execute a plan. They avoid the distractions that lead to misdirected and wasted effort, and they reach their goals without unnecessary or ineffective steps.

HOW DO WE GET THERE?

The way we get to high performance is an important choice. The standard choice is out there, and everyone's using it. "The fundamental paradox of any corporation is that even though it competes in the marketplace, it uses nonmarket instruments—plans, commands, controls—to accomplish its goals. As the British economist D. H. Robertson evocatively explained it, corporations are 'islands of conscious power in this ocean of unconscious co-operation.'... Companies want to retain the structure and institutional coherence of the traditional corporation."[6]

The problem is, this isn't a paradox, it's a *contradiction*. Many people like to talk about "alignment," but here is the granddaddy of misalignment: Organizations trying to operate with anti-free-market means in a free-market economy and world. The only reason this works at all is that everyone is benchmarking the competition and the competition is doing it the same way.

Few are building a *Thinking Organization*. The Thinking Organization learns, of course, and it teaches, but it does so much more. It *thinks*. It thinks with its head and it thinks with its heart. It discusses and debates. It invents and discards. It encourages healthy conflict and discourages unhealthy consensus. It finds ways to high-grade its information and knowledge and truth and wisdom. It respects authority without fearing it. It sees and hopes for better things even while welcoming the hard truth. It values the present and the future in equal measure. It understands that freedom is more powerful than control, even as it knows that boundaries are necessary for freedom to last and be effective. It finds a way to hold the core changeless, so it can change everything else.

Thinking people are the most fundamentally free people on earth, and freedom should and will produce more impact and wealth in a free market than does any ancient means of oppression.

"We look for really smart people who have tremendous passion," said the COO of Yahoo!, "great conviction and courage, and a little bit of willingness to go out there and take a risk."[7] The most important activity for really smart people is to think big, to take a risk on thinking differently.

"Those achieving the highest levels of performance," noted several experts, "do so through deftly balancing the conflicting demands or 'tensions' created by the paradoxes... [leaders] will acknowledge and overcome this chaos and complexity not with some set of formulae or rigid management doctrines but by working flexibly—and with uncommon intelligence; by managing paradox itself... Each is attempting to achieve enduringly superior performance by managing paradox."[8]

The paradox principle is designed for smart people who like to think and then convert that new thinking into results that are different in kind. Paradox-Based Leadership, if you've gotten this far, is for you.

SUGGESTED ACTION PLAN

There are many ways to apply the paradox principle in your organization. Just getting your team thinking in paradoxical terms will move your organization into a different kind of future than most organizations can expect. Here is a suggested action plan to get you started.

1. Eliminate either–or discussions—A very high percentage of supposed trade-offs are actually situations in which we can get some of each or the best of both. Is turnover good or bad? Is passion good or bad? The answer to these and many similar questions is "yes." Turnover is good if it leads to the departure of the people who don't believe or win, and it is bad if means that our stars are leaving. Passion is good if it is focused on building up and bad if focused on tearing down.
2. Change the nature of the conversation—After some opening discussions with your team about the concept of paradox, get them thinking about each of the twenty Power Paradoxes in this book.

Take a look at the table of contents. We thought you would like to know that most leaders and organizations tend to be stronger, or focus more, on the left side of each of these 20 paradoxes. A good place to start dialogue on this subject is to pick the two or three that are the most important to you and your team, look at the right side, and use the ideas in the chapter as a launching pad to discuss how that side can be enhanced.

If you have a weekly meeting, make one of the paradoxes the subject of at least a part of that meeting. Assign an individual or small group to prepare some challenging questions or recommended actions the team could take, given the specifics of your current opportunities or challenges. It will probably be a more vigorous conversation than you have had in other staff meetings.

3. Distribute the Power Paradoxes—These areas are too important to be left to our faulty memories and busy schedules. Find a way to assign these paradoxes, preferably one per person, to your team. If you have four senior direct reports, you could assign each one a category of paradoxes—those on leadership, culture, talent, and strategy (see the table of contents). Then they could assign each of the five paradoxes in that category to their direct reports. Each person can be "working" his or her paradox—thinking and reading about it, bringing in ideas from the related chapter in this book, suggesting possible applications, posing challenging questions, watching for places

where the team falls into the either—or trap on that paradox. You want someone to own each of these paradoxes.

4. Get the organization thinking about the value of paradox—The value to your organization of everyone thinking about how they can, for example, communicate more while using their right to filter information, is immense. Teaching your organization about the value of the paradox allows everyone to contribute to a richer, higher-impact communication that can give your organization a much better chance of creating wealth. One detailed analysis of high-performing people found that *"individuals are always paradoxical when they are performing at their best.*[9]

5. Assess the organization's ability to comprehend and willingness to use paradox—The goal of this process isn't to produce a "learning organization," it's to produce a *Thinking* Organization. This pushes people out of doing a job and into growing a job. You want to test both your team's understanding of paradox and its use of paradox in making better business decisions. Do they understand the types of communication that add the most value? Do they know how to identify the low-value or useless information that is choking your organization? At Luman Consultants International, we have developed assessment surveys to measure these skills, but regardless of the method you use, it's crucial for you to know whether this more robust way of organizational life is taking root and creating value.

6. Create an internal "best practices in paradox" site (or subset of your existing Intranet) —The principles and practices in this book are way off the radar screen of the management literature and standard organizational practice. As you begin to enrich your organization with paradox, find and use a place where ideas and applications can be noted, discussed, debated, and expanded. What mechanisms have people found to communicate more of the good stuff? What tools have they found effective at filtering the junk? This kind of corporate conversation is valuable on many topics but is especially so on the subject of paradox.

7. Set your sights high—"The greater danger for most of us," said Michelangelo, "is not that our aim is too high and we miss it, but that it is too low and we reach it." Don't let the paradox principle get away from you. You can use it to optimize your answers, decisions, solutions, innovations, communications, agreements, and thought. "We have to find ways to make sense of...paradoxes, to use them to shape a better destiny," Charles Handy encouraged us in *The Age of Paradox.*[10] We believe, and encourage you to believe with us, that

- The only great answers are those that destroy the questions
- The only great decisions are those that maximize impact and wealth
- The only great solutions are those that annihilate the problem
- The only great innovations are those that change the rules of the game
- The only great communications are those that add or create value

- The only great agreements are those that have mined all legitimate disagreement
- The only great thoughts are those that combine furious opposites

If you manage the paradox principle well, the results—no matter how high your hopes—may surprise you.

THE YELLOW BRICK ROAD

Speaking at the Kellogg School of Business at Northwestern University in 2004, I told the group that all leaders and organizations are on the Yellow Brick Road with Dorothy and her friends—looking for a brain, looking for heart, and looking for courage.[11]

- Brain—The scarecrow wanted to be able to think, and we want our organizations to be able to do the same. We call it "intellectual capital"—the total stock of knowledge and truth and wisdom that we have available for investment in our future. It has been said that individuals only access a small percentage of their brains; if so, given internal politics, organizations access even a smaller percentage. Many organizations don't even *expect* their people to think. The world of paradox is inviting you and your team to use much more of the brilliance that is already there.
- Heart—The Tin Man wanted to be able to experience life deeply, and we should certainly want the same for our people. While writing *The Passionate Organization: Igniting the Fire of Employee Commitment*, I came to see that a few organizations had a very high level of "passion capital"—the total stock of commitment and dedication that we have available for investment in our future. Few organizations tap into their passion capital. To invite people to think and discuss and debate is to invite them to be passionate, to use much more of the fire that is already there.
- Courage—The lion wanted to be what he and everyone else expected him to be—brave—and we most definitely want the same for our team. This is our "courage capital"—the total stock of determination and willpower and risk-acceptance that we have available for investment in our future. Almost no organizations tap into their courage capital, and many view it more as an uncontrollable pollutant than a valuable resource. To invite people to choose and act and take risks is to invite them to be courageous, to use much more of the desire to make a difference that is already there.

To maximize the value of our organization's head, heart, and courage, we have to blend them together. Applying the principles and practices in this book will go a long way toward getting you there.

Of course, we shouldn't forget Dorothy, who simply (and mainly) just wanted to go home. We want our organizations to "go home"—to fulfill their purpose and to get where they want to go. Wherever home is for your organization, there is no place like it. And if you learn to use the power of paradox in your organization, you will get there in style, bringing legacy and prosperity with you.

NOTES

CHAPTER 1

1. Jack Welch, "How to Be a Good Leader," *Newsweek*, April 4, 2005, 45–46. Taken from Welch's book *Winning* (New York: HarperCollins, 2005).

2. As quoted in Glenn Tinder, *Political Thinking* (New York: HarperCollins, 1991).

3. Derm Barrett, *The Paradox Process: Creative Business Solutions Where You Least Expect to Find Them* (New York: AMACOM, 1998), 117.

4. Quinn and Cameron, as quoted in Fletcher, Jerry and Kelle Olwyler, *Paradoxical Thinking* (San Francisco, CA: Berrett-Koehler Publishers, 1997), 7.

5. From *The Age of Paradox*, as quoted in The Price Waterhouse Change Integration Team, *The Paradox Principles* (Chicago, IL: Irwin Professional Publishing, 1996), 5.

6. Barry Johnson, *Polarity Management: Identifying and Managing Unsolvable Problems* (Amherst, MA: HRD Press, 1992, 1996).

7. Jerry Fletcher and Kelle Olwyler, *Paradoxical Thinking* (San Francisco, CA: Berrett-Koehler Publishers, 1997), 113.

8. Richard Farson, *Management of the Absurd: Paradoxes in Leadership*, as quoted in the American Management Association's workbook for the course, "Developing Executive Leadership." Interestingly, as of the last time I reviewed the materials for this course, it was full of "how-to-do-it formulas and techniques, if not...slogans and homilies, as the principle management guides."

9. Gabriel Garcia Marquez, *One Hundred Years of Solitude* (New York: Perennial Classics, 1998), 365. Even Marquez's writing style—"magical realism"—is a paradox.

10. *Oxford English Reference Dictionary*, edited by Judy Pearsall and Bill Trumble (New York: Oxford University Press, 2002), 1352.

11. Ibid.

CHAPTER 2

1. Ralph Peters, *Fighting for the Future* (Mechanicsburg, PA: Stackpole, 1999), 194.

2. See the cover story on happiness in *Time*, January 17, 2005.

3. *Oxford English Reference Dictionary*, edited by Judy Pearsall and Bill Trumble (New York: Oxford University Press, 2002), 1020.

4. Ibid.

5. David McCullough, *The Great Bridge* (New York: Simon & Schuster, 1972), 39–40.

6. "Why Companies Fail," *Fortune*, May 27, 2002, 54.

7. *Oxford English Reference Dictionary*, 1352.

8. "Oh Yeah? Says Who?" *The Wall Street Journal*, January 14, 2005, W11.

9. Ibid.

10. Ibid.

11. Larry Bossidy and Ram Charan, *Confronting Reality: Doing What Matters to Get Things Right* (New York: Crown Business, 2004), 9.

12. "Why Companies Fail," *Fortune*, May 27, 2002, 52.

13. Ibid., 53.

14. Ibid., 54.

15. Peter F. Drucker, *The Daily Drucker* (New York: HarperBusiness, 2004), 6.

16. These areas, covered in detail in my book *Fatal Illusions: Shredding a Dozen Unrealities That Can Keep Your Organization from Success* (Kansas City, MO: Quintessential Books, March 2001), are illusions about vision, priorities, quality, expectations, change, consequences, comparisons, people, openness, incentives, cooperation, and passion.

17. "Gospels of Failure," *Fast Company*, February 2005, 66.

18. Ibid.

19. Ibid., 67.

20. Gordon Livingston, *Too Soon Old, Too Late Smart* (New York: Marlowe & Company, 2004), 150.

21. "Accuracy of Battlefield News Often Hazy," *USA Today*, April 8, 2003, 7A.

22. Ibid.

23. "Don't Worry, Be Sorry," *Fortune Small Business*, February 2005, 29.

24. Carlo D'Este, *Eisenhower: A Soldier's Life* (New York: Henry Holt, 2002), 652.

25. "NBC's New Reality," *Time*, November 1, 2004, 63.

26. "The New Face of Confidence," *Inc. Magazine*, February 2003, 60.

27. "Intel's Andy Grove Tells How to Make It...Really Make It," *Bottom Line Personal*, September 15, 1997, 1.

CHAPTER 3

1. Peter F. Drucker, *The Daily Drucker* (New York: HarperBusiness, 2004), 38.

2. Former General Electric CEO Jack Welch and Former Hermann Miller CEO Max DePree, to name a few.

3. James Surowiecki, *The Wisdom of Crowds* (New York: Doubleday, 2004).

4. Peter F Drucker, *The Daily Drucker* (New York: HarperBusiness, 2004), 38.

5. See the book by that name written by my friend Annette Simmons (New York: AMACOM, 1999).

6. "Intel's Andy Grove Tells How to Make It...Really Make It," *Bottom Line Personal*, September 15, 1997, 2.

7. If you want some in-depth thinking and tools on this area of exposing the truth, see my book *Fatal Illusions: Shredding a Dozen Unrealities That Can Keep Your Organization from Success* (Kansas City, MO: Quintessential Books, 2001).

8. To see a sample reality check, go to http://www.lumanconsultants.com and click on "Fatal Illusions."

9. Geoffrey Parker, *Success Is Never Final* (New York: Basic Books, 2002), 67.

10. Both quotes in this paragraph are from *Forbes*, June 7, 1982, 212.

11. "Gospels of Failure," *Fast Company*, February 2005, 62–64.

CHAPTER 4

1. From "If," by Rudyard Kipling.

2. Peter L. Bernstein, *Against the Gods: The Remarkable Story of Risk* (New York: Wiley, 1996), 15.

3. Carleen Hawn, "What Money Can't Buy," *FastCompany*, December 2004, 71.

4. Carlo d'Este, *Eisenhower: A Soldier's Life* (New York: Henry Holt, 2002), 459–60.

5. Ibid., 239.

6. Quoted in *Forbes*, November 23, 1981, 236.

7. See D'Este, *Eisenhower*, 197.

8. "No Risk, No Reward," *Fast Company*, August 2002, 84.

9. Larry Bossidy and Ram Charan, *Execution* (New York: Crown Business, 2002), 192.

10. French philosopher and mathematician Blaise Pascal, as quoted in Bernstein, *Against the Gods*, 71.

CHAPTER 5

1. Benjamin Disraeli, speech, June 24, 1870, quoted in *Forbes*, Nov. 23, 1981, 236.

2. See Bevin Alexander, *How Generals Win* (New York: Norton, 1993).

3. In American football, KPIs for the offense are victories and total points and yards and first downs. You want to see them at very high levels. CSFs are red zone scoring strategies, turnover ratio improvement activities, and efforts to reduce missed blocking assignments. If we do these well, the KPIs should be achieved.

4. Stewart Levine, *The Book of Agreement: 10 Essential Elements for Getting the Results You Want* (San Francisco: Berrett-Koehler, 2002), xvi.

CHAPTER 6

1. Benjamin Nathan Cordozo, *Law and Literature*, ThinkExist.com Quotations, "Benjamin Cordozo quotes," August 2005, Online.

2. Jack Welch, *Jack: Straight from the Gut* (New York: Warner Books, 2001), 383.

3. Geoffrey Colvin, *Fortune*, March 6, 2000, F-9.

4. "Money and Morals at GE," *Fortune*, November 15, 2004, 178.

5. From *The Tao Te Ching* "Where Is Thy Sting" (New York: Vintage Books, 1997), 50.

6. Anne Sweeney, President, The Disney Channel. Quoted in "My Greatest Lesson," *Fast Company*, June 1998, 83.

7. See Malcolm Gladwell, *Blink: The Power of Thinking without Thinking* (New York: Little Brown Company and Time Warner Book Group, 2005).

8. Gordon Livingston, *Too Soon Old, Too Late Smart* (New York: Marlowe, 2004), 16.

CHAPTER 7

1. Jack Welch, "How to Be a Good Leader," *Newsweek*, April 4, 2005, 45–46. Excerpted from Welch's book *Winning* (New York: HarperCollins, 2005).

2. Larry Bossidy and Ram Charan, *Execution* (New York: Crown Business, 2002), 189.

3. "Gospels of Failure," *Fast Company*, February 2005, 64.

4. Ibid., 182, 186.

5. "Gospels of Failure," *Fast Company*, February 2005, 65.

6. John Keegan, *The First World War* (New York: Vintage Books, 2000), 404.

7. "The Fall and Rise of David Pottruck," *Fast Company*, September 2005, 62.

CHAPTER 8

1. As quoted in Derm Barrett, *The Paradox Process: Creative Business Solutions Where You Least Expect to Find Them* (New York: AMACOM, 1998), 182.

2. In a speech in 1943 at Harvard University. Quoted in *The Oxford Dictionary of Quotations* (New York: Oxford University Press, 1999), 215.

3. For example, in January 2005 the Hewlett-Packard board gave large quarterly bonuses to an array of executives—including CEO Carly Fiorina, right before they terminated her. This was especially ridiculous since the "good quarter" was in the midst of terrible multiyear economic performance, including a miserable acquisition of Compaq.

4. F. A. Hayek, *The Road to Serfdom* (Chicago: University of Chicago Press, 1994), 4.

5. See Ken Blanchard and Terry Waghorn, *Mission Possible* (New York: McGraw-Hill, 1997).

6. In the groundbreaking book *Bowling Alone* (New York: Simon and Schuster, 2000), 34, Robert Putnam writes, "If different generations have different tastes or habits, the social physiology of birth and death will eventually transform society, *even if no individual ever changes.*"

7. "Peter Drucker Takes the Long View," *Fortune*, September 28, 1998, 170.

CHAPTER 9

1. Seneca, *Epistles to Lucilius*, quoted in Lewis D. Eigen and Jonathan P. Siegal, *The Manager's Book of Quotations* (New York: AMACOM, 1989), 45.

2. "In Praise of Privacy," *Inc. Magazine*, March 2005, 116.

3. Bevin Alexander, *How Great Generals Win* (New York: Norton, 2002), 190.

4. For more on this, see my book *Fatal Illusions: Shredding a Dozen Unrealities That Can Keep Your Organization from Success* (Kansas City, MO: Quintessential Books, 2001), chap. 12.

5. James Surowiecki, *The Wisdom of Crowds* (New York: Doubleday, 2004), 183.

6. Ibid., 185.

7. Joe Posnanski, columnist for the *Kansas City Star*, in a presentation made on November 6, 2004.

8. "Gospels of Failure," *Fast Company*, February 2005, 67.

9. "Evolving from Information to Insight," *MIT Sloan Management Review*, Winter 2005, 55–56.

10. Ibid., 58.

CHAPTER 10

1. Abolitionist Henry Ward Beecher, quoted in James R. Lucas, *Balance of Power: Fueling Employee Power without Relinquishing Your Own* (Kansas City, MO: Quintessential Books, 2002), 31.

2. Ibid., 13.

3. For a full treatment of this concept of *power sharing* and the way to use all available power effectively, see Lucas, *Balance of Power*.

4. Robert Mueller, Director of the FBI, in a speech given at Northwestern University's Kellogg School of Management on November 17, 2004.

5. Ibid.

6. James Surowiecki, *The Wisdom of Crowds* (New York: Doubleday, 2004), 202.

7. "Fathers Know Best," *Inc. Magazine*, June 2004, 32.

8. At Luman Consultants International, we work with our clients to design six clearly defined levels of decision-making into the core of their organizational systems.

9. Carlo D'Este, *Eisenhower: A Soldier's Life* (New York: Henry Holt, 2002), 414.

10. "A Man on a Gray Horse," *The Atlantic Monthly* 294, no. 4, September 2002, 25.

11. "Why Leadership Is the Most Dangerous Idea in American Business," *Inc. Magazine*, June 2004, 94.

CHAPTER 11

1. Georg Wilhelm Hegel, *The Philosophy of History*, quoted at www.borntomotivate.com May 2004, "Famous Quotes by: Georg Hegel."

2. "Why Passion Pays," *Fortune Small Business*, September 2002, 58. Although we agree with this assessment, we find that the twelve statements Gallup uses to detect the level of employee engagement are too simplistic to get at core issues that destroy passion and commitment.

3. Jack Welch, *Jack: Straight from the Gut* (New York: Warner Books, 2001), 385.

4. Jim Collins and Jerry Porras, *Built to Last* (New York: HarperCollins, 2002).

5. Ibid., 385.

6. We have found in our research and practice that there are ten key elements of an environment in which passion can flourish. We have also found a strong correlation between this kind of environment and high levels of performance.

7. We have developed a radically different methodology that includes a twenty-category "Passion Scale" with supporting questions for each category. We have very different general questions and processing approach as well. This gets the search for passionate people and "hiring for attitude" past the "gut instinct" that can put such an emphasis on external observables rather than indwelling, durable, effective passion.

8. "The Case Against Loyalty," *Inc. Magazine*, April 2005, p. 144.

9. Czeslaw Milosz, Lithuanian poet and Nobel Laureate, quoted in *Bottom Line Personal*, January 1, 2005, 15.

10. We have also developed a methodology to (on a regular basis) allow leaders and organizations to restructure work. Unlike most of our approaches, ours lets each person be the initial driver and places little additional work on the leaders.

11. "The Great One Skates Away," *Time*, April 26, 1999. (See www.time.com.)

CHAPTER 12

1. Diogenes Laertius, *Lives and Opinions of Eminent Philosophers: Xenophanes*, quoted in Lewis D. Eigen and Jonathan P. Siegal, *The Manager's Book of Quotations* (New York: AMACOM, 1989), 325.

2. Peter Cappelli, "A Market-Driven Approach to Retaining Talent," *Harvard Business Review*, January–February 2000, 109.

3. "Recruit Your People Every Day," *Fast Company*, March 2001, 44, 102.

4. "Employees Better Their Working Environment," *The Edinburgh Press and Journal*, May 28, 2004.

CHAPTER 13

1. Thomas Beecham, quoted in Lewis D. Eigen and Jonathan P. Siegal, *The Manager's Book of Quotations* (New York: AMACOM, 1989), 452.

2. For a brilliant analysis of the path freedom has taken over the last five hundred years, see Jacque Barzun's *From Dawn to Decadence* (New York, NY: HarperCollins, May 2000).

3. James R. Lucas, *Balance of Power: How to Fuel Employee Power without Relinquishing Your Own* (Kansas City, MO: Quintessential Books, 2001).

4. I had to create this word while writing *Balance of Power*. "Empowerment" is a defective concept and word. It implies, inaccurately, that all power resides in the top but also suggests that enlightened despots will trickle a bit of it down to the masses. It's something you do *to* other people. "Power sharing" recognizes that all people have power—to care, to commit, to invest, to hurt, to do nothing—and seeks ways to get that power working for the good of the organization. It's something you do *with* other people.

5. Will Durant, *The Lessons of History* (Littleton, CO: KNC Books, 1968), 61.

CHAPTER 14

1. Suetonius, *Lives of the Caesars: Divas Augustus*, quoted in Lewis D. Eigen and Jonathan P. Siegal, *The Manager's Book of Quotations* (New York: AMACOM, 1989), 449.

2. Richard Nixon, with all of his flaws, knew something about tenacity.

3. Gordon Livingston, *Too Soon Old, Too Late Smart* (New York: Marlowe, 2004), 56.

4. "The Doctor Is Still In: Secrets of Health From a Famed 96-Year-Old Physician," *The Wall Street Journal*, March 8, 2005, D1.

5. *The Columbia World of Quotations*, Robert Andrews, Mary Briggs, Michael Seidel, et al., eds. (New York: Columbia University Press, 1996), quotation #56794.

CHAPTER 15

1. Benjamin Franklin, *Autobiography*, quoted in Lewis D. Eigen and Jonathan P. Siegal, *The Manager's Book of Quotations* (New York: AMACOM, 1989), 187–88.

2. "The Creative Campus: Who's No. 1?" *The Chronicle of Higher Education*, Oct. 1, 2004, p. 6.

3. Quoted in *Bottom Line Personal*, July 1, 1999, 7. Based on research done by Alan G. Robinson at the University of Massachusetts School of Management.

4. B. Thomas Golisano, "I Thought Small Business Should Have a Way to Get Payroll Done Just Like the Big Guys," *Fortune Small Business*, September 2003, 84.

5. Marcus Buckingham and Curt Coffman. *First, Break All the Rules* (New York: Simon & Schuster, 1999), 123.

6. "Ford's Famous Filly Turns 40," *USA Today*, April 16, 2004, 1B.

7. As quoted in *The Paradox Process: Creative Business Solutions Where You Least Expect to Find Them* (New York: AMACOM, 1998), 30.

8. Anita M. McGahan, *How Industries Evolve* (Boston: Harvard Business School Press, 2004), 6.

9. "Forward into the Past," *Time*, October 11, 2004, 80.

10. Pete Bicak, professor at Rockhurst University, in an e-mail to the author dated February 7, 2005.

11. "3M," *Fortune Small Business*, April 2003, 40.

CHAPTER 16

1. *Dynamic Administration: The Collected Papers of Mary Parker Follett*, edited by Harry Metcalf and L. Urwick (New York: Harper & Brothers Publishers, 1940).

2. At Luman Consultants International, we in fact offer these very courses as part of our cutting-edge leadership development program.

3. James Surowiecki, *The Wisdom of Crowds* (New York: Doubleday, 2004), 166.

4. *Dynamic Administration: The Collected Papers of Mary Parker Follett*.

5. One large consultant actually recommended this negative. See The Price Waterhouse Change Integration Team, *The Paradox Principles* (Chicago, IL: Irwin Professional Publishing, 1996), 87–88.

6. James R. Lucas, *Fatal Illusions: Shredding a Dozen Unrealities that Can Keep Your Organization from Success* (Kansas City, MO: Quintessential Books, 2001), 160. Originally published by AMACOM.

7. If you e-mail a request to www.clientcare@lumanconsultants.com, we will send you an essay on "10 Reasons Why Business Is a Lot Harder than Sports."

8. Lucas, *Fatal Illusions*, 161.

9. Alex Axelrod, *Patton on Leadership: Strategic Lessons for Corporate Warfare* (Paramus, NJ: Prentice Hall, 1999), 242.

CHAPTER 17

1. Lord Palmerston, speech in Parliament on the Polish question, March 1, 1848.
2. "Get Inside the Lives of Your Customers," *Harvard Business Review*, May 2001, 81.
3. *The Wall Street Journal*, November 4, 2004, 1.
4. Although this is not defined in psychiatric journals, it is very real and prevalent nonetheless.
5. For a full treatment of this subject, see my book, *Fatal Illusions: Shredding a Dozen Unrealities that Can Keep Your Organization from Success* (Kansas City, MO: Quintessential Books, 2001).
6. "Fire That Client!" *Fortune Small Business*, June 2005, 75.

CHAPTER 18

1. Lily Tomlin, *Omni*, April 1988, quoted in Lewis D. Eigen and Jonathan P. Siegal, *The Manager's Book of Quotations* (New York: AMACOM, 1989), 59.
2. *Oxford English Reference Dictionary*, 132.
3. For a deep analysis of the problems with benchmarking, see chapter 10 of my book, *Balance of Power* (Kansas City, MO: Quintessential Books, 2001).
4. "How Intel's Missteps Juiced Up Rival AMD," *The Wall Street Journal*, January 12, 2005, B1.
5. "Comcast Aims to Dial Up Profit—and Growth," *The Wall Street Journal*, January 11, 2005, C1.
6. Ibid., C3.
7. Most of these criteria are from Ram Charan's book, *Profitable Growth Is Everyone's Business* (New York: Crown Business, 2004).
8. A review of "Contagious Success," *Fast Company*, January 2005, 89.
9. "The 10 Lives of George Salk," *Fast Company*, February 2005, 49.
10. "Gospels of Failure," *Fast Company*, February 2005, 64

CHAPTER 19

1. Ralph Waldo Emerson, speech at the Mercantile Library Association, Boston, Massachusetts, February 7, 1844, quoted in "The Young American," Nature, Addresses, and Lectures (1849). Full text available at www.emersoncentral.com/youngam.
2. Nell Minow, co-founder of The Corporate Library, quoted in "Sprint Plans Big Bonuses," *The Kansas City Star*, January 22, 2005, C-2.

CHAPTER 20

1. James Poe, John Farrow, and S. J. Perelman, "Around the World in 80 Days," screenplay (1956), from narration by Edward R. Murrow.
2. "Tall Order: Coffee on the Double," *The Wall Street Journal*, April 12, 2005, B7.
3. "The Fabric of Creativity," *Fast Company*, December 2004, 59.

4. Michael Treacy, *Double-Digit Growth* (New York: Penguin Group, 2003), 44.

5. This was said of Larry Brown, the coach of the underdog Detroit Pistons in their incredible victory over the Los Angeles Lakers in the 2003 U.S. National Basketball Association finals, in the *Kansas City Star*, June 13, 2003.

6. Proverbs 16:32.

CHAPTER 21

1. Mark Twain, paper read in Hartford, Connecticut, 1884; reprinted in *Complete Essays*, ed. Charles Neider (New York: Da Capo Press, 1963).

2. Peter F. Drucker, *The Daily Drucker* (New York: HarperBusiness, 2004), 28.

3. "So Many Standards to Follow, So Little Payoff," *Inc. Magazine*, May 2005, 26.

4. "Rethinking the Quality-Improvement Program, *The Wall Street Journal*, September 19, 2005, B3.

5. Will and Ariel Durant, *The Lessons of History* (Littleton, CO: KNC Books, 1968), 36.

6. "Intel's Andy Grove Tells How to Make It, Really Make It," *Bottom Line Personal*, September 15, 1997, 1.

7. Gordon Livingston, *Too Soon Old, Too Late Smart* (New York: Marlowe, 2004), 99.

8. Ibid., 44.

9. The Price Waterhouse Change Integration Team, *The Paradox Principles* (Chicago, IL: Irwin Professional Publishing, 1996), 19.

10. Gordon Livingston, *Too Soon Old, Too Late Smart* (New York: Marlowe, 2004), 46.

11. Quoted by William Green in his article "I Spy" in *Forbes*, April 20, 1998.

12. Larry Bossidy and Ram Charan, *Confronting Reality* (New York: Crown Business, 2004), 10.

CHAPTER 22

1. As quoted in *Time* Magazine Review of *Kennedy's Secret Pain* by Lance Morrow, May 19, 2003, Vol. 161, No. 20.

2. *Philosophical Fragments by Søren Kierkegaard* (Princeton, NJ: Princeton University Press, 1936).

3. A phrase used by G. K. Chesterton

4. As quoted in Michael Treacy, *Double-Digit Growth* (New York: Penguin Group, 2003), 89.

5. As quoted in Mark Albion's book *Making a Life, Making a Living* (New York: Warner Business Books, 2000), 2.

6. James Surowiecki, *The Wisdom of Crowds* (New York: Doubleday, 2004), 195, 200.

7. Dan Rosensweig, "What I Know Now," *Fast Company*, February 2005, 96.

8. The Price Waterhouse Change Integration Team, *The Paradox Principles* 7.

9. Jerry Fletcher and Kelle Olwyler, *Paradoxical Thinking* (San Francisco, CA: Berrett-Koehler Publishers, 1997), X. The book itself treats paradoxes as personal traits.

10. Ibid.

11. With credit to L. Frank Baum for his wonderful story, *The Wonderful Wizard of Oz* (New York: Tom Doherty Associates, LLC, 1993, A Tor Book), and with thanks to R. Michael Mahoney for pointing out this analogy.

INDEX

discipline, 68
disillusionment, 21, 173
distractions, 148
diversity, 97, 99, 135
Drucker, Peter: on change and continuity, 170, 174, 175; on customers, 138; on hiring and results, 40; on performance, 69; on reality, 15, 19
Durant, Will, 109, 172

education, 4, 24, 130
80/20 rule, 143
Eli Lilly, 16
eliminate (paradox management step), 3
embrace (paradox management step), 3
Emerson, Ralph Waldo, 153, 170
emotional blackmail, 48
empathy, applied, 138
employees: benchmarks for, 149–50; categories of, during change, 176; character assumptions of, 107; commitment to, 118–19; cutting costs through, 154, 155; development of, 119; evaluations, 97, 132; importance of, 78; as investors, 90, 100; invisible spending and costs, 159; matching jobs to right, 48; pay for performance, 156; powersharing with, 83, 85; pressure response of, 112; promotions of, 116; rationally-skilled as leaders, 46; stress and, 114–19; termination of, 98–102, 163; truth-finding and, 15, 19–20. *See also* hiring
employment as a personal investment, 90, 100
empowerment, 81, 82
engagement, rules of, 57, 138
engage (paradox management step), 3
enhance (paradox management step), 3
enjoyment, promotion of, 65
entitlement mentality, 140
environments: building trust, 73; conducive to truth, 16; creating unified, 135; ineffective stress reducers in, 115; passion-friendly, 88, 89–90; as reason for job changes, 101; risk-friendly, 116; safe, 22–24, 30, 108, 118

envy, 132
errand running, 80
evaluations: customer, 142–43; employee, 97, 132; time-consuming reviews, 164. *See also* assessments
events, focusing on, 12, 14, 112
Excellencies, Core, 33, 61
excuse making, 12
exercise, physical, 115
expectations, 92–93, 113, 117–18
expenditures, 154
experience, as hiring criteria, 96
explore (paradox management step), 3
extortion, 22

facts, 15, 46, 48, 49, 156
failure: challenging, 113; and leading with heart, 49; learning from, 16, 25; of management training, 4; persistence with, 170; pressure and fear of, 113; reasons for organizational, 15
false cooperation, 133
false hopes, 88, 99, 113
false promises, 23
Fatal Illusions (Lucas), 21, 133
fear: behaviors producing, 106; of failure producing pressure, 113; of risk, 34–35; of truth-telling, 19–20; used to spark passion, 92
field of view, 148
filtering information, 74–77
firing. *See* termination
"first movers," 29
focused wandering (time-outs), 116, 118
Follett, Mary Parker, 129
formal authority, 80, 83, 85
forums, creating, 23, 76, 125, 133, 134
frailty, 32, 117
freedom, 103–4, 107–8
French Revolution, 82–83, 103
future, living in, 63–64, 65–69, 156

Garcia Marquez, Gabriel, 5
gatekeepers (screeners), 75, 163
General Electric, 34, 48
gifts, trinket, 89
goals, 89, 113

ABOUT THE AUTHOR

James R. Lucas is a recognized authority on leadership and organizational development. He is a groundbreaking author, thought leader, provocative speaker, and experienced consultant.

As President and CEO of Luman Consultants International, Inc., he is dedicated to developing passionate, thinking, high-performance leaders, people, teams, and organizations. Recent clients are from areas as diverse as oil and gas, chemicals, forest and paper products, computer hardware, diversified manufacturing, health care, pharmaceuticals, medical devices, consumer products, diversified business services, financial services, accounting, construction, state government, and federal government. They range from *Fortune* 1000 public companies and private for-profit organizations to not-for-profit organizations, and government agencies.

Prior to founding Luman Consultants International, Inc., in 1983, Jim has held managerial and executive positions at Hallmark Cards, VF Corporation, EMCI, and Black & Veatch Consultants.

Jim is an award-winning senior faculty member of the American Management Association and has taught in the School of Professional Studies at Rockhurst University. He has been honored with continuous listings in *Who's Who in America*, *Who's Who in the World*, and *Who's Who in Finance and Industry*.

He is the author of thirteen books, including *The Passionate Organization: Igniting the Fire of Employee Commitment*, *Balance of Power: Fueling Employee Power without Relinquishing Your Own*, and *Fatal Illusions: Shredding a Dozen Unrealities that Can Keep Your Organization from Success*. He has also written numerous curricula for business and leadership seminars, as well as many essays and articles.

WEB SITES FOR FURTHER INSIGHT

For more on the subject of paradox, including a look at some crucial assessment tools, please join us at: http://www.paradoxbasedleadership.com

Mr. Lucas is president and CEO of a provocative, thought-leadership consulting practice, which can be found at:http://www.lumanconsultants.com

More on other books and related ideas can be found at: http://www
.thepassionateorganization.com, http://www.powersharing.net, and http://www
.fatalillusions.com